Integrating
INQUIRY
Across
the CURRICULUM

Integrating
INQUIRY
Across
the CURRICULUM

Edited by Richard H. Audet and Linda K. Jordan

Foreword by Joseph Exline

CORWIN PRESS
A SAGE Publications Company
Thousand Oaks, California

For information:

Corwin Press
A Sage Publications Company
2455 Teller Road
Thousand Oaks, California 91320
www.corwinpress.com

Sage Publications Ltd.
1 Oliver's Yard
55 City Road
London EC1Y 1SP
United Kingdom

Sage Publications India Pvt. Ltd.
B-42, Panchsheel Enclave
Post Box 4109
New Delhi 110 017 India

Printed in the United States of America

Library of Congress Cataloging-in-Publication Data

Integrating inquiry across the curriculum / edited by Richard H. Audet, Linda K. Jordan.
   p. cm.
Includes bibliographical references and index.
ISBN 1-4129-0616-4 (cloth) — ISBN 1-4129-0617-2 (pbk.)
   1. Inquiry-based learning. 2. Active learning. 3. Curriculum planning.
I. Audet, Richard H. II. Jordan, Linda K.
LB1027.23.I58 2005
371.39—dc22   2004029802

This book is printed on acid-free paper.

05   06   07   08   09   10   9   8   7   6   5   4   3   2   1

Acquisitions Editor:	Rachel Livsey
Editorial Assistant:	Phyllis Cappello
Production Editor:	Diane Foster
Copy Editor:	Liann Lech
Typesetter:	C&M Digitals (P) Ltd.
Proofreader:	Cheryl Rivard
Indexer:	Teri Greenberg
Cover Designer:	Michael Dubowe

Contents

Foreword

Learning through inquiry has been, and continues to be, a much debated topic. One way to encapsulate the controversy surrounding this issue is to ask, "What would inquiry learning look like if I were to encounter it in a classroom?" The compilation of articles edited by Richard Audet and Linda Jordan in *Integrating Inquiry Across the Curriculum* provides valuable insights that explore and help to answer this confounding but significant question.

As one becomes immersed in this engaging book, the question posed in the provocative title of Chapter 3—"Science Inquiry: Is There Any Other Way?"—provides a powerful stimulus for addressing the myriad aspects of inquiry learning. Substitute any other content area for science, and this cross-cutting query retains its relevance. One comes away from the first section of the book wanting to take the question a major step further by asking "Inquiry: Is There Any Other Way to Better Learn Anything?"

What becomes clear as one delves deeply into the material of this book is that many of our current assumptions about education demand serious reconsideration. In contrast to the lingering past emphasis on "what we know," the rigors of living in today's modern society stress "how we come to know." A quote attributed to Jerome Bruner in the English Language Arts chapter points out that literature should involve "trafficking in human possibilities rather than in settled certainties." This type of instructional approach leads to discourse about literature that is dialogic and invites and allows for multiple student perspectives. Material in the book's second section emphasizes the important responsibility for creating classroom conditions that make such opportunities for inquiry available to all students.

The numerous vignettes and research-based examples found in *Integrating Inquiry Across the Curriculum* strongly support the argument for applications of inquiry across the entire curriculum. As discussed, geography standards propose that students learn content through the similar processes and tools of inquiry used by historians and social scientists. These same standards argue that problem-based or issue-based geographic inquiry offers the best chance for inspiring students to assume social responsibility and take action as citizens of the world. Another chapter indicates that the nature of history lends itself to inquiry and exploration, and encourages thinking, reflection, revision, and recognition of unfinished stories. In effective history learning, students "do history."

Jennifer, a student referred to in the geography chapter, who asked, "Is it possible to teach all subjects using an inquiry approach?" raised the central question explored in this book. Her question was reminiscent of decades of collegial discussions about inquiry that I have enjoyed with colleagues. I was not surprised to read that her fellow students' responses to Jennifer's question mirrored commonly expressed views in the ongoing debate about the efficacy of learning through inquiry.

Although consensus about the merits of inquiry as a means of supporting both effective instruction and meaningful learning may never be fully reached, *Integrating Inquiry Across the Curriculum* will contribute to thoughtful dialogue about this topic. The essential message that this well-researched and well-written book conveys is that students can and do learn about subjects in teacher-centered classrooms, but they learn best in a learner-centered environment that emphasizes inquiry. This book should be high on every educator's reading list and is destined to become an important reference for anyone who is seeking a fuller understanding about the nature of classroom inquiry.

—Joseph "Joe" Exline
Executive Director
Council of State Science Supervisors

Preface

Teaching, like learning, is fundamentally an enduring struggle for meaning and inquiry is the catalyst in this struggle.

—Weinbaum et al. (2004), p. xiii

R aquel, a preservice elementary school teacher, had just completed a long-term, in-depth observation in my science methods course. The purpose of this investigation was to familiarize her with the process of inquiry with the hope that she would develop a positive disposition toward this form of instruction in her own classroom. The assignment required her to first isolate a question she wanted to explore and then to develop an implementation plan. As is commonly the case for students at all educational levels, Raquel's biggest hurdle was identifying and clearly stating an answerable question. She eventually decided to monitor the surroundings she encountered during her daily lunchtime walk. What follows is the final entry in her science notebook for this semester-long task.

> Inquiry is the process of searching for patterns and observations in the world around us. This idea parallels the experience I've had with my long-term observation project. At first I wasn't sure what to expect. When I decided to simply take a walk for 20 minutes a day while on my lunch break, I remember being concerned that I wouldn't have enough "data" at the end of the project. I asked my professor about this and was met with a smile, a shrug of the shoulders, and a very pleasant "I'm not sure what you're going to find." The response challenged me to find data and perturbed me a little because I wasn't comfortable

with the uncertainty of not knowing exactly what the results of my long-term observation were going to look like.

What I didn't realize at the time was that this was the beginning of inquiry learning . . . it is student-centered. I had faith in the process and I stuck to it. What I discovered was that there was a lot of value to what I did. My daily walks brought continuity to my long-term observation. The investigation engaged me in learning.

Eventually, I began to think, "What can I learn from this experience and bring to my classroom?" This type of thinking transformed my long-term observation project into a full, meaningful, and rich experience. . . . I know I can learn to teach through inquiry because I've been able to take a simple, 20-minute daily walk and turn it into a valuable learning experience.

Raquel's essay vividly captures the fundamental aspects of teaching and learning through inquiry. She carefully observed her surroundings, detected peculiarities, asked questions, probed, and continually reflected on her growing understanding. This book advocates that all partners in the learning enterprise offer students the opportunity to actively investigate objects, events, text materials, people, places, and phenomena.

This book's central premise is that inquiry offers *unifying* process skills and a knowledge base that are equally relevant for guiding student learning across *all* major subject areas. A recent Internet search for "science/inquiry/K-12 education" yielded 18,200 hits. The raw, unanalyzed numbers from other comparable searches for inquiry identified 29,000 Web sites associated with geography, 82,000 for English, 98,400 for mathematics, and 117,000 for history. This oversimplified, nonscientific, data-gathering approach supported our contention that although inquiry is most commonly associated with science, it combines practices and understandings that are recognized and implemented across all disciplines. Inquiry should be embedded throughout the school experience.

The book is divided into two distinct sections. Experts from mathematics, geography, language arts, history, and science education authored chapters found in Part I: Teaching and Learning Through Inquiry in the Content Areas. Each follows a common framework that presents a research-based rationale for incorporating inquiry in that particular discipline, illustrates how inquiry can provide a focal point for developing and implementing the curriculum, offers ideas for assessing student performance, and identifies some important technological tools that support an inquiry classroom. The section on integrating the curriculum focuses on the case study approach and problem-based learning.

Content Chapters 2–7 conclude with Ideas From the Field curriculum materials that treat inquiry as the central feature of a learning environment and are grounded in the respective national curriculum standards. This collection of inquiry-based learning activities builds on the ideas, suggestions, and principles introduced in the content chapters and illustrates how questions can serve to both initiate and guide student learning. The ideas presented here and throughout the book can help readers to develop an inquiry stance and become better prepared to evaluate curriculum and instruction for the presence of inquiry.

Part II: Creating Conditions for Successful Student Inquiry adds to this inquiry in the content area mix by introducing information specific to concerns about assessment, special education, English language learners, and informal education. The assessment chapter introduces strategies that provide reliable data about how students are performing while engaged in inquiry. The special education and English-learner segments take forceful stances for making inquiry accessible to all student populations. The informal education piece illustrates how museums are uniquely positioned to provide leadership in content-based professional development for teachers. Each chapter in Part II helps to clarify the ancillary conditions for successfully implementing inquiry with all learners.

Although many books address the topic of inquiry, most target their coverage to specific content areas. Few, if any, approach the theme of inquiry from the overarching, thematic perspective presented here. The broad scope of *Integrating Inquiry Across the Curriculum* makes it a general starting place for any K–16 teacher who is interested in exploring instructional approaches from the perspective of student inquiry.

Integrating Inquiry Across the Curriculum can be used specifically as a textbook for undergraduates in K–12 teacher preparation programs and as a resource for practicing K–12 teachers across all curriculum areas. We envision that the book will be helpful to:

- Classroom teachers who are searching for ideas about incorporating inquiry-based experiences into their curriculum

- School or districtwide study groups that are exploring ways to integrate materials from a variety of content areas and investigating strategies to assess active learning
- K–12 district teams that are examining curricula for applications of inquiry and problem solving
- Professional developers and educational leaders who are helping inservice teachers to understand inquiry-oriented curriculum approaches
- College professors who are introducing information about inquiry to K–12 preservice teachers
- College faculty who are teaching about integrated curriculum and instruction

Concerns are mounting that instructional constraints associated with the mandated testing requirements of No Child Left Behind will drive teachers away from using inquiry-oriented approaches to student learning. The fear is that, in the interest of time and content coverage, direct instruction will become the dominant teaching approach found in the classrooms of the future. Proponents of inquiry must produce evidence that clearly demonstrates the importance of striking a proper balance between instruction focused on telling and instruction that is aimed at student discovery.

REFERENCE

Weinbaum, S., Allen, D., Blyther, T., Simon, K., Seidel, S., & Rubin, C. (2004). *Teaching as inquiry: Asking hard questions to improve practice and student achievement.* New York: Teachers College Press.

ACKNOWLEDGEMENTS

The contributions of the following reviewers are gratefully acknowledged:

Anne Roede Giddings
Curriculum Supervisor
Newington Public Schools
Newington, CT

David A. Squires
Associate Professor
Southern Connecticut State University
New Haven, CT

Margaret Barilla
Director of Curriculum and Instruction
Owen J Roberts School District
Pottstown, PA

Patricia R. Herr
Teacher
Smart's Mill Middle School
Loudoun County Schools
Leesburg, VA

About the Editors

Richard H. Audet, Coeditor, is Associate Professor of Science Education at Roger Williams University (Bristol, RI). After teaching high school science for more than 20 years, he completed his master's degree at Providence College and received an EdD in Curriculum and Instruction from Boston University. Richard coauthored *GIS in Schools* and *Standards in the Classroom: An Implementation Guide for Teachers of Mathematics and Science.* raudet@rwu.edu

Linda K. Jordan, Coeditor, is Science Coordinator for the Tennessee State Department of Education, Division of Curriculum and Instruction. She provides technical assistance to local education agencies and coordinated the recent revision of Tennessee's state science framework. She coauthored *Standards in the Classroom: An Implementation Guide for Teachers of Mathematics and Science.* Linda is active on the Council of State Science Supervisors and has extensive national and statewide experience as a professional development specialist. Before assuming her present position, she taught high school biology. She earned her MS and EdS degrees at the University of Tennessee, Knoxville. linda.k.jordan@state.tn.us

About the Contributors

Alan Canestrari is the coeditor (with Bruce Marlowe) of *Educational Foundations: An Anthology of Critical Readings.* He is a veteran social studies practitioner and Assistant Professor of Education at Roger Williams University. He has had a long career in public schools and universities as a history and geography teacher, department chair, adjunct professor at Rhode Island College, and mentor in Brown University's Masters of Teaching Program. In 1992, he was named the RI Social Studies Teacher of the Year. Alan earned his advanced degrees from Rhode Island College and Boston University. acanestrari@rwu.edu

Fred Dobb is Director of the English Learner Initiative for the California Science Project at the University of California, Los Angeles. His career in language minority programs was spent as a bilingual teacher, administrator, and staff development specialist. He collaborated on the California English Language Development Test and taught courses in linguistic and cultural diversity and second language acquisition at San Francisco State University. Fred received the California Language Teachers Association's President's Award and was a Fulbright scholar to Brazil. His advanced degrees were earned at Stanford and Temple Universities. fdcsp@sbcglobal.net

Galina Dobrynina, is Assistant Professor of Mathematics at Wheelock College, where she teaches a variety of mathematics courses including a problem-solving seminar, college algebra, linear algebra, calculus, and the history of mathematics. Her main interest is developing innovative programs for teaching mathematics to preservice teachers. Galina has presented professional development workshops and conducted mathematics content summer institutes for inservice and preservice teachers. Her research includes the study of elementary and middle school students' problem solving and algebraic reasoning. She received a master's degree from Moscow Pedagogical University and an EdD from Boston University. gdobrynina@ wheelock.edu

Patricia Fitzsimmons is the K–8 Science Curriculum Specialist for the Barre (Vermont) Supervisory Union. She facilitates the Vermont Science Leaders' Network and is actively involved in science assessment at both the local and the state levels. Pat has written a teacher guide, *Scientists and Inventors,* for the Learning Materials Workshop. She was instrumental in developing the Vermont Grade Cluster Expectations for Inquiry. Her MEd degree was awarded by Trinity College in Burlington, Vermont. phitzyp@aol.com

Bruce Marlowe is the author (with Marilyn Page) of *Creating and Sustaining the Constructivist Classroom* and coeditor (with Alan Canestrari) of *Educational Foundations: An Anthology of Critical Readings.* He earned his PhD in Educational Psychology from the Catholic University of America in Washington, DC, where he also completed 2 years of postdoctoral training in neuropsychological assessment. Bruce has taught at the elementary, secondary, and university levels and is currently Associate Professor of Educational Psychology and Special Education at Roger Williams University. bmarlowe@rwu.edu

Marilyn Page is Assistant Professor of Education at Penn State University. She began her career in education as a high school social studies teacher and has taught every grade from 7–12, at every academic level, in rural, suburban, and urban school systems. Marilyn received her EdD from the University of Massachusetts, Amherst, in Instructional Leadership: Secondary Teacher Education and in Educational Media and Instructional Technology. She began her university teaching in 1990 and is the coauthor, with Bruce Marlowe, of *Creating and Sustaining the Constructivist Classroom.* mlp23@psu.edu

Linda S. Shore is the Director of the Exploratorium Teacher Institute and is on the teaching faculty of the Exploratorium's Center for Informal Learning and Schools. She earned bachelor's and master's degrees in physics from San Francisco State University and a doctorate in science education from Boston University. Linda has expertise in science teacher induction, museum-based professional development, and inquiry-based teaching and learning. She is an

Adjunct Professor of Education at the University of San Francisco, where she teaches courses in constructivism, secondary science methods, and uses of technology to support inquiry. She coauthored the award-winning *Science Explorer, Science Explorer: Out and About* and *The Brain Explorer.* lindas@exploratorium.edu

Kathleen Anderson Steeves is Associate Professor of Secondary Education, Social Studies/History in the Graduate School of Education and Human Development at George Washington University. She formerly taught high school history, social studies, and foreign languages. Kathy was active in developing the history/social studies standards and provides technical assistance in assessment and curriculum for the American Historical Association, the National Council for the Social Studies, the Council of Chief State School Officers, and area public schools. She designed resource kits to accompany major exhibits at the Smithsonian Institution and the National Museum of American History. Her research interests include the history of American technology, technology and learning, history education, and teacher leadership. She received her MAT from the University of Massachusetts, Amherst, and her PhD from George Washington University. ksteeves@gwu.edu

Jane S. Townsend is Associate Professor in Language, Literacy, and Culture at the University of Florida in Gainesville. She was a classroom teacher in a variety of settings as well as co-owner and codirector of a small school. She teaches courses in language acquisition, inquiry, and composition. Her research interests are classroom discourse and students' and teachers' understandings of linguistic diversity. Her publications have appeared in *English Education, English Journal,* and *Language Arts,* among others. Jane coedited *Teaching Language Arts: Learning Through Dialogue* for the National Council of Teachers of English. She earned her master's and doctorate degrees from the University of Texas, Austin. jst@coe.ufl.edu

Jenny Tsankova is Assistant Professor of Mathematics Education at Roger Williams University, where she teaches mathematics methods courses for preservice teachers. She is also Director of Mathematics Teacher Training for Teachers 21, a major professional development provider in the New England area. She specializes in helping teachers diagnose student learning difficulties and selecting developmentally appropriate interventions. Her research focuses on the algebraic reasoning of elementary and middle school students, and the adoption of international best practices in preservice and inservice programs. Jenny coedited a National Council of Supervisors of Mathematics monograph and coauthored a K–1 textbook, *The Number Crew.* Her advanced degrees were earned at Sophia University, Bulgaria, and Boston University. jtsankova@rwu.edu

David White is the Science Assessment Coordinator for the Vermont Department of Education. He oversees the development and implementation of the statewide science assessment program, Vermont-PASS. He was a codirector of Vermont's Grade Expectation project. David is a former Senior Research Associate with WestEd and a classroom teacher for 15 years. In his current work, he develops strategies for using Vermont's Grade to design and implement local comprehensive science assessment systems. His master's degree was earned at the University of Vermont. dwhite@doe.state.vt.us

PART I

Teaching and Learning Through Inquiry in the Content Areas

It is error only, and not truth, that shrinks from inquiry.

—Thomas Paine

C an you recall the first time you heard the term *inquiry* used to describe an approach to teaching and learning? For me (Richard Audet), the memory is still vivid. It was during the late 1960s, and I was part of a huge wave of eager new teachers determined to change the face of education. At this time, proponents of inquiry were at their ascendancy. Educators call this the alphabet soup era because of the explosion of innovative curriculum projects with acronyms such as MACOS, IPS, SCIS, and PSSC. My high school was caught up in this tide of reform and adopted textbooks produced by the Biological Sciences Curriculum Study (BSCS) project. BSCS was, and still is, among the leaders in developing instructional materials that feature an exploratory approach.

Despite their high quality and orientation toward investigation, such student-centered materials failed to gain a substantive and permanent foothold in most schools. My brief story, told from the perspective of an unaccomplished novice from that time period, may explain why such materials failed to meet the original high and widely held expectations.

During the early stages of my development as a teacher, I was heavily dependent on BSCS's vision of effective biology instruction. Because of my lack of experience, I had few other choices. Never in my K–12 education, except for mandatory science fairs, was I offered challenging opportunities to learn through inquiry. Never in the 7 years spent obtaining my biology degrees had I heard the word *inquiry* used to describe this scientific way of knowing. Never in the early stages of my teaching career did I receive professional development to prepare me for this new style of instruction. Because I was forced to rely exclusively on my own naïve interpretation of the BSCS model, most of my instructional decisions were based solely on intuitive hunches. The unfortunate yet fully predictable ending of this tale was that several years later, my department abandoned BSCS curricula in favor of more traditional textbooks and approaches—another illustration of "the discrepancy between beliefs about the importance of inquiry teaching and actual school practice" (DeBoer, 1991, p. 109).

Surprisingly, these pioneering curriculum movements proved to have an enduring impact on the educational community. True believers of inquiry persevered, and, like fine wine, their ideas and understandings continued to improve and mature over time. Aided by formal research and considerable trial and error, more finely tuned approaches and deeply rooted personal philosophies about inquiry appeared in the literature. Eventually, national content standards emerged that included strong and clear statements about inquiry.

Today, an ever-increasing number of inquiry-based classrooms from all areas of study suggest that educators learned from these lessons of the past. Such settings are supported by rich curricula that incorporate cognitive research findings, research-based instructional models, strategies for differentiating among learners, and technologies that offer immediate access to information and data. Inquiry *teachers* possess an inquiry "stance" (Cochran-Smith & Lytle, 1999), a disposition toward teaching that assigns more value to a good question than a correct answer. Inquiry *learners* are curious and eager to search for explanations, and they accept responsibility for their learning. Inquiry-based *curriculum* materials incorporate open-ended invitations to explore and accommodate alternative explanations and interpretations. Inquiry *assessment* is authentic and carefully aligned with the goals for student learning. Inquiry *classrooms* are noisy, semichaotic places populated by students and teachers wearing happy, quizzical, and satisfied expressions.

This book's major sections were shaped by the contributors' contemporary beliefs, ideas, and understandings about inquiry. Part I begins with an overview of inquiry as an overarching theme for teaching and learning that cuts across all areas of the K–12 curriculum. In the five chapters that follow, content area experts examine inquiry from the unique perspectives offered by geography, science, history, mathematics, and English language arts. This section's final chapter examines inquiry in terms of its potential for supporting seamless curriculum integration.

REFERENCES

Cochran-Smith, M., & Lytle, S. (1999). Relationships of knowledge and practice: Teacher learning in communities. *Review of Research in Education, 24*(8), 249–305.

DeBoer, G. E. (1991). *A history of ideas in science education: Implications for practice.* New York: Teachers College Press.

CHAPTER ONE

Inquiry

A Continuum of Ideas, Issues, and Practices

Richard H. Audet

Inquiry is not a "method" of doing science, history, or any other subject in which the obligatory first stage in a fixed, linear sequence is that of students each formulating questions to investigate. Rather, it is an approach to the chosen themes and topics in which the posing of real questions is positively encouraged whenever they occur and by whoever they are asked. Equally important as the hallmark of an inquiry approach is that all tentative answers are taken seriously and are investigated as rigorously as the circumstances permit.

—Wells (1999)

DIFFERENCES AND SIMILARITIES

Distinctions among academic disciplines arise from their principal elements of interest. Unique approaches and tools help answer the special brand of questions that puzzle its disciples. Geographers investigate spatially referenced objects with modern technologies such as global positioning systems. Scientists study phenomena with equipment that extends the senses. Historians seek to understand events using evidentiary documents, historic narratives, and forensic instruments. Symbolic representations and high-speed computers are integral features for understanding the mathematical domain. For students of language, answers are found through private and public interpretations of text. People are the stuff of universal and eternal curiosity. Inquiry—the practice of extracting meaning from experience—is the habit that binds. It drives the pursuit of understanding across all areas of study. Every chapter in Part I explores this dichotomy between the common practice of inquiry among the disciplines and the special approaches and tools that support inquiry within each content area.

Ideas

References to seminal educational thinkers such as John Dewey, Lev Vygotsky, Jean Piaget, and Jerome Bruner appear throughout this book. These foundational figures offered their perspectives on inquiry and explained why problem solving provides an all-important context for actively engaging students in meaningful learning. Their combined work created an impetus for grounding classrooms in inquiry across all areas of the curriculum.

The legion of ideas, beliefs, definitions, and descriptions of inquiry all boil down to one: *Inquiry is any activity aimed at extracting meaning from experience.* Whether it is a fire marshal sifting though a pile of smoldering ashes, a team of geologists analyzing Mount St. Helen's seismic data, or students asking probing questions about the lingering impact of the Civil War based on their reading of *Confederates in the Attic* (Horwitz, 1998), all of these preoccupations share the characteristic of being a search for understanding.

Although most commonly associated with science, inquiry includes an overarching set of principles, process skills, and a comprehensive information base that is relevant for thinking about effective classroom practice in all fields of study. As Dow (1999) stated, "Inquiry has its roots in the inherent restlessness of the human mind" (p. 5). All bodies of knowledge emerge from collective attempts to answer a discipline's core questions.

DeBoer (1991) presented an excellent overview of how inquiry teaching evolved. He noted that over time, inquiry teaching came to be associated with a set of instructional practices that [is] . . . inductive in nature. Inductive approaches are based on the premise that students can be inquirers in classrooms and generate meaning more or less independently by examining a variety of available learning materials. (p. 208)

Inquiry is often falsely equated with having students perform hands-on activities. Students who are engaged in mathematical inquiry might be doing *gedanken,* or thought experiments. History students could be analyzing online primary source documents. Conversely, a set of highly engaging activities about Egypt could have the look and feel of inquiry. But as pointed out by Marlowe and Page in Chapter 9, unless these learning experiences foster significant understanding of geography concepts, they constitute "sham" inquiry. What distinguishes inquiry from other classroom events is the attempt to draw meaning out of experience. Without driving, answerable questions and an emphasis on sense making, no classroom experience has a true connection with the process of inquiry.

Inquiry is not an all-or-nothing proposition. Like most practices and habits of mind, it manifests itself along a continuum that shifts according to time, place, and circumstance. As the inquiry model presented in the science chapter illustrates, the principal factor that determines the level of inquiry is the relative amounts of student versus teacher control over an activity. The skills, processes, tools, and elements of inquiry are developmental. Skillful teachers know that choosing the most appropriate instructional strategy is influenced by the time of year, age level, amount of experience, and nature of the learning activity. Gradual release of control over classroom events is how most teachers phase inquiry into their programs.

Issues

Chapter 7, which addresses curriculum integration, points out that elementary school teachers have the monumental task of helping students achieve standards-setting performances across the entire range of disciplines. Despite the fact that there are so many standards and so little time, teachers must fulfill this responsibility as a condition of their continued employment. Integrated approaches to delivering curriculum may be the only viable means of addressing the multitude of standards that students must meet during their K–12 education.

A crosswalk is a systematic procedure for generating and representing cross-comparison data. In the matrix given in Figure 1.1, the science-as-inquiry standards serve as anchor points for comparing how standards from different content areas treat the topic of inquiry. Science was chosen as the basis for comparison because the National Science Education Standards (National Research Council, 1996) make such a strong commitment to inquiry. The science standards divide inquiry into Abilities to Do Inquiry and Understandings About Inquiry, and treat it as a distinct content standard area.

In preparing the crosswalk, national standards from all major disciplines were reviewed and technology standards were added. The information in Figure 1.1 is my own interpretation of how different standards address the topic of inquiry.

As these data indicate, elements of inquiry cut across all of the national standards. This offers compelling evidence that teaching and learning through inquiry is a natural and coherent way to simultaneously approach standards from a multitude of disciplines, and to do so with strong intention. Such an approach is one way to address Fogarty's (2002) claim that "the only way the compendium of standards can possibly be met is by clustering standards into logical bundles and addressing them in an explicit and integrated fashion" (p. 1).

Practices

Delisle (1992) maintained that "all education involves either problem solving or preparation for problem solving" (p. 1). Teachers from across the full K–16 spectrum are increasingly using open-ended, in-depth explorations to create rich educational contexts in which the artificial barriers between disciplines are reduced or eliminated. Any novice-to-expert shift is apt to be stressful. Teachers who are moving toward inquiry commonly experience an initial sense of unease during the period when questions remain unanswered and children are adapting to the unfamiliar roles of question posers and problem solvers.

Creating conditions that reinforce inquiry must be systemic and sustained. Inquiry-based teaching and learning pay special attention to motivational factors, provide opportunities for social interaction, and create active learning environments. In such settings, traditional classroom roles for students and teachers are blurred, and formats for assessment are multiple, varied, and carefully aligned with the relevant content standards.

Figure 1.1 Standards Crosswalk

SCIENCE	GEOGRAPHY	ENGLISH/ LANG. ARTS	HISTORY	MATHEMATICS	TECHNOLOGY
ABILITY: Ask a question about objects, organisms, and the events in the environment.		7. Students conduct research on issues and interests by generating ideas and questions, and by posing problems . . .	3. **Historical Analysis and Interpretation** A. Formulate questions to focus their inquiry or analysis. 2. **Historical Comprehension** C. Identify the central question(s) the historical narrative addresses. 4. **Historical Research Capabilities** A. Formulate historical questions.	1. **Problem Solving** B. Solve problems that arise in mathematics and in other contexts.	
ABILITY: Plan and conduct a simple investigation.		3. Students apply a wide range of strategies to comprehend, interpret, evaluate, and appreciate texts . . .	4. **Historical Research Capabilities** D. Marshal needed knowledge of the time and place, and construct a story, explanation, or historical narrative.	1. **Problem Solving** C. Apply and adapt a variety of appropriate strategies to solve problems. D. Monitor and reflect on the process of mathematical problem solving.	
ABILITY: Employ simple equipment and tools to gather data and extend the senses.	How to use maps and other geographic representations, tools, and technologies to acquire, process, and report information.	8. Students use a variety of technological and information resources . . .	1. **Chronological Thinking** D. Measure and calculate calendar time.		7. Routinely and efficiently use online information resources to meet needs for collaboration, research, publications, communications, and productivity.

(Continued)

Figure 1.1 (Continued)

SCIENCE	GEOGRAPHY	ENGLISH/ LANG. ARTS	HISTORY	MATHEMATICS	TECHNOLOGY
ABILITY: Use data to construct a reasonable explanation.	How to use mental maps to organize information about people, places, and environments.	7. . . . they gather, evaluate, and synthesize data from a variety of sources.	**1. Chronological Thinking** E. Interpret data presented in time lines. G. Explain change and continuity over time. **2. Historical Comprehension** F. Draw upon data in historical maps. G. Draw upon visual and mathematical data presented in graphs. H. Draw upon the visual data presented in photographs, paintings, cartoons, and architectural drawings. **4. Historical Research Capabilities** B. Obtain historical data. C. Interrogate historical data.	**5. Representation** A. Create and use representations to organize, record, and communicate mathematical ideas. B. Select, apply, and translate among mathematical representations to solve problems. C. Use representations to model and interpret physical, social, and mathematical phenomena.	
UNDERSTANDING: Scientific investigations involve asking and answering a question and comparing the answer with what scientists already know about the world.	How to analyze the spatial organization of people, places, and environments on Earth's surface.	3. . . . Students draw on their prior experience, their interactions with other readers and writers, their knowledge of word meaning and of other texts, their word identification strategies, and their understanding of textual features.			

10

SCIENCE	GEOGRAPHY	ENGLISH/LANG. ARTS	HISTORY	MATHEMATICS	TECHNOLOGY
UNDERSTANDING: Scientists use different kinds of investigations depending on the questions they are trying to answer. Types of investigations include describing objects, events, and organisms; classifying them; and doing a fair test.			5. **Historical Issues-Analysis and Decision-Making** A. Identify problems and dilemmas in the past. B. Analyze the interests and values of the various people involved. C. Identify causes of the problem or dilemma. D. Propose alternative choices for addressing the problem. E. Formulate a position or course of action on an issue. F. Identify the solution chosen. G. Evaluate the consequences of a decision.	1. **Problem Solving** A. Build new mathematical knowledge through problem solving.	
UNDERSTANDING: Simple instruments, such as magnifiers, thermometers, and rulers, provide more information than scientists obtain using only their senses.					8. Select and apply technology tools for research, information analysis, problem solving, and decision making in content learning.

(*Continued*)

Figure 1.1 (Continued)

SCIENCE	GEOGRAPHY	ENGLISH/ LANG. ARTS	HISTORY	MATHEMATICS	TECHNOLOGY
UNDERSTANDING: Scientists develop explanations using observations (evidence) and what they already know about the world (scientific knowledge). Good explanations are based on evidence from investigations.		8. . . . Students gather and synthesize information and create and communicate knowledge.	3. **Historical Analysis and Interpretation** B. Compare and contrast differing sets of ideas, values, personalities, behaviors, and institutions. C. Analyze historical fiction. D. Distinguish between fact and fiction. E. Compare different stories about a historical figure, era, or event. F. Analyze illustrations in historical stories. G. Consider multiple perspectives. H. Explain causes in analyzing historical actions. I. Challenge arguments of historical inevitability. J. Hypothesize influences of the past.	2. **Reasoning and Proof** A. Recognize reasoning and proof as fundamental aspects of mathematics. B. Make and investigate mathematical conjectures. C. Develop and evaluate mathematical arguments and proofs. D. Select and use various types of reasoning and methods of proof.	

12

SCIENCE	GEOGRAPHY	ENGLISH/ LANG. ARTS	HISTORY	MATHEMATICS	TECHNOLOGY
UNDERSTANDING: Scientists make the results of their investigations public; they describe the investigations in ways that enable others to repeat the investigations.		7. . . . communicate their discoveries in ways that suit their purpose and audience.		10. Collaborate with peers, experts, and others to contribute to a content-related knowledge base by using technology to compile, synthesize, produce, and disseminate information, models, and other creative works.	5. Use technology tools and resources for managing and communicating personal/ professional information.
UNDERSTANDING: Scientists review and ask questions about the results of other scientists' work.				4. **Connections** A. Recognize and use connections among mathematical ideas. B. Understand how mathematical ideas interconnect and build on one another to produce a coherent whole. C. Recognize and apply mathematics in contexts outside of mathematics.	

Some people do not routinely wonder about the unknown. Strong inquiry teachers do. They possess an inquiry stance (Cochran-Smith & Lytle, 1999). This refers to a general way of thinking about teaching characterized by a preference for asking instead of answering questions and an eagerness to move away from center stage. Learning to tolerate ambiguity in the classroom can be difficult for everyone. Children need constant support and reassurance that they are fully equipped to meet the challenge of taking charge of their own learning. The essential features of an inquiry-based classroom are engagement in activities that are congruent with the developmental readiness of students, frequent opportunities to ask and answer questions, a gradual but steady movement toward student control over the learning environment, and a growing record of successful accomplishments. Watching children as they solve problems or clarify issues is like observing a muddy suspension change over time. What first appears as cloudy or even opaque gradually clears as understanding emerges.

As an instructional framework, classroom inquiry is often depicted as a set of recurring learning events commonly referred to as the inquiry cycle. Although they differ in detail, most models include stages during which students

- Ask an answerable question or identify a researchable problem
- Develop a plan and take some form of action
- Gather resources; analyze and summarize information
- Draw conclusions and report findings
- Reflect on the process

Because learning through this type of format is highly responsive to the context, the process is dynamic rather than linear, rigid, and prescriptive. And a particular inquiry experience may include only portions of the complete cycle.

The following chapters demonstrate that using inquiry approaches to teach and help children learn is fully consistent with student-centered, activity-based, and constructivist models of instruction. Enduring dispositions are the principal goal of inquiry-based learning experiences because these "habits of mind and tendencies" are what students need "to respond to categories of experiences across classes of situations" (Katz & Chard, 1994, p. 30). Adept problem-solving adults have the cognitive flexibility needed to successfully apply what is learned in one context to a myriad of novel circumstances.

REFERENCES

Cochran-Smith, M., & Lytle, S. (1999). Relationships of knowledge and practice: Teacher learning in communities. *Review of Research in Education, 24*(8), 249–305.

DeBoer, G. E. (1991). *A history of ideas in science education: Implications for practice.* New York: Teachers College Press.

Delisle, R. (1992). *How to use problem-based learning in the classroom.* Alexandria, VA: Association for Supervision and Curriculum Development.

Dow, P. (1999). Why inquiry? A historical and philosophical commentary. In *Foundations, Volume II, A monograph for professionals in science, mathematics, and technology education: Inquiry, thoughts, views, and strategies for the K–5 classroom* (pp. 5–8). Arlington, VA: National Science Foundation.

Fogarty, R. (2002). *How to integrate the curricula.* Arlington Heights, IL: SkyLight Professional Development.

Horwitz, T. (1998). *Confederates in the attic.* New York: Random House.

Katz, L. C., & Chard, S. C. (1994). *Engaging children's minds: The project approach.* Norwood, NJ: Ablex.

National Research Council. (1996). *National science education standards.* Washington, DC: National Academy Press.

Wells, G. (1999). *Dialogic inquiry in education: Building on the legacy of Vygotsky.* Cambridge, UK: Cambridge University Press.

CHAPTER TWO

Social Studies and Geography

Beyond Rote Memorization

Alan Canestrari

> *Isn't telling about something—using words . . . already something of an invention? Isn't just looking upon this world already something of an invention? . . . The world isn't just the way it is. It is how we understand it, no? And in understanding something, we bring something to it, no? Doesn't that make life a story?*
>
> —Martel (2001)

Imagine that the correct answer to the following question will break the tie between you and your toughest competitor and secure you a $25,000 college scholarship, a lifetime membership to the National Geographic Society, a trip to Sea World, and the prestigious title of 2003 National Geographic Bee Champion. "Goa, a state in southwestern India, was a possession of which country until 1961?" Alex Trebek, the host of *Jeopardy!* and moderator of the Bee, keeps time as the clock ticks down the 12 seconds you have to respond. Tick, tick, tick . . . the pressure is on. Goa? 1961? Couldn't be Great Britain, could it? Suddenly, your thought pattern is interrupted when Alex says, "Sorry, your time is up. Your answer please."

. . . Silence. Your nemesis, James Williams, 14, of Vancouver, Washington, isn't silent. He gets the correct answer, the membership, the money, the trip, and the title (Vernon, 2003). You can find the answer toward the end of the chapter.

The National Geographic Bee is a wonderful event and a yearly testament to teachers, students, and those committed to geographic literacy, high standards, and the development of a geographically informed citizenry. James and his peers are certainly brainy and very well prepared. But how did they become so knowledgeable? What informed the instructional approaches used by their geography teachers? How were their classrooms engaged in learning geography?

The success enjoyed by the Geographic Bee may conceal the answers to these important questions. At first glance, given the content, structure, and protocol of the Bee, one might infer that the geography instruction James received emphasized rote memorization, and a style of teaching focused on transmitting a vast array of bits and pieces of information. This assumption may be correct in some cases. Imagine classrooms where instruction consists primarily of Bee-like questions: In March 2003, thousands of endangered sea turtles returned to the Bay of Bengal to nest on beaches in the state of Orissa in which country? What Asian country organized its citizens into a strict caste system related to Hinduism? Maharashtra borders the Arabian Sea and is one of the most urbanized states of which Asian country? Yes, the answer to all of these questions is India ("Test Yourself," 2003). But in what context were these questions asked? Did the students ask the questions? In what ways were students involved in discovering answers? In what ways were students encouraged to learn?

RITUALS, ROUTINES, AND ROTE

To contrast the difference between learning geography in order to compete in a Bee and learning that targets the geography content standards, let us consider Mr. Baker's approach to teaching and learning. Mr. Baker teaches in the eighth grade and uses a world geography survey textbook to guide the organization of the curriculum and the content of his instruction. For example, on a particular day, Mr. Baker might assign the students a section of the chapter on India. Students read, take notes, and answer the section review questions. Each lesson begins with Mr. Baker, grade book in hand, moving up one aisle and down another checking student homework. A check or check plus is entered for the dutiful students, and a check minus or zero is entered for the less dedicated students.

Then, Mr. Baker calls on students who have raised their hands to provide answers to the section review questions. If a student responds incorrectly, the teacher or another student provides the correct answer, then Mr. Baker moves on to the next question. Sometimes, Mr. Baker offers explanations, extends the discussion, or makes clarifications with wall maps, charts, and photographs in the text. Occasionally, Mr. Baker implements an instructional suggestion made in the teacher's edition, which typically calls for completing a worksheet from the teacher's resource manual. Students are allowed to work in groups provided the noise level remains within reasonable limits. Mr. Baker usually complements this form of instruction with an occasional trip to the computer lab, videos, special map assignments, or projects. But generally, Mr. Baker conducts class in a lecture-discussion format.

On this day in Mr. Baker's class, students have completed reading the following excerpt from a packet of reproducible worksheets and are about to answer the questions aloud.

The Bengal tiger is one of the best-known and larger cat species in India. It is usually about 10 ft. long including its tail, and weighs more than 400 pounds. The Bengal tiger, a carnivore well camouflaged by its rich tawny color and dark stripes, lives on blackbuck deer, livestock, and fish. It can be found in the savanna, wetlands, and forests of central and southern India. Tigers have seen their forest sanctuaries disappear, and poachers have hunted them to near extinction.

1. What does the Bengal tiger look like?
2. What is a carnivore?
3. Where in India can the Bengal tiger be found?
4. Why has the Bengal tiger been placed on the endangered species list?

Here is what a typical exchange between Mr. Baker and his students sounds like: "Attention . . . I trust everyone has completed the worksheet. Who would like to begin?" Sarah dutifully raises her hand, and after a nod from Mr. Baker, she reads question #1 and her answer. "What does the Bengal tiger look like? The Bengal tiger is a large animal about 10 feet long from its nose to the tip of its tail and it weighs more than 400 pounds. It has a rich tawny color with dark stripes." Mr. Baker acknowledges her response with, "Good job, Sarah," and then continues in the same manner until all the questions on the worksheet are answered.

Every Friday, Mr. Baker administers a test that consists of some multiple-choice questions, true or false questions, fill in the blanks, and short answers. A few students fail, but most earn passing grades. Even though he will not return to the content on India for the remainder of the year, Mr. Baker feels confident that the generally strong test scores indicate that he has adequately covered the content and that his students have learned the material. This "traxoline" approach, a euphemism for fact-based busy work, coined by Judith Lanier of Michigan State University, works for Mr. Baker. But during this unit, Mr. Baker clearly wasted the opportunity to deliver instruction in a more meaningful, empowering way. He and his students missed the chance to investigate the connection between the disappearance of Bengal tigers and humans and animals vying for the same space. Mr. Baker is regarded as competent by the administration, faculty, staff, and parents and is well liked by students. But is his model of teaching and learning a powerful approach for stimulating student interest in geography? What do you think? What questions would you ask of Mr. Baker? What questions could he have used to truly engage his students?

POWERFUL SOCIAL STUDIES

The notion of powerful social studies is discussed extensively in the National Council for the Social Studies's (1994) position statement, *A Vision of Powerful Teaching and Learning in the Social Studies: Building Social Understanding and Civic Efficacy.* The following questions, which are adapted from the position statement, might provide a departure point for our analysis of Mr. Baker's instruction:

- Is the teaching and learning *meaningful*? Are students simply required to memorize facts? Is the teacher concerned more with coverage than understanding, appreciation, and life application? Is the teacher a reflective practitioner?

- Is the teaching and learning *integrative*? Are students involved in activities that incorporate essential skill development? Are students experiencing lessons that demonstrate interdisciplinary connections?
- Is the teaching and learning *value-based*? Are students applying value-based reasoning when addressing issues and problems? Are students encouraged to take social responsibility and action?
- Is the teaching and learning *challenging*? Is the teacher a problem-poser? Are students thinking critically and creatively about issues? Is the teacher modeling thoughtful inquiry? Are students exposed to a variety of sources and multiple perspectives?
- Is the teaching and learning *active*? Are students involved in the active construction of knowledge and meaning? Are the students functioning as a learning community? (pp. 162–170)

Unfortunately, much of the teaching and learning that takes place in our schools is altogether reminiscent of what we observe in Mr. Baker's classroom. All too often, children are exposed to this traditional, authoritarian ritual and routine that creates conformity, compliance, and passivity—experiences that are considerably less than powerful. But what is the alternative? What theory of learning and methodological approaches support powerful social studies teaching? What ideas and innovations can make the learning experience more powerful for students?

THE "NEW" SOCIAL STUDIES

Questions about what constitutes effective teaching and learning are hardly new, having been posed and discussed since the latter part of the 19th century and into the present. Possible answers have been examined and reexamined, and they continue to fuel dialogue and debate. Recently, there has been a renewed interest and reexamination of the ideas of progressive educators such as reformer Francis Parker and philosopher John Dewey.

In the late 19th century, Francis Parker, in his books *Talks on Teaching* and *Talks on Pedagogics,* suggested that the study of geography could be accomplished more effectively through field trips during which children used their observational skills to study and map the land around them. He encouraged teachers to help students ask questions, speculate, and make generalizations. He recommended using a variety of classroom resources instead of limiting students to information found in a single textbook (Zarrillo, 2004, pp. 8–9).

John Dewey, in *Experience and Education* (1972), argued that some classroom experiences are "mis-educative" and may hinder the development of understanding rather than promote it. Here is how Dewey framed the issue:

The belief that all genuine education comes through experience does not mean that all experiences are genuinely or equally educative. Experience and education cannot be directly equated to each other. For some experiences are mis-educative. Any experience is mis-educative that has the effect of arresting or distorting the growth of further experience. An experience may be such as to engender callousness; it may produce lack of sensitivity and responsiveness. Then the possibilities of having richer experience in the future are restricted. (pp. 25–26)

Dewey made a case for the abandonment of authoritarian teaching methods in favor of an emphasis on child-centered experiences. The progressive approaches of the latter part of the 19th century and early 20th century enjoyed brief success but fell from grace because critics perceived them as flimsy, permissive, and lacking rigor.

The Soviet Union's launch of Sputnik in 1957 fueled an already growing fear that American students were not keeping pace with the challenges of the cold war. In the fall of 1959, the National Academy of Sciences—with support from the U.S. Office of Education, the National Science Foundation, the RAND Corporation, and the military—hosted a conference in Woods Hole, Massachusetts, to discuss how science education could be improved at all grade levels. Attending the conference were many prominent university scholars, including Jerome Bruner. According to Bruner (1961),

The history of science is studded with examples of men "finding out" something and not knowing it. I shall operate on the assumption that discovery, whether by a schoolboy going it on his own or by a scientist cultivating the growing edge of his field, is in its essence a matter of rearranging or transforming evidence in such a way that one is enabled to go beyond the evidence so reassembled to new insights. (p. 22)

Bruner's views would influence the direction of science, math, language arts, and social studies education. His report's findings prompted a new wave of reform and government and private funding for university studies, curriculum development, and inservice projects based on discovery learning or the inquiry method. The inquiry method, once the exclusive domain of scholars to generate new knowledge and ideas, was now being promoted as the best way for students to learn.

In the social studies—or the New Social Studies, as it was labeled by Edwin Fenton (1961)—discovery also took on a distinctly Brunerian flavor. Bruner featured his ideas in his own curricular project titled "Man: A Course of Study (MACOS)." Bruner believed that all instruction should be organized around the contextual structure of the discipline, and that knowledge and understanding can be discovered through the structure of the discipline. In the case of social studies, students should learn content through the same processes and tools of inquiry used by historians and social scientists. To illustrate, teachers should engage their students in activities that are used by historians, anthropologists, political scientists, geographers, and so forth. He coined the term *spiral curriculum* to explain his idea that any concept or principle could be taught to any child at any age. At higher grade levels, ideas would unravel as students revisited topics at increasingly sophisticated levels. He believed that student learning ought to be dominated by inquiry—the process of solving problems and answering questions—and that this inductive method should be positioned within a constructivist theory of learning.

Moving Toward a Constructivist Classroom

Teachers who perceive themselves as progressives often invoke the term *constructivist* to describe their own practice. But are they truly constructivists? Teachers seeking to create and sustain constructivist classrooms might reflect on their practices by considering the following picture of constructivism offered by Marlowe and Page (1998):

The main proposition of constructivism is that learning means constructing, creating, inventing, and developing our own knowledge. Others can give us information, we can find information in books, and we can get information from the media, but as important as information is—and it is very important—receiving it, getting it, and hearing it does not necessarily equal learning. Learning in constructivist terms is:

- both the process and result of questioning, interpreting, and analyzing information;
- using this information and thinking process to develop, build, and alter our meaning and understanding of concepts and ideas; and
- integrating current experiences with our past experiences and what we already know about a given subject. (p. 10)

This description should strike a cautionary note with teachers who believe that instruction sprinkled with cooperative learning, alternative seating arrangements, computer-aided instruction, videos, and field trips makes for a constructivist learning environment. Successful constructivist practices depend on a deep understanding of how children learn. Helping students to develop determination and critical thinking requires more than the superficial use of "snappy" activities or "stir and serve" techniques. Teachers invested in constructivism must be courageous in their advocacy for children and steadfast in their commitment to meaningful instructional and assessment practices. This is particularly challenging given what Brooks and Brooks (1999) observe about the narrowing of curricula to match what is covered on high-stakes and statewide assessments. But in this era of accountability, what principles must teachers seek to promote and sustain? Brooks and Brooks suggest the following:

- Keeping essential principles and recurring concepts at the center of curriculum and instruction.
- Keeping the assessment of student learning within the context of daily instruction.
- Using assessments to guide teaching.
- Keeping students free to think, question, reflect, and to interact with ideas, objects and others. (p. 8)

Do you recall Mr. Baker's geography class? Examine Figure 2.1 below. What is the effect of teacher talk on students? What is lost in the traditional teacher-dominated classroom? What is gained in the

Figure 2.1   Teacher-Dominated Instruction Versus Student-Centered Instruction

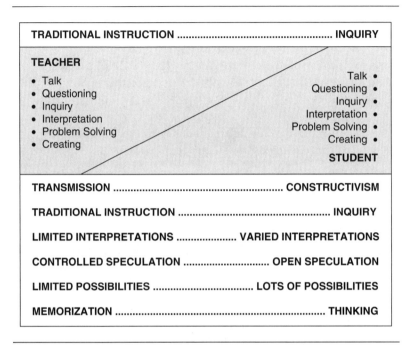

TRADITIONAL INSTRUCTION .... INQUIRY

TEACHER
- Talk
- Questioning
- Inquiry
- Interpretation
- Problem Solving
- Creating

Talk •
Questioning •
Inquiry •
Interpretation •
Problem Solving •
Creating •

STUDENT

TRANSMISSION .... CONSTRUCTIVISM

TRADITIONAL INSTRUCTION .... INQUIRY

LIMITED INTERPRETATIONS .... VARIED INTERPRETATIONS

CONTROLLED SPECULATION .... OPEN SPECULATION

LIMITED POSSIBILITIES .... LOTS OF POSSIBILITIES

MEMORIZATION .... THINKING

constructivist classroom when students have time to investigate and create meaning and knowledge? Where on the continuum are you?

Geographers on Geography

What does it mean to be a geographer? How do geographers define geography? What is geography about? What principles and concepts occupy the center of geography curriculum and instruction? What does the "geographically informed person" know and understand? The document "Geography for Life, National Geography Standards" (1994) provides answers to these questions and a compass for those seeking direction, credibility, and legitimacy in geography curriculum and instruction. The National Council for Geographic Education (1994) subscribes to the definition of geography as a "discipline that integrates the physical and human dimensions of the world in the study of people, places, and environments" (p. 1). Geography, as the progressives pointed out long ago, has much to do with questions and problem solving, issues-based or problem-based inquiry, and little to do with factual recall, rote memorization, and chasing the right answer.

The National Geography Standards provide guidance in the matter of essential elements, standards, perspectives, and skills of the "geographically informed person" (see Figure 2.2). The ultimate goal of the national standards is to help develop geographically informed people who

- See meaning in the arrangement of things in space
- Recognize relationships among people, places, and environments
- Use geographic skills
- Apply spatial and ecological perspectives to life situations (Geography for Life, 1994)

For students to successfully observe patterns, associations, and spatial order, these skills must be practiced in context. These skills are the necessary tools and techniques that enable us to think geographically. Geography for Life identifies five sets of geographic skills:

- Asking geographic questions
- Acquiring geographic information
- Organizing geographic information
- Analyzing geographic information
- Answering geographic questions

Overall, the standards and the related content suggested by the document are helpful in informing curriculum and instruction and particularly accurate in capturing the structure of geography. However, a critical examination of the information reveals that the standards are somewhat antiseptic, decontextualized, and depoliticized. These factors may not be problematic for seasoned social scientists and veteran geographers, but may well pose difficulties for the typical classroom teacher, especially if standards are solely relied on for making curricular and instructional decisions. Standards may pose problems for teachers who have little experience interpreting them, who are seeking teacher-proof prescriptions for effective instruction, or whose worldview encourages literal interpretation of the standards and who do not entertain a thematic or problem-based approach to content.

Teachers must be careful not to misuse the standards. Posting standards around the classroom does little to improve learning or

Figure 2.2   The National Geography Essential Elements and Standards

ESSENTIAL ELEMENTS	STANDARDS
THE WORLD IN SPATIAL TERMS	1. How to use maps and other geographic representations, tools, and technologies to acquire, process, and report information. 2. How to use mental maps to organize information about people, places, and environments. 3. How to analyze the spatial organization of people, places, and environments on Earth's surface.
PLACES AND REGIONS	4. The physical and human characteristics of places. 5. That people create regions to interpret Earth's complexity. 6. How culture and experience influence people's perception of places and regions.
PHYSICAL SYSTEMS	7. The physical processes that shape the patterns of Earth's surface. 8. The characteristics and spatial distribution of ecosystems on Earth's surface.
HUMAN SYSTEMS	9. The characteristics, distribution, and migration of human populations on Earth's surface. 10. The characteristics, distributions, and complexity of Earth's cultural mosaics. 11. The patterns and networks of economic interdependence on Earth's surface. 12. The process, patterns, and functions of human settlement. 13. How forces of cooperation and conflict among people influence the division and control of Earth's surface.
ENVIRONMENT AND SOCIETY	14. How human actions modify the physical environment. 15. How physical systems affect human systems. 16. The changes that occur in the meaning, use, distribution, and importance of resources.
THE USES OF GEOGRAPHY	17. How to apply geography to interpret the past. 18. How to apply geography to interpret the present and plan for the future.

guarantee student achievement. Even citing standards as goal statements adds little to the inquiry-based constructivist classroom (or any classroom, for that matter). Both of these practices simply add to the nominal memorization of people, places, and processes. It is best to think of the geography standards from a holistic perspective in the same way that events, both physical and cultural, occur in a complex, connected, and interrelated world. Rather than using the geography standards as a departure point for geography instruction, standards and the principles and concepts they represent ought to emerge over time from the context of the instruction and investigations, and as students themselves make observations, connections, realizations, discoveries, and predictions, and solve problems like practicing geographers. Knowledge discovered through inquiry within the constructivist classroom has permanence because it is a function of the educative experience, a function of induced generalizations, conclusions . . . standards.

Inquiry, Involvement, and Investigation

Given the tentative conclusions that might now be brewing about teaching and learning geography, consider Ms. Andrews's approach. Here is a glimpse of an exchange between Ms. Andrews, an eighth-grade geography teacher, and a group of students that has been reading *Gandhi Great Soul* (1997) by John B. Severance. The book is biographical, with numerous snapshots that depict Gandhi, India, and its people. The students just finished viewing a few photographs and reading the following passages:

At the same time that Gandhi was helping the mill workers, he was coping with another problem at home. Plague had broken out in Kochrab shortly after Gandhi returned to the ashram. In his autobiography he wrote, "It was impossible to keep ourselves immune from the effects of the surrounding insanitation, however scrupulously we might observe the rules of cleanliness within the Ashram walls." Unable to persuade the villagers to adopt good sanitary procedures and afraid for the health of the children in the ashram, Gandhi decided to move it to a location on the Sabarmati River.

One of the crops grown at the new Sabarmati Ashram was cotton, which was hand woven into a coarse cloth called khadi. Gandhi's idea was to avoid buying more expensive cotton woven in England and also to encourage a village industry so Indian peasants could try to pull themselves out of poverty. He decided to create even more self-sufficiency by hand spinning of cotton yarn. He knew nothing about spinning, but a wealthy widow located an antique portable spinning wheel, or charkha, and he began to learn. In time, caps and shirts made of khadi became sort of a rough uniform for Gandhi's followers. The rhythmic hum of the charkhas became heard all over India, and Gandhi used his own wheel to make a sort of soothing music for meditation in his simple study at Sabarmati. (pp. 64–66)

Ms. Andrews visits the Gandhi group and asks, "What have you discovered?" The children respond with a flurry of ideas. Michael says, "A plague broke out in Kochrab, and Gandhi moved the ashram to a place on the Sabarmati River." Sonia adds, "The people of the village were poor, and Gandhi showed them how to spin cotton yarn to make cloth called khadi." Ms. Andrews asks, "Do you have any questions that you would like to investigate? "I do," says Laura as she inspects a world atlas to find the exact location of Kochrab and the Sabarmati River so that the locations can be transferred to a large student map of India. "Why did the peasants have to buy cotton cloth woven in England?" Toni asks, "What did the charkha sound like?" "Those are great questions. Let's record your questions and develop some hypotheses for each and think about some strategies for investigation," responds Ms. Andrews. Then she visits another group to check on their progress.

Later, Ms. Andrews, as she often does, convenes a whole-class conference where students have the opportunity to ask questions, speculate, and describe understandings. In the conferencing session, Traci shares her questions: "How long was India controlled by Great Britain? Why did the English go to India? Did the people accept the British?" "What do you think, Traci?" asks Ms. Andrews. Traci collects her thoughts and replies, "Maybe the British were a lot stronger than the people of India and had no real choice. Lots of people in India speak English." "I wonder what other things changed?" adds Tom. "What if the British were never in India?" wonders Shayla.

The school district has provided Ms. Andrews's students with textbooks, but she and the students do not consider the text as their primary source of information. Instead, Ms. Andrews chose a literacy-based approach to inform much of the teaching and learning in her classroom. Students are encouraged to read and examine a variety of sources; locate information; and especially develop their ability to ask questions, plan investigations to answer those questions, and design and deliver classroom presentations. Student presentations are used almost exclusively by Ms. Andrews to assess student performance. She believes that this practice helps to create and sustain a culture of inquiry in her geography class. In addition, Ms. Andrews insists that students assume authentic roles as they ask questions, locate information, synthesize sources of information, and communicate their ideas.

Luis and his group of "conservationists" are constructing a map, one of several, along with a number of charts and graphs that will be part of their presentation called "Lots of Land But Not Enough Space." Ms. Andrews watches and listens. "This is great. Look how little green there is on the map," observes Luis. "Yeah," adds Hunter. "This really shows how little forest cover is left for animal habitats." Annie nods her head in agreement but asks, "How are we going to show how close people are to these spots?" Jack, paper waving in hand, answers, "Maybe we can combine this population distribution map with the forest cover map." The students examine the new piece of information. "Look at the pattern," says Luis. "People and animals are all mixed together in some places. Let's use red for the people population." "Wow, in the future, there's going to be lots more red and the green might disappear," observes Ben. "How are we going to represent wildlife sanctuaries on the map?" asks Jennie. Ms. Andrews smiles and moves on.

For teachers like Ms. Andrews, questions offer points of departure for further investigation. Ms. Andrews often applies a cooperative jigsaw approach to instruction, preferring to act as a facilitator rather than the primary dispenser of information. She has students working in a number of investigative groups organized around fields of inquiry designed to uncover big ideas, or what might be thought of as geographic elements and standards. As the investigations and preparations continue for the presentations, students often make observations and reach conclusions that are exactly or very close to the standards established by national organizations. The students are thinking geographically about human activity; the distribution of resources; and interrelationships that shape the past, present, and future of our world. The students are not accidentally stumbling on these understandings or the standards. Big ideas are emerging from a set of intentional planning actions taken by Ms. Andrews and by active student inquiry.

Think back to the exchange between Ms. Andrews and her students and compare it to the chart below. What National Geography Standards do you think the students have uncovered? How close have the students come to the notion of distribution that informs geographers' spatial perspectives? What observations have you made about Ms. Andrews's approach to teaching geography? What hypotheses can you make about her curricular and instructional decision making?

Problem-Based Inquiry Brainstorming

Prepackaged lesson plans do not fare well with constructivists committed to making geography curriculum and instruction problem-based. Our problem-based inquiry begins with brainstorming. Let's test our ability to apply what we have learned, our understanding of the structure of geography, and the constructs of inquiry.

Imagine yourself as a high school geography teacher who has chosen to ground student geographic investigation in contemporary events—in this case, one of India's most daunting problems . . . the impoverished Indian farmer. As you read the selection below, pay close attention to the secondary conversation going on in your head, not so much the content comprehension one (although that is very important) but the reflective one, the one that so readily and automatically evokes potential images of your own constructivist classroom. Also, imagine how differently Mr. Baker and Ms. Andrews would approach this material. Here is the content material that provides a field of inquiry for our brainstorming.

The Face of Reform: New Prime Minister Manmohan Singh Faces Immense Challenges in His Bid to Lift Up India's Rural Poor (edited; Adiga, 1994)

On April 20, impoverished farmers in the village of Potaram voted overwhelmingly for Sonia Gandhi. Yet days after the results were announced, the news still hadn't reached many of the rural voters responsible for her triumph. "Will Sonia become Prime Minister?" asks Kumari Satamma, a 58-year-old villager, surprised and excited. She praises Gandhi's mother-in-law, former Indian Prime Minister Indira Gandhi, while neighbors nod in agreement. "We had more food and better clothes then," one woman remembers. Says Satamma: "Sonia is Indira Gandhi's daughter-in-law. She'll take care of farmers and the poor."

Now, however, the people of Potaram must grapple with a new and equally startling development in this remarkable election: it's not Gandhi but a quiet, self-effacing technocrat who will be their next Prime Minister. On May 18, Gandhi announced that she would follow an "inner voice" and renounce the post of Prime Minister. Her decision cleared the way for her handpicked nominee, Manmohan Singh, a former Finance Minister, to fill her place. The country's future now rests primarily on Singh, who comes to the job with an unprecedented résumé. He is an Oxford-trained economist and a Sikh (not a Hindu)—both firsts for an Indian Prime Minister. Singh, a former governor of India's reserve bank, began the process of opening up the economy to competition and foreign investment. A cool-headed, analytical thinker with a fondness for Urdu poetry, he is trusted by the Gandhi family for his loyalty and is respected across the political spectrum.

In his first major press conference since the election, Singh emphasized that his priority will be "to wage the battle against poverty. . . . We need reforms but with a human face." India's economy has never been stronger, but the boom—driven by tax cuts, privatization of state industries and cutting red tape—has been narrow, failing to help most of the 650 million Indians who live off the land.

One of the biggest problems facing India's farmers is inadequate irrigation. In states such as Andhra Pradesh, Karnataka and Punjab, farmers have tried to boost their incomes by switching to cash crops like cotton and sugarcane, which require a great deal of water. Although Andhra Pradesh has several rivers, the state has only a partial system of irrigation to channel river water for agriculture. In large areas, the state has provided no irrigation at all, so farmers must find water themselves—an expensive, haphazard proposition. Adavayya, a farmer in the village of Boppapura in Andhra Pradesh, says he dug 16 boreholes and 15 of them were dry. "It was pure luck," he says, "that even one hit water." To take out loans for their boreholes, farmers can rarely count on banks. If crops fail, these debts tend to be catastrophic.

Intensifying the woes of rural Indians, the government has also cut its spending in other key areas. "Delivery systems of primary education, health care, rural roads and drinking water are rusty and decrepit," says former Finance Minister Chidambaram. For India's new Prime Minister, the challenge of fixing these problems is immense.

As you read this passage, I suspect that some of the questions below blended in with your thoughts, images, and perceptions. Consider these questions and your own as departure points for your investigation into problem-based inquiry.

- How will I organize curriculum and instruction around this material? How will I engage my students?
- What sorts of problem-based/inquiry-based activities will engage my students?
- How will I assess the students?
- What geography standards are likely to emerge from student discovery?

ADDITIONAL THOUGHTS

Geographic understanding is crucial to our existence on Earth. This body of knowledge has contributed to a greater emphasis on landscapes and the people and cultures that occupy them in the curriculum. But teaching geography sometimes resorts to an overreliance on measuring students' ability to locate and name places. These outcomes fall short of what is needed to ensure that students understand that the world's resources are finite, and that only through human cooperation can problems be solved on a global scale. How can teaching geography become more transformative? Problem-based or issue-based geographic inquiry offers the best chance for inspiring students to assume greater social responsibility and take action as citizens of the world.

As is often the case in my own social studies methods course, the class generates more questions than could ever possibly be answered in the allotted time. We are comfortable with this circumstance and do not mind (some students still mind!) carrying around unfinished business. One evening, during one of our extended follow-up discussions about inquiry in social studies, Jennifer asked, "Is it possible to teach all subjects using an inquiry approach?"

The class was split in its opinion. Some students viewed inquiry as applicable to any and all disciplines. Others recognized its applicability across all areas of the social studies, including geography. But some students were unable to fully accept this idea. I wonder about this and look forward to what the students will say when we convene again. I know that disagreements about inquiry will continue to exist, and this is fine. But I suspect that a wide range of beliefs about inquiry also prevails in our schools. How can we explain this?

The key to continual development as a teacher is lifelong learning. The best teachers are those who constantly strive to examine and reexamine their work in an ongoing effort to provide the best possible instruction for their students. They have not become linear and complacent, like the Mr. Bakers of the profession. Like Ms. Andrews, they embrace inquiry and have discovered that it gives teachers and students the freedom to think, act, and transform.

The inquiry classroom is rich with variety and alive with possibilities for teaching and learning. But inductive approaches are not easy to implement. They take time to plan and may encounter resistance from students, parents, and colleagues. Some of your students might have had vastly different experiences from the ones they encounter in your classroom. They may have learned to be passive receivers of information—a tough behavior to change. Some parents and colleagues may view inquiry as wasting precious allocated time, especially for those who are overly concerned with standardized test performance. Indeed, inquiry takes time, but that is because students become deeply immersed in the curriculum, rather than finishing the day's work as quickly as possible.

In the tradition of the Socratic method, constructivism, inquiry, and the unfinished business of education, I challenge you with one more question: How can we create and sustain a broad culture of inquiry in our schools?

The winning answer: Portugal. Incidentally, Goa is somewhat different now from when it was a Portuguese colony. Check out http://www.Photoguide.to/Goa to investigate.

IDEAS FROM THE FIELD

RAILS, REALTY, AND RISK

Rails, Realty, and Risk, an instructional framework for a 3-week guided inquiry unit for 10th–12th graders, is designed to integrate science, geography, and U.S. history. Western development in post–Civil War America provides a rich era of study in terms of geography; national growth; and expansive study of the physical, psychological, and domestic factors of how and why the West developed. The unit features a variety of learning experiences that rely heavily on technology, incorporate the study of maps and the study of the U.S. Census for demographic research, and involve the investigation of primary sources. Inquiry provides the opportunity for students to apply principles of investigation and exploration to develop their capacity for historical thinking. A set of essential questions helps to drive student discussion, exploration, and assessment. Student entrepreneurs design and develop an authentic marketing presentation as the culminating activity.

Getting on Track

As the people of the United States began to move westward, the need for adequate surveying and mapping activities flourished. The influx of settlers to the undeveloped land created a demand for agricultural products and new ways to move goods and people. At this time, the railroad industry was reaching its maturity and was ready to tackle the task of creating a continental railway. Risk, adventure, and an entrepreneurial spirit captured the imagination of the young captains of the railroad industry, and through hard work, determination, expertise, and much luck, they opened the West to new patterns of settlement.

Ties to Critical Thinking

The following focus questions provide the critical guide for teaching and learning. Teachers and students are encouraged to revisit these questions throughout the unit and add their own essential questions to this list.

- How did a combination of historical and geographical factors, along with a vision for America's future, help create a stage for westward expansion and national development?
- How did the opening of the West provide opportunities for imaginative entrepreneurs?

- How did the development of continental railways benefit America's growth?
- Is the use of technology such as GIS more efficient than the traditional surveying methods employed in the past?

Gauging the Standards

The following standards are the guideposts for this inquiry-based unit.

National Geography Standards

- Use maps and other geographic representations, tools, and technologies to acquire, process, and report information from a spatial perspective.
- Describe the physical and human characteristics of places.
- Explain how social, cultural, and economic processes shape the features of places.
- Apply geography to interpret the present and plan for the future.
- Use geography knowledge and skills to analyze problems and make decisions within a spatial context.

National History Standards

- How the rise of corporations, heavy industry, and mechanized farming transformed the American people so that students

    - Understand the connections among industrialization, the advent of the modern corporation, and material well-being

    - Compare various types of business organizations in production and marketing

    - Evaluate the careers of prominent industrial and financial leaders

    - Explain how business leaders sought to limit competition and maximize profits in the late 19th century

National Science Education Standards

- Abilities necessary to do (scientific) inquiry, so that students

    - Recognize and analyze alternative explanations

    - Communicate and defend a (scientific) argument

    - Understand natural and human-induced hazards and the need to assess potential danger and risk

Project 2061 Benchmarks for Science Literacy

- Value of evidence, logic, and good argument
- Human inventiveness brings new risks as well as improvements to human existence
- To be convincing, an argument has to have both true statements and valid statements among them
- Use of tables, charts, and graphs in making arguments and claims in oral and written presentations

A Plan for Learning

Lesson 1: Nothing Like It in the World

As amateur historians investigating westward expansion, students read *Nothing Like It in the World* by Stephen Ambrose (2000). Students select excerpts from the book to examine and discuss, and they generate a list of important events, topics, and questions from the reading. Students then embark on a WebQuest based on the questions that they have generated. Students might be directed to the Railroads portion of the American Memory Collection at the Library of Congress or other Web sites. Students bring history alive through the construction of a living time line that dramatizes the major events of this era.

Lesson 2: Suppose There Were GIS Back Then

This lesson introduces students to Geographic Information Systems (GIS) technology and the practice of using the Global Positioning System (GPS). Following an investigation of GIS, the students will speculate on how it might have aided westward expansion and the development of continental railways. Student groups formulate their own "what if" scenarios to present to the class.

Lesson 3: Getting Your Own Railroad Company on Track

Introduce the following performance assessment task to the students.

The Situation

Imagine it's the late 1870s, and America's western frontier lies wide-open before you. As the newly promoted director of the "Mississippi to Pacific" (invent your own name) railroad company, you believe that the western frontier offers the company its best chance at growth and prosperity. You and your colleagues have a vision of a rail line to the Pacific

Ocean, but in order for the vision to become reality, you must engage in an extensive study of the history and geography of the frontier. The frontier offers considerable opportunity but also formidable risks.

The Challenge

As an entrepreneur, you must plot and plan the most cost-efficient and advantageous stops for your railroad. Your advantage, which railroad entrepreneurs of the past did not have, is the luxury of GIS/GPS technology. This pinpoint satellite guided system of mapping has eliminated the need for months of tedious, costly, and often dangerous land surveys. To secure investors for the enterprise, your group must design and develop a formal marketing presentation that will convince venture capitalists to supply funds to develop your railway.

Lesson 4: Tracks, Cow Catchers, and Topography

Students examine archival maps and primary sources that profile the West during the latter part of the 19th century. Students speculate about the challenges that faced railroad enterprises. Students should consider the following questions: What are the natural contours and borders of the region? How does the topography determine where railroads would be built? How might the discovery of natural resources create economic opportunity? How might a continental railway affect agricultural practices in the region? What is the potential impact on Native American settlements?

Lesson 5: What Does the Census Have to Do With It?

Given U.S. census records from 1820 to 1890, students investigate the demographics of a changing and developing West. Based on this information, students, acting as railroad entrepreneurs, decide on the most sensible and profitable location for railroad junctions. Students present and support their itineraries using maps and other pertinent data. Students might, for example, construct a PowerPoint presentation. This could also be used as the format for the final presentation.

Lesson 6: Sharp Money Men: The Captains of the Railroad Industry Examine the PBS *American Experience* Web Site (http://www.pbs.org/wgbh/amex/iron/)

Have students view the video *The Iron Road* by Neil Goodwin. Have students compile a list and construct biographies of railroad entrepreneurs mentioned in the video. Students might cite the Big Four and others. Students should examine and discuss the positions and motives of these tycoons. Have students contrast these perspectives by investigating the social history of the transcontinental railroad reflected through the lives of the Chinese, Irish, and other immigrants and the roles they played in its construction. Have students examine photographs and newspaper headlines. Organize students into groups for generating scripts. Students select roles and perform group productions to demonstrate their understanding.

Lesson 7: Marketing in the Wild West

Have students contact local chambers of commerce to obtain publications used by these organizations to promote their region's suitability for business and commerce. Have students compare current media to the actual advertisements and newspaper articles of the railway period. Have students reflect and brainstorm ideas that would entice Americans to move west. What stories about the West would attract them? What kind of an impact would the Gold Rush have had on pioneers? Have students create their own advertisements and newspaper articles.

Lesson 8: Making the Pitch

Each student group will have 30 minutes to deliver its marketing presentation. Remember that the Big Four would want

- Historical, geographic, and scientific quality and accuracy
- A clear, well-organized, and grammatically correct presentation
- Skillful use of charts, maps, graphs, and other visuals
- A persuasive and substantiated argument for decisions made by the group concerning costs, risks, and profitability
- A presentation format that relates to and extends understanding of the unit's content and purpose

The panel of judges will use the following scoring guide to score the presentations (Figure 2.3).

Figure 2.3   Rails, Realty, and Risk Scoring Guide

	You are one of the "Big Four"!	You have been invited to the Promontory Point Ceremony.	You have been awarded a gold "plated" spike.	You thought you knew where Promontory Point was.
Historical, Geographic, and Scientific Quality	Exemplary . . . understanding of the historical, geographic, and scientific contexts research and use of primary sources analysis and interpretation of data	Good . . . understanding of the historical, geographic, and scientific contexts research and use of primary sources analysis and interpretation of data	Reasonable . . . understanding of the historical, geographic, and scientific contexts research and use of primary sources analysis and interpretation of data	Inadequate . . . understanding of the historical, geographic, and scientific contexts research and use of primary sources analysis and interpretation of data
Clarity of the Presentation	Very effective . . . organization grammar, spelling, and mechanics	Effective . . . organization grammar, spelling, and mechanics	Somewhat effective . . . organization grammar, spelling, and mechanics	Ineffective . . . organization grammar, spelling, and mechanics
Skillful Use of Visuals	Very skillfully . . . constructed charts, photographs, maps, etc.	Skillfully . . . constructed charts, photographs, maps, etc.	Reasonably well . . . constructed charts, photographs, maps, etc.	Poorly . . . constructed charts, photographs, maps, etc.
Persuasiveness of the Argument	Excellent argument . . . very logical, convincing, and much substantive support	Good argument . . . logical, convincing, and substantive	Reasonable argument . . . minor confusion, errors in logic, and less than substantive support	Unpersuasive argument . . . lots of confusion, illogical, lack of substantive support
Overall Quality of the Presentation and Format	Excellent . . . application of the presentation format transitions cohesiveness collaboration	Good . . . application of the presentation format transitions cohesiveness collaboration	Reasonable . . . application of the presentation format transitions cohesiveness collaboration	Ineffective . . . application of the presentation format transitions cohesiveness collaboration

CONCLUSION

Inquiry-based experiences like the one offered here afford students the opportunity to take charge of their own learning by constructing their own knowledge and meaning. Like all instructional plans, Rails, Realty, and Risk is a work in progress. Teachers and students can use it to guide learning, as a departure point for extended study, or as a framework for future investigation and speculation. Inquiry provides an authentic contextual base and an opportunity for students to apply the principles of investigation and exploration to develop their capacity for historical thinking.

ACKNOWLEDGEMENT

Rails, Realty, and Risk: A Framework for Guided Inquiry was designed by Sean Colley, Valerie Frezza, Michael Karwin, and Thomas O'Keefe, all future secondary history teachers enrolled in the Roger Williams University School of Education. Dr. Alan Canestrari, Assistant Professor of Education, advises these students.

REFERENCES

Adiga, A. (2004, May 31). The face of reform: New Prime Minister Manmohan Singh faces immense challenges in his bid to lift up India's poor. *TIME Asia.*

Ambrose, S. (2000). *Nothing like it in the world.* New York: Simon & Schuster.

Brooks, M. G., & Brooks, G. B. (1999). The courage to be constructivist. *Educational Leadership, 57*(3), 18–24.

Bruner, J. (1961). The act of discovery. *Harvard Educational Review, 31*(1), 21–32.

Dewey, J. (1972). *Experience and education.* New York: Collier Books. (Original work published 1938)

Fenton, E. (1961). *Teaching the new social studies in secondary schools: An inductive approach.* New York: Holt, Rinehart & Winston.

Marlowe, B. A., & Page, M. L. (1998). *Creating and sustaining the constructivist classroom.* Thousand Oaks, CA: Corwin.

Martel, Y. (2001). *Life of Pi.* New York: Harcourt.

National Council for Geographic Education. (1994). *Geography for life: National geography standards.* Retrieved June 12, 2004, from http://www.ncge.org/publications/tutorial/standards/

National Council for the Social Studies. (1994). *A vision of powerful teaching and learning in the social studies: Building social understanding and civic efficacy.* Retrieved from http://www.socialstudies .org/positions/powerful/

Severance, J. B. (1997). *Gandhi great soul.* New York: Houghton Mifflin.

Test yourself: A selection of questions asked at the national-level preliminary competition. (2003). Retrieved June 4, 2004, from http://news .nationalgeographic.com/news/2003/05/0520_030520_beeprelimques tions.html

Vernon, J. (2003, May 21). Washington state eighth grader wins National Geographic Bee. Retrieved June 4, 2004, from http://news.national geographic.com/news/2003/05/0520_030521_geobee2003.html

Zarrillo, J. J. (2004). *Teaching elementary social studies: Principles and applications.* Upper Saddle River, NJ: Pearson Education.

CHAPTER THREE

Science Inquiry

Is There Any Other Way?

Linda K. Jordan

> *Inquiry into authentic questions generated from student experiences is the central strategy of teaching science. Teachers focus inquiry predominantly on real phenomena in classrooms, outdoors, or in laboratory settings . . .*
>
> —National Science Education Standards (NRC, 1996)

Every reader should know that the immediate answer to the question posed in the title is a resounding yes. Science teachers routinely lead students through meaningful investigations using a wide variety of instructional techniques and experience good results. However, since the advent of national standards, the pendulum has switched from an orientation toward how to deliver instruction to an emphasis on student learning (National Research Council [NRC], 1996). The National Science Education Standards (NSES), in which inquiry is treated as a distinct and unique content area, provides a compelling argument for how learners should be introduced to scientific concepts and ideas. Although inquiry may not be the only way to teach science, many science educators believe that it may be the best way for students to *learn* science. This fundamental belief underscores the premise of Chapter 3.

THE WETLANDS CONNECTION

As a new and energetic science teacher, I employed every pedagogical skill at my disposal to engage students. In the biology classes, students thrived under my tutelage; however, my level of success was considerably less in a course titled "Chemistry and the Community." My naive assumption that successful teaching techniques from biology would transfer well to this new course was unfounded. Things went quickly awry. Long before Christmas, to paraphrase James Lovell, I found myself thinking, "Jordan, we have a problem."

Because many of these students were seniors who had previously taken my biology course, I felt comfortable asking their opinions about how the class was progressing. Their responses were both surprising and annoying. ChemCom, the alternative choice to traditional Chemistry, attracted students who planned to attend college but not major in science. Consequently, my students were anticipating a less rigorous course, demanding that it be practical and fun, and expecting me to provide the entertainment. Because I never considered myself a rousing entertainer, I was disappointed that they expected me to adopt a teaching style that I found unnatural.

Their brutally honest feedback left me with much to ponder over the long holiday break. Despite this time for reflection, I returned to school still searching for inspiration or even divine intervention. Unless something drastic happened, we were all facing business as usual. It was everyone's good fortune that I received a call from the director of our Community Design Center. He offered to help me transform the wetland near our middle school into an outdoor learning center. The first step in preparing a wetland master plan, he said, was to complete a plant and animal inventory. Because I lacked the personal time and resources to address this task, I asked him if students could help. He replied that this would be acceptable, as long as the work was completed by a spring deadline.

The most logical choice for completing the inventory was my second-year biology class ... the bad news was that they showed no interest in the project. In desperation, I struck a deal with my ChemCom students. We would move forward with the regular curriculum, but one day a week would be devoted to studying wetlands. As a class, we brainstormed what we should explore and how. Questions arose, and groups self-assembled to analyze soil conditions, examine water quality issues, and complete transects for surveying the plant and animal communities. The plant team eventually identified more than 100 species. The animal group was frustrated with being able to observe only the daytime wetland residents, and they were eager to learn more about the nocturnal inhabitants. A local naturalist taught them how to bait and set appropriate traps. Trapped animals must be released quickly. This required that additional time be spent studying the wetland. The snowball began to gather momentum.

Water quality emerged as the most interesting aspect of the project. A team of students tested water before, during, and after its passage through the wetland on its journey to the town creek. Something in the data seemed to be wrong. Water quality was poorer before it entered the mire than when it resurfaced at the other end. Students were convinced that they had made an error. When the tests were repeated, similar findings resulted.

The project was scheduled for completion by the last week of school, and the class report was to count as the major part of their semester grade. Knowing that they would be presenting their data to the school board added another dimension to the mounting stress. Tension was running high when I suggested that they compare their water quality findings with those conducted by chemistry classes in previous years. All of the results were consistent. The data were in, but students continued to have little success interpreting the results. On the last day for seniors, I initiated a discussion about conditions at the nearby farm and how wetlands functioned. Because students had yet to associate these two ideas, I was almost ready to help them connect the dots. Suddenly, a student who had not been living up to expectations interrupted and said, "You mean the swamp cleaned up the water that was contaminated by the cattle before it entered the creek?" There were audible sighs of relief. Associations were finally made, and grades were no longer in jeopardy.

Almost 20 years later, I recall this event as if it happened yesterday. I realize that if I had asked better questions, students would have been able to make quicker sense of the water quality data. The wetlands project provided me with the crystal-clear revelation that giving students the opportunity to discover answers for themselves represents teaching in its most powerful form.

The impetus for inquiry teaching and learning, as evidenced by my students' wetland encounter, is generally attributed to Schwab, who, in the 1960s, argued persuasively for the supremacy of teaching science through process skills. Schwab submitted that science should be presented to students and practiced by them in a manner consistent with the way scientists go about their work. Science educators soon realized that Schwab's recommendations posed serious practical limitations. The consensus was that there need not be a one-to-one correspondence between science as practiced in the laboratory and science as experienced in the classroom. Although student inquiry today is seldom equivalent to original scientific investigation, the approach introduces the unique ways of knowing that characterize the scientific enterprise. Frequently, these central attitudes and dispositions are referred to as the nature of science. Layman, Ochoa, and Heikkinen (1996) reviewed important similarities between practicing scientists and students engaged in inquiry. The reader may notice that many of the tenets of science mentioned by Layman et al. were integral features of the wetland project.

- The world is understandable.
- Scientific ideas are subject to revision.
- Scientific knowledge is durable.
- Science cannot provide complete answers to all questions.
- Science is inquiry.
- Science demands evidence.
- Science is a blend of logic and imagination.
- Science explains and predicts.
- Scientists try to identify and avoid bias.
- Science is not authoritarian.
- Science is a complex social activity.
- There are generally accepted ethical principles in the conduct of science.
- Scientists participate in public affairs.

So much has been written about science as inquiry that it is impossible to cover the topic fully within this limited space. This chapter summarizes my research and selected thoughts about science as inquiry. I begin by comparing widely accepted definitions of science as inquiry with widespread myths about inquiry.

MISCONCEPTIONS ABOUT INQUIRY

According to Colburn (A. Colburn, personal communication, January 2000), "Perhaps the most ambiguous thing about inquiry lies in simply defining the term." Here is how some of the leading science and educational organizations have described this slippery concept.

National Science Education Standards

Scientific inquiry refers to the diverse way that scientists study the natural world and propose explanations based on the evidence derived from their work. Inquiry also refers to the activities of students in which they develop knowledge and understanding of scientific ideas, as well as an understanding of how scientists work. (NRC, 1996, p. 23)

Science for All Americans

Scientific inquiry is not easily described apart from the context of particular investigations. There is simply no fixed set of steps that scientists always follow, that leads them unerringly to scientific knowledge. There are certain features of science that give it a distinctive character as a mode of inquiry. (AAAS, 1989, p. 4)

Exploratorium Institute for Inquiry

Inquiry is an approach to learning that involves exploring the natural or material world that leads to asking questions and making discoveries in search for new understandings. (Exploratorium Institute for Inquiry, n.d.)

Council of State Science Supervisors (NLIST Project)

Inquiry is the process scientists use to build an understanding of the natural world based on evidence. Students can also learn about the world using inquiry. Although they rarely discover knowledge that is new to humankind, current research indicates that when engaged in inquiry learners build knowledge new to themselves. (Council of State Science Supervisors [CS3], n.d.)

Contrast these carefully worded descriptions of inquiry with the misconceptions presented in the section below. Note that these ideas were merely cited by these authors and do not represent their personal perspectives on inquiry. Other impressions have been drawn from my own teaching and professional experience.

- Inquiry is soft science and is not based on rigorous science content.
- Doing hands-on science is the equivalent of doing inquiry (Moscovici & Nelson, 1998; Thier, 2001).
- Inquiry is an either/or proposition (Rankin, 1999).
- There is a clear distinction between science content and science process (Rankin, 1999).
- Inquiry involves a step-by-step sequence commonly referred to as the scientific method (AAAS, 1989; NRC, 1996).
- Inquiry means asking students lots of questions.
- Inquiry requires the teacher to know all of the answers.
- Inquiry is unstructured and chaotic (Rankin, 1999; Sumrall, 1997).
- Materials and equipment needed to teach science as inquiry are readily available in most K–12 classrooms.
- Inquiry is fine for elementary and middle-level students, but high school teachers lack sufficient time to use this approach.
- Inquiry is for high-achieving students and does not work with students who have learning disabilities (Colburn, 2000; DeBoer, 1991; Welch, Klopfer, & Aikenhead, 1981).
- Inquiry oriented instruction precludes the use of textbooks or other instructional materials (Haury, 1993).
- Inquiry-based learning cannot be properly assessed.
- Inquiry is just the latest fad in science education.

Despite Llewellyn's (2002) claim that "A common thread to (all) organizational recommendations has been the citation of inquiry-based instruction as a central strategy for teaching science" (p. ix), DeBoer (1991) noted that "There is a considerable discrepancy between beliefs about the importance of inquiry teaching and actual school practice" (p. 209). Perhaps some of the erroneous ideas about inquiry are partially responsible for the gap between theory and practice.

In my experience as a professional developer, I have heard many of these ideas expressed by teachers. Despite the general agreement among teachers that inquiry enhances student learning, attitudes and/or beliefs can contribute to a reluctance to implement this approach. Only after inquiry is demystified do workshop participants understand how their prior understanding handicaps or prevents them from moving toward inquiry-based instruction.

NLIST: THE ESSENTIAL FEATURES OF CLASSROOM INQUIRY

Schwab (1969) maintained that all educational settings consist of four commonplaces: learner, subject matter, teacher, and milieu or context. The Council of State Science Supervisors (CS3) adopted a similar conceptual framework to design their NASA-supported Networking for Leadership and Systemic Thinking (NLIST) project. I selected the NLIST program and their definition of science as inquiry to frame this section because of my work on the project and my belief in the integrity and value of NLIST tools. In developing their materials, NLIST teams drew from the experiences of all of the major reform initiatives and the major science as inquiry projects. The CS3 Web site (http://www.inquiryscience .com) contains a detailed description of the NLIST Science as Inquiry program.

One segment of the NLIST definition states,

As a result of participating in inquiry, learners increase their understanding of science subject matter, gain an understanding of how scientists study the natural world, develop the ability to conduct investigations, and develop the habits of mind associated with science.

These four essential features of inquiry provide the framework for the Instructional Practices and Instructional Materials scoring guides. NLIST scoring guides are analytical tools that provide a lens with which to assess teaching and curriculum materials for the presence of science inquiry. Such scrutiny can provide an evidence base for modifying instruction or changing curriculum materials to make them more consistent with the features of inquiry.

The NLIST project also includes a student self-assessment scoring guide constructed from the following language in another section of the NLIST definition of inquiry:

Student inquiry is a multifaceted activity that involves making observations; posing questions; examining books and other sources of information to see what is already known; planning investigations; using tools to gather, analyze, and interpret data, reviewing what is already known in light of the learner's experimental evidence; proposing answers, explanations, and predictions; and communicating results. Inquiry requires identification of assumptions, use of critical and logical thinking, and consideration of alternative explanations.

This tool generates self-assessment data that students and teachers can use to chart appropriate courses for inquiry-based learning.

In essence, the NLIST scoring guides are teacher tools for "inquiring" about their own practice. Teachers can apply scoring guide data to make informed decisions about curriculum and instruction (Fitzgerald & Byers, 2002). For this reason, it is possible and reasonable to think about the goal of moving toward inquiry as a systematic process that can be implemented over time.

DIMENSIONS OF INQUIRY: ALL OR NOTHING?

In an elementary science methods course, one of my colleagues asked prospective teachers to review a collection of science learning activities and rate them according to how well they addressed teaching and learning through inquiry. As a rule, preservice students fall into the either/or camp. In other words, they believe that a learning experience either incorporates full inquiry or is not authentic inquiry. A much different opinion prevails within the science education community.

NSES adopted a developmental perspective to describe appropriate levels of inquiry for children at different grade ranges. Their recommendations were based on the premise that prior knowledge, past educational events, and personal dispositions determine what students should be experiencing and how they interpret and learn from these experiences. Some of the important distinctions made in the NSES (NRC, 1996) are the following:

- K–4: Students should be provided with opportunities to investigate earth materials, living organisms, and properties of common objects. Children in this age group can apply simple inquiry skills, such as "ask questions, investigate aspects of the world around them, and use observation to construct reasonable explanations for questions posed . . . and communicate about their investigations and explanations" (p. 121). Teachers can expect that children will have difficulty making the connection between experimentation and using evidence to reach conclusions.

- 5–8: The distinction between full and partial inquiry is introduced. Partial inquiry is when selected abilities and understandings are targeted. Students in this grade range begin to recognize the difference between evidence and explanation. The student's background knowledge base is the principal influence on the design of investigation, types of observations, and methods for interpreting data.

- 9–12: The knowledge and experience base is rapidly expanding. At the high school level, students are generally capable of reflecting on the concepts that guide inquiry. Full inquiry is a viable option for high schoolers.

Over the past ten years, a spate of articles has been published that examine inquiry in terms of levels, degrees, or along continua (Bonnstetter, 1998; Colburn, 1997; Sutman, Hilosky, Priestley, & Priestley, 1999). Kluger-Bell (1999) described three types of conventional activities: guided worksheet with brief teacher directions, challenge activity with minimal teacher direction, and open with a teacher-led brainstorming discussion. *Structured, guided,* and *open* are the terms Colburn (2000) used to portray the inquiry options. Barman (2002) applied the expression *coupled inquiry* to describe situations where the teacher chooses the question and students design the research procedure. All of these inquiry models share the position that quality science instruction engages students in a broad variety of learning experiences. Thinking experiments, interactions with real-time scientific Internet data, and even thought-provoking lectures can provide equally rich opportunities for applying elements of inquiry.

Perhaps the most widely recognized model is the inquiry continuum (Bonnstetter, 1998). Like any well-designed graphic organizer, it has enormous explanatory power. Bonnstetter described five categories of science learning activities ranging from traditional hands-on, through structured, guided, student-directed, and student research inquiry. What distinguishes an activity in terms of inquiry is the relative amount of teacher versus student input and control. After my colleague introduced the continuum to the prospective teachers mentioned earlier, their understanding of inquiry changed considerably. They could easily apply Bonnstetter's model to characterize an activity according to its level of inquiry and apply the continuum framework to move a lesson toward a higher level of student exploration. Preservice students began to realize that such models provide a framework for general discussions about inquiry. However, artificial constructs are not prescriptions for teaching science, because the nature of inquiry is heavily dependent on the context that surrounds the learner.

Schwab (1963) advocated science teaching that incorporated historical explanations of how scientific ideas originate. He recommended laboratory investigations of authentic problems that "invite the students to use his information and intelligence in an effort to find the answer" (p. 51). The multiple and varied perspectives on inquiry offered by the NLIST project, the National Science Education Standards, and the inquiry continuum give teachers an expansive range of options for moving toward this kind of science instruction. These reflective self-assessment tools give teachers the means for carefully examining their own practices and provide the evidence needed to move instruction in the direction of inquiry.

REVISITING THE WETLAND PROJECT

Reflecting on the past in terms of what is presently understood can be bittersweet. As I look back on the wetland project, I vividly recall the energy and excitement we all brought to the task. I also remember the deep frustration that stemmed from my inexperience with teaching through inquiry. My teacher preparation program did not provide me with good models of inquiry instruction. I stumbled onto inquiry. Most of the decisions I made were based on intuition instead of any deep-seated beliefs or understandings about inquiry. Fortunately, my ideas about teaching and learning continued to evolve, following the adage that experience, combined with reflection, is a prescription for personal growth.

Despite its original rocky start, the wetland project continued to thrive. Successive years resulted in the development of the 10-acre site as an outdoor resource for all district students. Collaborations with other high school departments resulted in an interpretive trail guide, removal of exotic species, marked and mulched trails, and construction of elevated boardwalks and activity stations. Because many of these improvements required resources that were not available through the school, students carried out creative fundraising projects. This project garnered considerable recognition for the school and the students who worked diligently to make this wetland an outdoor study area and a place for the community to enjoy.

If I had the opportunity to begin the project anew, my approach would be much different. The following sections present my current thinking about how the wetlands experiment could have been transformed into student learning through inquiry.

Standards

Years ago, no standards existed to guide the selection of student learning experiences or clarify the elements of inquiry. Textbooks and the teacher's own interests generally dictated what was taught. Teachers in standards-based classrooms begin their instructional planning with a topic in mind, identify the related standards, and develop assessments and lessons that carefully align with these goals for student learning (Audet & Jordan, 2003). Today, the wetland unit would be aimed at standards drawn from the following NSES content areas: inquiry; life science (nutritional relationships, life cycles); physical science (water chemistry, properties of matter); earth and space science (soil composition, water cycle); and standards associated with humans' impact on the environment.

Assessment

The past 20 years have been revolutionary in terms of how educators assess student understanding. Formerly, teachers were most concerned with constructing tests and quizzes that would accurately measure what kids knew. Today, a variety of methods are used to determine if students have met the standards that are targeted through instruction. The final report that my students generated was a performance assessment, in current educational language. Had the project been implemented now, I would use a backward design approach and develop the assessment soon after selecting the content standards. The task would include a scoring guide that lists all the criteria for measuring student performance (Audet & Jordan, 2003). I would review the assessment with my students prior to beginning the project to ensure that they were clear about the learning expectations.

I would also incorporate some aspects of phased assessment in which separate abilities and understandings were evaluated at different stages of the student investigation (Champagne, Kouba, & Hurley, 2000). The NLIST tools (CS3, n.d.) and NSES Inquiry Standards (NRC, 1996) would direct me toward specific types of evidence to assist in monitoring student performance.

Lesson Design

Much has been discovered about effective instructional planning and design since my original attempt to build a curriculum around this wetland resource. Conceptual change models that are consistent with ideas about how people learn, such as the learning cycle (Llewellyn, 2002) and 5Es (Bybee, 1997), offer more effective frameworks for structuring the learning environment. My current understanding of the inquiry continuum offers me a more holistic perspective for thinking about alternative levels of inquiry. I have become keenly aware of the importance of building on my students' prior understanding of and experience with inquiry. This gives me a clearer indication of students' readiness to exercise greater control over their own learning.

Questions occupy the core of inquiry. However, "Many of the questions children ask spontaneously are not profitable starting points for science" (Jelly, 1987, p. 47). Participating in the Exploratorium's Institute for Inquiry improved my understanding of how to generate and answer researchable questions. Brainstorming generates a broad range of possibilities. It is important to narrow this sample to questions that students can reasonably be expected to answer and to those that promote deeper understanding of a concept after the investigation has been completed. In the wetland experience, my students' questions were initially all over the lot (no pun intended). Too much time was spent following potential lines of investigation that proved to be unrealistic or impractical. For example, students were very curious about transients who visited during the evening. There was evidence that more than just rodents trespassed at night, but we had to limit ourselves to what could actually be verified. Another group wanted the investigation to include birds, but bird populations are notoriously difficult to track. Today, we could access projects such as the Cornell Project FeederWatch Web site for information about monitoring wetland bird populations (http://www.birds.cornell.edu/ pfw/news/feedercam/).

Technology

The opportunities that would have been afforded to my students by embedding modern technological tools into the wetland study are mind-boggling. Instead of test kits, we would use electronic probes to monitor water quality. We would pinpoint and record the exact location of the plant and animal populations with handheld GPS units. Returning to the lab, we would enter GPS coordinates on a spreadsheet, plot the data, and investigate the same information using our GIS software. Students would conduct much of their research on the Internet and use a word processing program for the final report. I imagine that they would prepare a PowerPoint presentation for the school board and display it with a computer projector or a Smart Board. This is just a small sampling of the amazing array of technological tools that is currently available to support K–12 student inquiry.

Safety

No conversation about science as inquiry is complete without discussing the responsibility teachers have for providing a safe learning environment. Inquiry, standards, and safety form what I refer to as an "essential partnership" (Figure 3.1) that drives student learning in the science classroom. Inquiry provides the instructional approach, standards offer guidelines for selecting content, and proper attention to safety establishes the necessary classroom preconditions.

The National Science Education Teaching Standards (NRC, 1996) most relevant to the essential partnership are included in Standard D:

> Teachers of science design and manage learning environments that provide students with the time, space, and resources needed for learning science. . . . To meet this standard, teachers are expected to create a setting that is flexible and supportive of science inquiry, and ensure a safe working environment. (p. 43)

Figure 3.1   The Essential Partnership

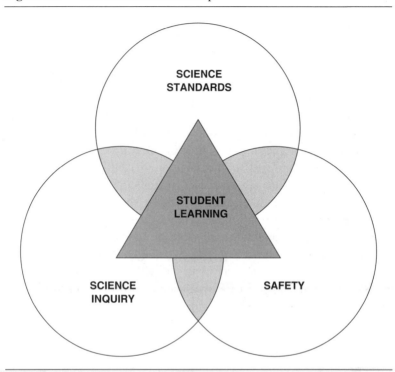

The NSES recommendations illustrate the importance attached to both inquiry and safety as the principal ingredients of science instruction.

The National Science Teachers Association's Position Statement on Safety (2000) and recent safety publications (Kwan & Texley, 2002; Texley, Kwan, & Summers, 2004) implicitly reference this "essential partnership." Kwan and Texley's framework embeds safety within the context of a standards-based classroom in which there is a commitment to science as inquiry. The authors state that

> today's students need hands-on experience in science more than ever. . . . We can still provide the investigative and observational activities that are essential to helping students understand the content and methods of science . . . that produce the "Aha!" so essential to engendering true understanding and love of the scientific endeavor . . . in a safe learning environment. (p. vi)

The NRC (2000) offers an important caveat about using inquiry to guide student learning. It cautions that "cost or safety concerns might weigh against doing a particular investigation ... not all investigations are worth pursuing" (p. 132). Fortunately, such decisions are assisted by an abundance of online and print lab safety resources. Some of the more popular science safety Web sites are NSTA (http://www.nsta.org); Council of State Science Supervisors (http://www.cs3.org); American Chemical Society (http://www.acs .org); Laboratory Safety Institute (http://www.labsafety.org); JaKel, Inc. (http://www.netins.net/showcase/jakel); and Flinn Scientific (http://www.flinnsci.com).

CHALLENGES OF TEACHING AND LEARNING THROUGH INQUIRY

According to the National Science Education Teaching Standards (NRC, 1996), teachers of science should

- Structure the time available so that students are able to engage in extended investigations
- Create a setting that is flexible and supportive of science inquiry
- Ensure a safe working environment
- Identify and use resources outside the school
- Engage students in designing the learning environment
- Make the available science tools, materials, media, and technological resources accessible to students

Arguably, even the most ardent supporters of standards would concede that achieving these goals demands a sustained commitment. After his review of the literature on inquiry, Anderson (1999) concluded that "barriers associated with putting inquiry ideas into practice were closely associated with teachers' basic values and beliefs about teaching and learning" (p. 17). Anderson also believed that successful changes in instruction require substantial professional development. Other science educators have reservations about wholesale and rapid changeovers to inquiry-based classroom practice and expressed the following concerns:

- Scientific inquiry is not as tidy as the frequently referenced process of scientific method (Bybee, 1997).
- Success with inquiry demands developmental readiness (AAAS, 1993; NRC, 1996).

- Past experience influences how students react to inquiry. Osborne and Freyberg (1985) suggested that "within very broad developmental categories and ability-related limits, children will process information differently according to their experiences rather than their age" (p. 85).
- There is a tendency to overemphasize process over content (DeBoer, 1991). Conversely, pressures associated with preparing students for the next grade level and doing well on standardized tests shift the emphasis toward content (Collette & Chiapetta, 1994).
- Discovery learning takes more time than teaching through transmission (Koballa & Tippins, 2004).
- Many teachers are uncomfortable with open-ended investigation because it generates unpredictable and varied student questions (Collette & Chiapetta, 1994).
- Students left to discover information for themselves might reach erroneous conclusions (Collette & Chiapetta, 1994).
- Working in an inquiry-based setting creates new types of classroom management issues (Collette & Chiapetta, 1994).
- Teachers may have difficulty obtaining the necessary materials and equipment (Collette & Chiapetta, 1994).
- Developing a safe learning environment can exert considerable demands on material resources (Kwan & Texley, 2002).

Instances abound in which such obstacles to implementing inquiry have been successfully overcome. The rewards for persevering have been significant. Anticipating and addressing challenges in advance is key to overcoming the hurdles that teachers encounter as they move toward inquiry. For prospective teachers, this probably will require substantive changes to the preservice program. Both novice and experienced teachers will need high-quality professional development. Success with science as inquiry will demand unwavering commitment to this approach and a full awareness of the relevant educational research. Administrative and collegial support, as well as access to community and grant resources, may be needed to obtain appropriate materials and equipment. As with my wetland example, the answer to most major teaching conundrums can be found when a teacher possesses the same habits of mind that we seek to encourage in students: curiosity; openness to new ideas; and a healthy, informed skepticism (AAAS, 1989).

IDEAS FROM THE FIELD

ALIEN INVADERS

This is an inquiry-based middle school unit on invasive species. This problem is second only to habitat destruction in terms of its threat to biodiversity and economic impact. The problem of invasives is global in scope and expanding rapidly as the spatial and geographic boundaries that once separated natural populations continue to weaken and fall.

Invasion Ecology (Krasny, 2003) offers an outstanding set of activities that incorporates inquiry. The book's ecological approach offers a cross-disciplinary perspective that addresses all science areas. Many of the ideas in this 5E learning cycle (Bybee, 1997) were drawn from this book.

Portions of the unit can be adapted for elementary and secondary school students. The materials include both laboratory and field components. Fall is a great season to conduct these lessons because so many fruits and seeds ripen at this time of year. Our current awareness of this global problem makes this topic ideally suited for inclusion in wetland projects.

Alien Invaders

Engage: Hitchhikers Beware

A simple question like "How do seeds spread from place to place?" can serve as a great launching pad for guided student inquiry. Use a silent demonstration for this engagement. Students observe you displaying seed specimens and later describe the exact steps completed during your demonstration. Select fruits and seeds that have fairly obvious adaptations for spreading seeds. The maple samara, dandelion, touch-me-not, acorn, blueberry, and burdock are excellent examples. After the demonstration, a set of focusing questions can guide children to identify the salient elements of seed dispersal and generate ideas about how such features benefit plants. Students enter a summary statement in their science notebooks based on their prior understanding of seeds and insights triggered by this demonstration to consider the relationship between form and function.

Explore: Designer Seeds

In this guided discovery activity from the Access Excellence Web site, students use their prior knowledge to design, build, and test wind-dispersed "seeds." They test their seed's dispersal potential by dropping it in front of a fan and recording the distance traveled. Different design features are evaluated and then compared with properties that contribute to seed spreading in nature. The complete lesson is available at http://www .accessexcellence.com/AE/AEC/AEF/1995/taylor_seeds.html.

Explain: Deadly Plant Invaders

Science teachers can draw from the following resources to prepare an inquiry-based instructional plan that targets the essential information needed to understand the invasive species problem.

- The National Park Service offers an interactive simulation called *The Deadly Plant Invaders Game* that enables student to grasp the fundamental ecological issues associated with nonnative plants (http://www.nps.gov/piro/lp05.htm).
- *America's Least Wanted: Alien Species Invasions of U.S. Ecosystems* (http://www.conserveonline.org/2001/06/s/amleast) is a terrific reading that gives a comprehensive overview of the problem.
- Two videos devoted to invasive species are available free to school libraries: Bill Nye's *Aquatic Invaders* (http://www.sgnis.org/av/ video/aquatic.htm) and *Plants Out of Place* (ecoservices@dnr.state .mn.us).
- The Nature Conservancy offers a compendium of materials called *Invasives in Your Backyard* (http://nature.org/initiatives/invasive species/features/).

Extend: Invaders in Our Midst

The teacher searches the Internet for invasive plant lists for his or her state or region. Selected pictures are downloaded to prepare a laminated identification sheet (preferably in color) for each student (http://www.blm .gov/education/weeds/hall_of_shame.html has an example). Ask students to scour their neighborhoods for instances where alien plants have gained a foothold. Create a Local Invasive Species Sightings sheet in which students can record information about plant species, location, description of the site, approximate size of area affected, and so on. Have students describe their findings to the class and post their sightings on a community map in specific locations where they were discovered. After sufficient time has elapsed, have students summarize their findings in their science notebooks.

Another great extension activity, *Unwanted Travel Partners*, accompanies a program from the Scientific American Frontiers series called *The Silken Tree Eaters*. Students simulate an alien invasion by studying population changes that occur after an *Elodea* sprig is added to a tube of sterile water (http://www.pbs.org/saf/1204/teaching/menu.htm).

Evaluate: Let's Take Action

Ask the class to prepare a community awareness campaign aimed at reducing the incidence and local impact of invasive species. The performance assessment can involve preparing brochures, editorials, maps, videos for local cable programs, jingles, petitions, bumper stickers, wanted posters, commercials, and so on. A scoring guide with clear expectations for students should accompany the evaluation. Be sure that the guidelines for the task require that students provide evidence that demonstrates a clear understanding of the science content associated with this topic.

Literacy Connections

- *Kudzu: The Vine to Love or Hate* (Hoot & Baldwin, 1996) describes the impact of this nasty invader from Japan on the habitat of the southern United States.
- *Hawaii's Natural Forests* explains the threat to Hawaii posed by alien plants from around the world (Orr & Boynton, 2000).
- *When Animals and Plants Invade Other Ecosystems* (Batten, 2003) offers thought-provoking descriptions of how ecological balances are threatened by the accidental or intentional introduction of organisms such as the gypsy moth.

BIBLIOGRAPHY

American Association for the Advancement of Science (AAAS). (1989). *Science for all Americans.* New York: Oxford University Press.

American Association for the Advancement of Science (AAAS). (1993). *Benchmarks for science literacy.* New York: Oxford University Press.

Anderson, R. A. (1999). Inquiry in the everyday world of schools. *Focus, 6*(2), 16–17.

Audet, R. H., & Jordan, L. K. (2003). *Standards in the classroom: An implementation guide for teachers of science and mathematics.* Thousand Oaks, CA: Corwin.

Barman, C. R. (2002). How do you define inquiry? *Science and Children, 39*(10), 8–9.

Batten, M. (2003). *When animals and plants invade other ecosystems.* Atlanta, GA: Peachtree Press.

Biological Science Curriculum Study (BSCS). (1993). *Developing biological literacy.* Dubuque, IA: Kendall/Hunt.

Bonnstetter, R. J. (1998). Inquiry: Learning from the past with an eye on the future. *Electronic Journal of Science Education.* Retrieved July 6, 2004, from unr.edu/homepage/jcannon/ejse/ejse.html.

Bransford, J. D., Brown, A. L., & Cocking, R. R. (2000). *How people learn: Brain, mind, experience, and school.* Washington, DC: National Academy Press.

Bybee, R. W. (1997). *Achieving scientific literacy: From purposes to practices.* Portsmouth, NH: Heinemann.

Bybee, R. W. (2002). *Learning science and the science of learning.* Arlington, VA: NSTA Press.

Champagne, A. B., Kouba, V. L., & Hurley, M. (2000). Assessing inquiry. In J. Minstrell & E. H. van Zee (Eds.), *Inquiry into inquiry learning and teaching in science* (pp. 456–461). Washington, DC: American Association for the Advancement of Science.

Colburn, A. (1997, Fall). How to make lab activities more open ended. *California Science Teachers Association Journal,* pp. 4–7.

Colburn, A. (2000). An inquiry primer. *Science Scope, 23*(3), 42–44.

Collette, A. T., & Chiapetta, E. L. (1994). *Science instruction in the middle and secondary schools.* Columbus, OH: Merrill.

Council of State Science Supervisors (CS3). (n.d.). http://www.inquiry science.com/

DeBoer, G. E. (1991). *A history of ideas in science education: Implications for practice.* New York: Teachers College Press.

Exploratorium Institute for Inquiry. (n.d.). http://www.exploratorium.edu/ IFI/

Fitzgerald, M. A., & Byers, A. (2002). A scoring guide for selecting inquiry-based activities. *Science Scope, 25*(9), 22–25.

Haury, D. L. (1993). Teaching science through inquiry. *ERIC CSMEE Digest,* ERIC Document No. ED 359048.

Hoot, H., & Baldwin, J. (1996). *Kudzu: The vine to love or hate.* Kodak, TN: Suntop.

Jelly, S. (1987). Helping children to raise questions—and answering them. In W. Harlen (Ed.), *Primary science* (pp. 47–57). Portsmouth, NH: Heinemann.

Kluger-Bell, B. (1999). Recognizing inquiry: Comparing three hands-on teaching techniques. In *Foundations, Volume II: A monograph for professionals in science, mathematics, and technology education: Inquiry, thoughts, views, and strategies for the K–5 classroom* (pp. 39–50). Arlington, VA: National Science Foundation.

Koballa, T. R., & Tippins, D. J. (2004). *Cases in middle and secondary science education.* Upper Saddle River, NJ: Pearson Prentice Hall.

Krasny, M. E. (2003). *Invasion ecology.* Arlington, VA: NSTA Press.

Kwan, T., & Texley, J. (2002). *Exploring safely: A guide for elementary teachers.* Arlington, VA: NSTA Press.

Layman, J. W., Ochoa, G., & Heikkinen, K. (1996). *Inquiry and learning: Realizing science standards in the classroom.* New York: College Entrance Examination Board.

Lazarowitz, R., & Tamir, P. (1994). Research on using laboratory instruction in science. In D. L. Gabel (Ed.), *Handbook of research on science teaching and learning* (pp. 94–128). New York: Macmillan.

Llewellyn, D. (2002). *Inquire within: Implementing inquiry-based science.* Thousand Oaks, CA: Corwin.

Minstrell, J., & van Zee, E. H. (Eds.). (2000). *Inquiry into inquiry learning and teaching in science.* Washington, DC: American Association for the Advancement of Science.

Moscovici, H., & Nelson, T. H. (1998). Shifting from activitymania to inquiry. *Science and Children, 35*(4), 14–17, 40.

National Research Council (NRC). (1996). *National science education standards.* Washington, DC: National Academy Press.

National Research Council (NRC). (2000). *Inquiry and the national science education standards: A guide for teaching and learning.* Washington, DC: National Academy Press.

National Science Teachers Association (NSTA). (2000). *NSTA position statement on safety.* Arlington, VA: Author.

Orr, K., & Boynton, D. (2000). *Hawaii's natural forests.* Waipahu, HI: Island Heritage.

Osborne, R., & Freyberg, P. (1985). *Learning in science.* Portsmouth, NH: Heinemann.

Rankin, L. (1999). Lessons learned: Addressing common misconceptions about inquiry. In *Foundations, Volume II: A monograph for professionals in science, mathematics, and technology education: Inquiry, thoughts, views, and strategies for the K–5 classroom* (pp. 71–77). Arlington, VA: National Science Foundation.

Schwab, J. J. (1963). *Biology teachers' handbook.* New York: Wiley.

Schwab, J. J. (1969). The practical: A language for curriculum. *School Review, 78,* 1–23.

Schwab, J. J., & Brandwein, P. F. (1962). *The teaching of science.* Cambridge, MA: Harvard University Press.

Sumrall, W. J. (1997). Why avoid hands on science? *Science Scope, 20*(1), 16–19.

Sutman, F. X., Hilosky, A., Priestley, W. J., & Priestley, H. (1999, March). *Defining inquiry oriented laboratory instruction during professional enhancement experiences using the inquiry matrix.* Paper presented at the annual meeting of the National Association of Research Into Science Teaching, Boston.

Texley, J., Kwan, T., & Summers, J. (2004). *Investigating safely: A guide for high school teachers.* Arlington, VA: NSTA Press.

Thier, H. D. (2001). *Developing inquiry-based science materials: A guide for educators.* New York: Teachers College Press.

Welch, W. W., Klopfer, L. E., & Aikenhead, G. E. (1981). The role of inquiry in science education: An analysis and recommendations. *Science Education, 65*(1), 33–50.

CHAPTER FOUR

History

Uncovering the Past Through Inquiry

Kathleen Anderson Steeves

People learn when they seek answers to questions that matter to them.

—Dewey (1933)

Who we understand ourselves to have been plays a power-ful role in shaping our ideas of who we might yet become.

—Holt (1990)

Picture a typical high school lunchroom. Imagine yourself over-hearing the following conversation between a pair of history teachers.

Teacher 1: Why do so many students always say that history is their least favorite subject? How can I motivate my students to enjoy studying history?

Teacher 2: Engage them in the *realia* of history. Give them objects and documents to analyze so they can create their own questions and tell you how they reached their conclu-sions. We can motivate students by encouraging them to ask questions; create answers; justify them with data; and, most of all, think.

Teacher 1: Sounds great! I love history, and I want to engage students in that kind of study, but our students have to pass narrowly focused state tests. That doesn't leave much room for students to explore topics in depth.

This hypothetical scenario depicts the very real dilemma faced by teachers who use inquiry in today's standards-based classrooms. Thoughtful learning or teaching for understanding through inquiry requires careful planning, alters the scope of material that can be covered, and can create significant demands on classroom time. The accountability movement has exerted a profound effect on what gets taught and how it gets taught. Any practice that reduces the amount of content coverage has to be considered in light of its potential impact on student performance on standardized tests. This chapter offers compelling evidence that structuring history teaching and learning around inquiry or seeking answers to interesting questions can address both concerns successfully. Good teaching acknowledges the value of the history content standards and simultaneously develops learners who can and do perform well on various assessments, including state and national standardized tests.

DEFINING INQUIRY

The dictionary definition of inquiry as a systematic investigation of a matter of public interest clearly implies a history connection. Critical thinking skills such as curiosity, reflection, and raising and exploring questions are all essential ingredients of inquiry. Inquiry as discussed here is conceived both broadly, to include cognitive processes and thinking strategies that include decision making and problem solving, and more narrowly on the data gathering and analysis that functions within the decision-making process.

Teaching for understanding is the common goal for all who teach history. How students understand history depends not only on material selected or what is assessed, but more importantly on what we know about how students learn. Research on cognitive processing reinforces the importance of inquiry teaching for student understanding.

Research Into Student Learning

Arguments about the most effective way to teach history are drawn from an understanding of how people learn. A number of cognitive scientists influenced the way that we organize to present history in a manner that encourages thinking, exploration, and in-depth learning. Learning theorists such as Jean Piaget produced the knowledge base for much of the current constructivist thinking. Piaget believed that the "knowledge acquired by memorizing is not real knowledge that can be used" (Resnick & Klopfer, 1989, p. 3). Instead, he encouraged teachers to allow students to explore objects or situations until their understanding of concepts or language created disequilibrium. This state of dissatisfaction with their own explanations would spur further inquiry and ultimately lead to deeper understanding. Piaget's ideas encouraged curriculum developers to design learning approaches based on students' readiness to conceptualize language and ideas (Renner et al., 1976).

Although the direct age-to-intelligence link was later disputed, the process for asking students to examine new materials reinforced the Expanding Horizons curriculum used in many schools. Social studies learning for elementary students should begin with the study of concrete, familiar things, such as school or community, and expand in later grades to the study of state, nation, and world as students' abstract cognitive ability increased (National Center for History in the Schools, 1994; Parker, 1991).

In the 1940s and 1950s, Gestalt psychologist Max Wertheimer emphasized the importance of conceptual understanding and analytical thinking. He noted that "practiced performance in school often masked failure to understand why procedures worked and inability to adapt to modifications in how problems were presented" (Resnick & Klopfer, 1989, p. 3). If what is learned is used only as a one-time response to a test item, the enduring impact will be minimal. But the long-held belief in the United States that history knowledge was important because of its value in building citizenship reinforced the applied nature of learning.

In his theory about learning called the Zone of Proximal Development (ZPD), Soviet psychologist L. S. Vygotsky maintained that learners gain knowledge within a social framework that includes culture, daily experiences, and the history of the learner. Whereas Piaget believed that learning developed naturally, Vygotsky felt that mediators or mentors to guide the learner within that cultural setting were essential for learning. The desired outcomes for learning are strongly influenced by the political/social culture and directed by the teacher in his or her role as mentor. The ZPD emphasizes the importance of the students' existing situation and surrounding culture in building learning activities to which they can respond most effectively.

Recognizing that society surrounds the learner, Dewey emphasized how students can apply their educational experiences to current learning, thus building a base for application to later life situations. According to Glassman (2001), "Dewey used individual inquiry as a tool to assist students in creating a social history or culture; an understanding that might potentially recognize a need for change in society" (p. 5).

Teaching history through inquiry varies according to what priority is assigned to each of these two main theories. In Dewey's project approach, the process itself serves as the principal goal of the activity. Students build skills for lifelong application. According to Dewey, teachers should encourage students to explore their personal environments and reach their own conclusions. Vygotsky would maintain that inquiry is, by nature, embedded within the culture. Teachers should become aware of the ZPD of their students and create learning experiences that move them forward within this societal structure. For Vygotsky, process was significant, but not as important as drawing students closer to socially defined goals. In this context, Bruner's description of scaffolding helps explain how students process new ideas. Commenting on Vygotsky's approach, Bruner (1986) said, "I think he provides the still needed provocation to find a way of understanding man as a product of culture as well as a product of nature" (p. 78).

Whereas Piaget believed that growth in learning occurs naturally and that children change the environment through the very act of learning, Vygotsky focused on the nature of the materials available to the developing mind. The mind does not develop in a vacuum, nor does the intellect develop without assistance from others who already possess cultural knowledge. Learning involves culturally transmitted knowledge and processes and is embedded in a clearly defined sociocultural context (Bruner, 1986; Resnick, 1987; Rogoff, 1990; Vygotsky, 1978; Wertsch, 1998).

Cognitive psychologists have written extensively about the distinction between experts and novices (Chi, Feltovich, & Glaser, 1981; Sternberg & Horvath, 1995). The level of understanding about key concepts and the skills needed to successfully apply these concepts distinguishes the two groups. Experts have more intricately organized *schemas,* or mental representations of knowledge (Levstik & Barton, 2001). Acquiring these conceptual frameworks involves understanding concepts unique to a particular discipline. Nelson Goodman, founder of Project Zero at the Harvard Graduate School of Education, introduced the proposition that "much of knowing, acting, and understanding in the arts, sciences, and life in general involves the use—the interpretation, application, invention, revision—of symbol systems" (Goodman, 1984, p. 152). In specific subject areas such as history, students may need to understand additional symbolic systems to explore the subject effectively. That knowledge is integrated into the culture and central concepts of that discipline.

Each of the ideas presented above contributes to educators' beliefs about student learning. A central feature of these theories is that meaningful learning is better supported through activity than by passive exposure to information. Dewey believed that developing student learning through inquiry should happen in the early stages of schooling. Vygotsky tied this inquiry learning to conceptual development during adolescence (Glassman, 2001). Some models of teaching focus on the use of language; others apply culture as the defining framework. However, all inquiry-based approaches encourage active participation by the learner. To acquire knowledge sufficient for competency in any field, learners must explore the subject, learn its language, and engage frequently in its essential processes.

COGNITIVE RESEARCH AND INQUIRY-BASED HISTORY: THEORY INTO PRACTICE

The curriculum heavily influences what is expected of students and, thus, what is demanded of teachers. The cultural elements that Vygotsky addresses, Dewey's applied projects, Wertheimer's equilibrium/disequilibrium dichotomy, Piaget's developmental stages, and language and symbol systems are essential elements of an inquiry-based curriculum. The idea that students benefit by creating their own knowledge presents curriculum developers with a particular set of questions and conditions. Developers must probe into how much of the culture is already known and what information is necessary for students to analyze and interpret new information at higher levels. The content sequence and structure of the learning experiences should complement this theoretical perspective.

In history, translating these theories into practice results in a constructivist view of learning, and a curriculum that affirms that individuals are not just recorders of information, but also builders of knowledge. Students occupy the center of learning. Understanding requires more than simple introduction to information. Opportunities must be provided that help integrate new ideas with preexisting knowledge. Skillful students will know how to complete a certain task and when applying a newly learned skill is appropriate. They can ultimately apply the skill in circumstances that differ from those surrounding the original introduction to the task.

Such a curriculum must have recognizable schema, or conceptual frameworks, driven by an understanding of likely prior learning. The K–12 content standards are important sources of this information base. Recognition of what students learned in earlier grades and how new information becomes integrated into previously developed schema facilitates new and more in-depth learning. Curriculum implementation then becomes a dynamic delivery system instead of a process aimed at successfully memorizing blocks of information.

Bruner (1986), in describing a process of building on previously acquired knowledge called *scaffolding*, noted that when an answer to a question is too simple or a situation is already clear and recognizable, students respond quickly and with ease. When placed in unfamiliar situations, students need additional time and greater support to reach accurate conclusions or desired outcomes. He suggested asking students to invent new hypotheses instead of investigating questions posed by the teacher or the text. This practice bridges the gap between what is known and the world of possibilities. The value of inquiry, especially for implementing history curricula, is that it enables students to develop a deeper understanding of human events and "a sense of the alternativeness of human possibility" (Bruner, 1986, p. 53).

Where does mastery of factual information fit in an inquiry-based curriculum? History is built on a known body of knowledge that creates the context for conceptually integrating new ideas. Striking a proper balance between information that students are provided and what they gain through questioning and inquiry is the ultimate factor that determines the lasting impact of a learning experience. When students are told information and never asked to apply it, they are unlikely to connect it successfully with future events. Curriculum is the place where subject matter and invitations to practice meet. Both elements are essential. When students are superficially exposed to topics, told stories, or given facts, it is unreasonable to expect that they will later successfully apply that information to a project related to that topic. Content and method must be seamlessly integrated to create a thinking curriculum.

But as John Goodlad (1984) found in his exhaustive study of schools and schooling, students are seldom expected to apply critical thinking skills. He concluded that "preoccupation with the lower intellectual processes prevails in social studies and science as well. An analysis of topics studied and materials used gives not an impression of students studying human adaptations and explorations but of facts to be learned" (p. 236). This practice continues to hold in systems where high-stakes testing requires mostly factual recall. For curriculum development in general and the taught curriculum (what actually happens in classrooms) specifically, such forms of testing present an ongoing problem. The nature of history lends itself to inquiry and exploration. History, effectively taught, encourages thinking, reflection, revision, and recognition of unfinished stories. Yet too often, the observed teaching addresses none of these approaches.

Inquiry and the National History Standards

Contemporary curricula emerge from the agreed-upon content standards within a discipline. Consensus statements about this generative knowledge—that which is used to interpret new situations, solve problems, think, reason, and learn in history—surfaced from diverse groups within the history education community in documents such as the National History Standards (National Center for History in the Schools, 1994) and the National Assessment of Educational Progress (NAEP) Standards (National Assessment Governing Board, 1994). Within these frameworks, the use of inquiry is regarded as critical to studying history. Patrick (2002) argued that "lessons that stimulate questions and criticism in pursuit of truth, which are commensurate with the cognitive and personal development of students, should be encouraged in the schools of a free society" (p. 8). Doing so illustrates for students a basic tenet of American heritage: the freedom to think and openly express ideas.

The periodization structure of both the National History Standards and the NAEP documents provided the anchor for school systems and textbooks that used this device for decades to structure the presentation of history. These history framework documents recognize the interdependence between content standards and those associated with historical thinking. All of the standards are framed as questions that lend themselves logically to inquiry teaching and learning.

Although the formulation of the National History Standards has an uneven history, the materials address the concerns of both cognitive theorists and historians. The content standards encourage and support higher-order thinking and recognize the importance of a chronological frame. These standards "make explicit the goals that all students should have the opportunity to acquire" (National Center for History in the Schools, 1994, p. 2). The National Standards integrate Historical Thinking Standards across the content standards and grade levels to encourage multiple approaches to learning history. The writers established that Historical Thinking (skills) and Historical Understandings (content) are interdependent. Developing an in-depth understanding of history hinges on successful application of historical thinking skills and vice versa.

Historical thinking includes five skill sets that proceed developmentally through the grade levels: Chronological Thinking (e.g., create temporal structures); Historical Comprehension (e.g., read narrative imaginatively; interpret data from maps, photographs, cartoons); Historical Analysis and Interpretation (e.g., formulate questions to focus inquiry, consider multiple perspectives); Historical Research Capabilities (e.g., interrogate historical data, gather knowledge of time and place to construct a story); and Historical Issues-Analysis and Decision-Making (e.g., identify causes of a problem, evaluate consequences of a decision).

These standards recognize the importance of data (facts, names, dates, etc.) but emphasize that genuine historical understanding requires that students be able to raise questions, read primary documents, use data to support their conclusions, and have opportunities to create their own historical narratives. These aspects of student learning reinforce the idea that successful learning of history occurs when students view it as a discipline in which they participate in meaningful and productive ways. In *Thinking Historically,* Thomas Holt (1990) argued that history should not be presented as a story of known facts, all told and decided upon, but one that develops and accepts alternative perspectives. Such an approach fosters purposeful learning and provides opportunities for students to ask meaningful questions, find information, draw conclusions, and reflect on their own learning. Their engagement in the topic is genuine.

The National History Standards provide a clear rationale for teaching and learning history, reinforce the value of in-depth examination, and make the goals for learning clear, but they do not prescribe a curriculum for addressing these goals. It is the task of those most familiar with the school culture—namely, teachers—to mediate learning through the selection of appropriate instructional materials and assessment tools.

Implementing an inquiry-based history curriculum is not easily accomplished within the current climate of school reform. Contemporary measures of student learning rely heavily on rote recall of facts and dates and seldom require students to demonstrate their ability to discuss, analyze data, or integrate ideas. Teachers have to be wondering if there are any genuine benefits to creating and maintaining learning communities that are actively involved in inquiry. Several compelling reasons support this approach.

In effective history learning, students "do history" and explore the process of constructing historical accounts so that they derive their own understandings of past events. Students pose questions, investigate, offer tentative answers to historical questions, and develop historical explanations and interpretations. History standards expect analysis, exploration, comparison, and explanation—the essential skills for interpreting historical data. When practiced in history classrooms, inquiry develops skills needed to analyze narratives and answer questions that can be translated to data from different places and times. History taught through inquiry requires students to build their own narratives and supports the development of important writing, listening, and speaking skills. Inquiry helps to develop the language and frames of reference needed to recognize and create stories of the past. But as noted by James Baldwin in a speech to teachers, the ultimate importance of historical stories is that they help children

know that just as American history is longer, larger, more various, more beautiful and more terrible than anything anyone has ever said about it, so is the world larger, more daring, more beautiful and more terrible, but principally larger—and that it belongs to him [the child]. (Baldwin, 1988, pp. 12–13)

In-depth study invites students to critique myths, rewrite stories, and develop multiple accounts of events. It asks them not just to memorize someone else's interpretation, but to develop their own; not just to accumulate information, but to ask themselves and each other, "So what?" (Levstik & Barton, 2001). Holt (1990) insisted that the historical record has been too narrow, too simply political, and too exclusive. Students are shortchanged when teachers or textbook writers make all the decisions about what is taught; fail to include original source materials such as letters, photos, and diaries; or rely solely on activities that are merely verification exercises.

Inquiry is a practice, not a product. To paraphrase an old proverb, give a man a fish and he will eat for a day, show a man how to fish and he will live for a lifetime. This adage reflects the ultimate goal of using inquiry to teach and learn history. By creating classroom environments in which students learn how to inquire, we build the knowledge and skills for now and the future. Students also gain a deeper appreciation of the content that history values.

The merit of moving toward an inquiry curriculum is that it can cause students to change their perception about understanding history. By focusing on questions, students can see themselves as makers/interpreters of history, not just consumers of predetermined facts. Using the artifacts or objects of history motivates student learning and, by increasing their interest, helps to build knowledge. Although the benefits of history as inquiry are difficult to quantify, we argue vigorously for its use. The impact of presenting a carefully designed curriculum that is oriented toward inquiry *can* be assessed. How inquiry is assessed in our current climate of efficiency and accountability is described in the next section.

Assessing Student Inquiry

With few exceptions, the high-stakes testing now in place in many schools and states is not aligned with an inquiry-based curriculum. Assessments that compare students and schools are rooted in assumptions about the nature of learning developed by behavioral psychologists and not by cognitive researchers. The typical standardized test relies on the belief that knowledge is a collection of data that can be measured accurately through multiple-choice decisions about specific, discrete packets of information that have little connection to broader ideas, concepts, and principles. This approach may be appropriate for some areas of study, but it is inadequate and ineffective when applied to history.

Teachers who present an inquiry-based curriculum must recognize this current reality, but doing so does not preclude the use of other assessments. Normative assessments, as well as formative and summative assessments that focus on what the learner has accomplished, provide a more complete picture of student learning. Formative assessments might include written reports, chart and photographic analyses, or responses to oral questioning. Data derived from such methods provide the teacher with important information for monitoring student progress. Normative assessments of specific information about people, eras, events, or concepts elicit different information from students and are what teachers and schools expect, but they reflect only part of student learning. Summative assessments, often student driven, may include aspects of both aforementioned types of assessment. When students write their ideas and interpretations, they gain the opportunity to think carefully about the material; when students select the right answer from a set of choices, they practice test-taking skills required by their system. Summative projects or written assignments enable students to demonstrate how they made sense of multiple, discrete pieces of information. In this way, they integrate their new knowledge into schemas that, ideally, can be applied to later situations. Multiple forms of assessment can be used successfully to increase student interest and demonstrate learner gains and in-depth thinking when history is presented through inquiry.

Key Ideas That Guide Historical Inquiry

Inquiry learning has theoretical and practical classroom foundations that are important to bear in mind when teaching history through this approach.

Knowledge and skills must be thoroughly integrated. Successful inquiry requires that teachers account for students' content and skill levels. Students need guidance in how to practice inquiry. Although asking questions may be natural for students, they may lack the ability to answer them through a process of inquiry. The historian's craft must be introduced in steps.

Building a community of inquiry is essential. Students need frequent opportunities to observe others doing the same kind of work that is expected of them. Collaboration with peers enhances the likelihood of successful learning through inquiry.

Inquiry must center on questions and tasks that are worthy of sustained exploration. In-depth study should include opportunities for students to apply both prior knowledge and newly acquired information to build understanding.

Inquiry is a dynamic process in which outcomes are not always predictable.

Teachers, like historians, model and have students practice "classroom thoughtfulness." They take the time to think carefully and thoroughly before responding to questions or attempting to solve problems. Thinking aloud, that is, sharing the personal process of discovery with students, encourages their own successful thought processes.

Teachers must be aware of bias in developing inquiry lessons. Successful interpretation of historical material depends on recognizing the fact that language is not neutral. For example, interpretations of data may change, not because the data are different, but because society has changed and the questions being asked may no longer be relevant.

To successfully accomplish the goal of using inquiry to learn history, students must be given opportunities to reflect on the learning process and be able to justify their conclusions with evidence.

ADDITIONAL THOUGHTS

What are the true implications for students who participate in an inquiry-based history curriculum? The answers will differ from student to student and across situations. One class may reach different conclusions about why immigrants came to the United States. But if the data are accurate and the student thinking process is reasonable, multiple conclusions may be acceptable. After all, there are different stories and different interpretations of information. That recognition itself is an important conclusion for students to reach about the study of history.

Standards were meant to provide guidelines for teachers and curriculum developers. They are descriptive and not prescriptive. Standards describe broad goals for student understanding, not lists of facts to be memorized. This leaves ample room and freedom for teacher-mediated learning and for selecting a variety of approaches to support student learning.

Although teachers are guided by standards and design their curriculum within that framework, they are also increasingly influenced by state and federally mandated tests. Unfortunately, teachers often react to these extrinsic forces by adopting teaching styles that complement this narrow interpretation of student learning. Teaching to this type of test is a terrible disservice to all students, particularly those who are most oriented toward in-depth understanding through inquiry.

Common sense and the historical processes dictate that critical inquiry is an essential tool for understanding history. Results from the National Assessment of Educational Progress (NAEP) exam in U.S. History (Patrick, 2002) also support this view. Although students did not score as well as hoped, some encouraging trends were evident.

Eighth graders spending more time using primary source materials fared better on the exam than those who reported less or no use of this type of material. Twelfth graders who read biographies and other kinds of stories in history performed better than those who never experienced this kind of classroom assignment. (Patrick, 2002, p. 17)

Some students who believe that all the answers are already known find the study of history boring and too directed. Standards offer teachers choices and structures for student learning that inspire; that draw students into the challenge of searching data for the story that is history. Teachers cannot ignore the required student assessments in their schools. However, they should use the vast storehouses of increasingly available rich historical data to lead students to truly examine history beyond the level of repeating or recognizing factoids. As Bruner (1986) stated, "It is in hypothesis generating (rather than hypothesis falsification) that one cultivates multiple perspectives and possible worlds to match the requirements of those perspectives" (p. 52). When students become part of making, investigating, challenging, or retelling the story, they develop a greater chance of understanding the tale that must be passed on to following generations.

History is not tidy. It contains conflicting narratives. Not all of the answers are known. Understanding requires active thinking. This is the brand of history that students want to inquire, discover, and make their own.

IDEAS FROM THE FIELD

A COUNTRY OF MANY COUNTRIES:
50 YEARS OF IMMIGRATION

Movement of peoples has had a major impact on the history of the world. This lesson employs statistical data to study changes in the U.S. population during the 20th century. Students investigate historical census data and manipulate and interpret numbers to draw conclusions about causes and effects of immigration. This integrated activity strengthens students' historical knowledge and thinking skills, mathematical ability, and writing proficiency.

Inquiry in history falls into the information-processing model and, depending on how it is structured, incorporates either deductive or inductive reasoning. Effective history inquiry lessons incorporate the following key ideas:

- Standards, questions, and the culture of classroom and school are the foundations of the curriculum.
- Learning outcomes are often unpredictable, difficult to control, and usually open-ended.
- Choices of primary sources are significant. The perspectives of the chosen documents matter (e.g., slave vs. owner).
- Presenting multiple perspectives is important. There is seldom one answer that we want students to know about history.
- Interpretation cannot be value neutral or totally objective. This is why reflection is such a vital part of the inquiry process.
- Practicing inquiry builds skills that have broad application to other subjects and to future study.

Lesson Overview

Immigration of peoples from around the world has had a significant impact on U.S. history. This lesson employs statistical data to examine the origins of the U.S. population over time. It enables students to draw conclusions and investigate history content through manipulation of numbers. It strengthens students' historical knowledge and thinking skills, mathematical skills, and writing ability. This lesson could be used several times during the study of U.S. or world history (e.g., at mid-20th century and at the end of the 20th century). In each instance, predictions made in earlier studies could be checked. Spiraling the topic of immigration reinforces the inquiry process and the notion of history as a timeless story. Using one topic and returning to the same questions in different eras provides students with an increasing depth of understanding about the topic and its connection with the broader story of history.

History Standards

U.S. History Standards: Era 6, Standard 2A, Student understands sources and experiences of the new immigrants; Era 10, Standard 2B, Student understands the new immigration and demographic shifts.

World History Standards: Era 7, Standard 6, Student understands major global trends from 1750–1914; World History Across Eras, Standard 1, Student understands long-term changes and recurring patterns in world history (e.g., major changes in world population over time).

Historical Thinking Standards

Students use visual and mathematical data in graphs to increase historical comprehension, interrogate historical data, gather knowledge of time and place to construct a story.

Assessment

1. Students answer questions about immigration before analyzing chart.

2. Students write their hypotheses in their notebooks and share with class.

3. Students write statements about each decade illustrated in the chart or create a visual representation or illustration of the graph's data.

4. Student Exit Card with predictions for following decades.

5. Lesson organization

6. Opening the lesson (20 minutes)

7. Introduce topic to students with warm-up questions such as: Why would people want to come to the United States from other countries? Why would you leave the country in which you were born to move to a new country?

8. Students share answers and the teacher records. Post these in sight for later use. Introduce concept of *push factors* (reasons to leave a country) and *pull factors* (reasons for voluntarily moving to another place). Ask students to determine which items on their list are push factors and which are pull factors.

9. Have students divide a piece of paper into two columns labeled "Reasons to Enter U.S." and "World Events." Add a list of decades for the rows. Work with a partner to answer the following questions:
   - What would make people want to come to the United States during this decade?
   - What world events during this time period might make people want to leave their native countries?

10. Ask students to share their answers. Record responses on an overhead or chart.

11. Developing the lesson (50 minutes)

12. Ask students to review the lists and, in pairs, hypothesize about time periods that might have brought the most immigrants and when people might have left the United States. Explain the hypotheses.

13. Distribute the chart titled "Immigration and Emigration by Decade: 1901–1990" from the U.S. Bureau of the Census. Present only 1901–1950 data. Have students examine the data and answer any questions about how to interpret this information. Make sure that students can distinguish between immigrants and emigrants. Check for understanding of the Ratio and Net columns.

14. Working in pairs, students examine the data and write a sentence that describes the pattern for each decade, beginning with 1901–1910. They can also graph immigration/emigration data using figures on the chart "U.S. Immigration/Emigration by Decades."

15. Students compare their conclusions with their original hypotheses. They should search for examples of when the data matched their guesses and cases in which there was no match.

If the data support their hypotheses, ask students how they generated their hypotheses. If the data do not match, ask students what events or issues they did not consider that may have had an influence. Encourage them to think aloud to explain the process used to reach their conclusions.

Discuss the class findings.

1. Were there any decades in which you were surprised about the data? Why?

2. What events did you suggest would make people come to the United States?

3. Did you expect these large changes? Why? Why not?

4. Closing the lesson (5–10 minutes)

5. Have students answer the following questions in their Exit Card to summarize what they learned.

6. What information did the chart provide to you about U.S. (or world) history?

7. How do you think immigration/emigration might affect the future story of the United States (or another country)?

Teaching Resources

Emigration: Immigration and Emigration by Decade: 1901–1990 (http://uscis.gov/graphics/shared/aboutus/statistics/300.htm)

All census data are available online, indexed by location and topic (http://www.fedstats.gov/aboutfedstats.html).

Each department within the government collects data (e.g., Health and Human Services on health issues, Department of the Treasury on incomes/employment, Department of the Interior on parks and environment, etc.). For the study of immigration, the Immigration and Naturalization Service collects and publishes data. Questions about immigration can be searched on the census site: http://wscis.gov

Enrichment Activities

Have students hypothesize about what they would have expected to happen to immigration from 1950–1990. Repeat the above activity for these four decades.

There are many other ways to explore U.S. Census Bureau data. County of origin is another revealing source of information related to this activity on immigration (http://uscis.gov/graphics/shared/aboutus/statistics/299.htm).

Develop a WebQuest to explore the changing makeup of the local community by gathering data from state sources (also available through the Fedstats Web site).

This activity can be used to integrate mathematics and English language learners to the curriculum and encourage further inquiry.

Accommodations for Special Learners

Graphic data may require explanation and will certainly require teacher awareness of students' prior knowledge about this type of analysis.

It may be very helpful for this type of activity to check with the mathematics teachers for information about student experiences with graphic material.

Because there is little reading required, this type of activity may require less attention to reading ability, although expressing student learning in writing is encouraged. Writing conclusions drawn from graphs reinforces a goal across all disciplines to write mathematically and historically.

REFERENCES

Baldwin, J. (1988). A talk to teachers. In R. Simonson & S. Walker (Eds.), *Multi-cultural literacy* (pp. 3–12). St. Paul, MN: Graywolf.

Bruner, J. S. (1986). *Actual minds, possible worlds.* Cambridge, MA: Harvard University Press.

Chi, M. T. H., Feltovich, P., & Glaser, R. (1981). Categorization and representation of physics problems by experts and novices. *Cognitive Science, 5,* 121–152.

Dewey, J. (1933). *How we think: A restatement of the relation of reflective thinking to the educative process.* Boston, MA: D. C. Heath.

Glassman, M. (2001). Dewey and Vygotsky: Society, experience, and inquiry in educational practice. *Educational Researcher, 30*(4), 3–14.

Goodlad, J. (1984). *A place called school: Prospects for the future.* New York: McGraw-Hill.

Goodman, N. (1984). *Of mind and other matters.* Cambridge, MA: Harvard University Press.

Holt, T. (1990). *Thinking historically: Narrative, imagination, and understanding.* New York: College Entrance Examination Board.

Levstik, L. S., & Barton, K. C. (2001). *Doing history* (2nd ed.). Mahway, NJ: Lawrence Erlbaum.

National Assessment Governing Board. (1994). *U.S. history framework for the 1994 National Assessment of Educational Progress.* Washington, DC: Author.

National Center for History in the Schools. (1994). *National standards for history.* Los Angeles: Author.

Parker, W. (1991). *Renewing the social studies curriculum.* Alexandria, VA: Association for Supervision and Curriculum Development.

Patrick, J. (2002). *The 2001 NAEP in U.S. history.* Bloomington, IN: ERIC Clearinghouse for Social Studies/Social Science Education. (ERIC Document No. ED465707)

Renner, J. W., Stafford, D. G., Lawson, A. E., McKinnon, J. W., Friot, F. E., & Kellogg, D. H. (1976). *Research, teaching, and learning with the Piaget model.* Norman: University of Oklahoma Press.

Resnick, L. B. (1987). *Education and learning to think.* Washington, DC: National Academy Press.

Resnick, L. B., & Klopfer, L. E. (Eds.). (1989). *Toward the thinking curriculum: Current cognitive research.* Alexandria, VA: Association for Supervision and Curriculum Development.

Rogoff, B. (1990). *Apprenticeship in thinking: Cognitive development in social context.* New York: Oxford University Press.

Sternberg, R. J., & Horvath, J. A. (1995). A prototype view of expert teaching. *Educational Researcher, 24*(6), 9–17.

Vygotsky, L. S. (1978). *Mind in society: The development of higher psychological processes.* Cambridge, MA: Harvard University Press.

Wertsch, J. V. (1998). *Mind as action.* New York: Oxford University Press.

CHAPTER FIVE

Mathematics

Developing Curious Students

Jenny Tsankova
Galina Dobrynina

"Today is a special day," Mrs. Oliver announces to her kindergarten class. "We'll go on a 'Shape Hunt.' We will look around our classroom to discover shapes. I wonder what shapes we can find?"

Kindergarten students are full of curiosity and eager to explore the environment around them. They are impatient to name and find circles, squares, and balls. They are excited to learn that a diamond-shaped object actually has a first and a last name—"Rom" "Bus"—and are happy to pronounce "rectangular prism"—or was it "rectangular present"? And when Mrs. Oliver shows her students what a cylinder looks like, George comes up to her and says, "Can I take your pen? It is a cylinder."

The effective mathematics teacher discovers what students already know and moves them closer to acquiring new knowledge. They are engaged, motivated, and interested in learning mathematics. But what classroom ingredient keeps students focused for a longer period of time than expected? Is it the activity, the teacher, the students, or just the enthusiasm inherent in 5- or 6-year-old children? Quality teaching includes all of these ingredients and more. The teacher's ability to involve students in mathematical inquiry and connect it with students' interests; the students' habits of investigation, persistence, and natural curiosity; and the enthusiasm that is present in children of all ages are all part of the picture. Capitalizing on students' interests, leading students through a process of exploration and discovery, and challenging and supporting their reasoning efforts are central to developing students' mathematical curiosity. These practices form the heart and soul of learning with understanding and are essential for developing a lifelong positive disposition toward mathematics.

MATHEMATICAL INQUIRY: HISTORICAL PERSPECTIVES

For the past half century, the movement toward inquiry in the mathematics curriculum has been influenced heavily by historical events. After the Soviet Union launched Sputnik in 1957 and demonstrated its superiority to the world's mathematical and scientific communities, the United States initiated major curriculum reforms. Traditional curricula that emphasized computational procedures were infused with more challenging mathematical content and topics generally offered only in college courses. However, this so-called new math failed to produce the desired outcome of raising mathematical knowledge and skills for *all* students. New math presented challenges for teachers and students and fostered an elitist notion of mathematical literacy. The failure of the new math initiative caused the pendulum to shift toward the "back to basics" movement of the 1970s. Applications and investigatory activities were de-emphasized, and computational procedures once again became the principal focus of the mathematics classroom.

The results of the second National Assessment of Educational Progress (NAEP, 1970) and of the Second International Mathematics and Science Study (Robitaille & Travers, 1992), however, exposed the lack of students' understanding and again challenged the status quo of mathematics instruction. The National Council of Teachers of Mathematics (NCTM), in *Agenda for Action* (1980), recommended that (a) problem solving be the centerpiece of school mathematics; (b) mathematical reasoning rather than computational skill become the focal point; and (c) mathematics curricula encourage students to question, explore, and discover mathematical ideas. In its 1983 report, *A Nation at Risk: The Imperative for Educational Reform,* the National Commission on Excellence in Education called for sweeping changes in K–12 curricula. Mathematics education was singled out and challenged to radically modify its curriculum and improve teaching for all students.

The turning point in our nation's movement toward reform of school mathematics was initiated by NCTM's publication of *Curriculum and Evaluation Standards for School Mathematics* (1989). This document provided guidelines for implementing significant changes in the major content areas of school mathematics and, for the first time, directed major attention to mathematical process standards, such as reasoning, communication, connections, and problem solving. The mathematics classroom was pictured as a place for communicating, questioning, and applying mathematical concepts. Teaching and learning were described as processes of inquiry, discovery, and exploration. Excellence in mathematics education was founded on high expectations and promoted as being attainable by *all* students. The *Principles and Standards for School Mathematics* (NCTM, 2000) confirmed the need for dedicated and committed mathematics educators to improve school mathematics and turn this vision into reality.

The call for dramatic change in school mathematics coincided with an increased emphasis on assessment at the national and state levels. Results of the International Mathematics and Science Studies (Robitaille & Travers, 1992), NAEP tests (1980–2004), and state assessments showed some improvement in mathematics achievement over the past 15 years. However, international comparisons showed that U.S. students generally lack conceptual understanding of mathematical ideas. The 1995 and 1999 TIMSS studies (National Center for Education Statistics, 2003; TIMSS, 1996) also revealed that despite the purported changeover toward mathematical inquiry, which led to new curriculum materials and assessment practices, the most prevalent form of teaching and learning in U.S. mathematics classrooms still focused on computational procedures.

Efforts to implement the principles and standards, to promote exploration of challenging problem situations, reasoning, and communications in classrooms on an everyday basis, have yet to produce discernible results. Convincing arguments exist for supporting the goals of the principles and standards in general and for implementing mathematics inquiry. These positions tend to conflict with the widespread beliefs that inquiry-based teaching and learning are too challenging for students, too time-consuming, and too unrealistic to apply on a regular basis. In this chapter, we define and describe mathematical inquiry and its ingredients, and suggest how teachers and learners can explore problem-solving situations in existing curricular contexts to promote deep conceptual understanding.

MATHEMATICAL INQUIRY AND ITS PLACE IN THE CLASSROOM

> And how many hours a day did you do lessons? said Alice.
> Ten hours the first day, said the Mock Turtle: nine the next, and so on.
> What a curious plan! exclaimed Alice.
> That's the reason they are called lessons, the Gryphon remarked: because they lessen from day to day.
>
> Lewis Carroll, *Alice's Adventures in Wonderland*

For any mathematical term to be successfully applied and connected through reason with other mathematical entities, the definition must be correct and the term applied in an appropriate context. For this reason, in discussing mathematical inquiry, it is critical to properly contextualize the term, clarify its meaning, and describe and demonstrate its potential applications in the mathematics classroom.

The National Council of Teachers of Mathematics (NCTM, 2000) identified conceptual understanding through problem solving as a highly desired outcome of teaching and learning mathematics. Mathematics, if defined as a science of patterns and as a language for describing such patterns (National Research Council, 1990), infers that mathematical understanding emerges when students investigate and describe relationships among concepts, patterns, and ideas. To promote the construction of mathematical understanding, teachers need to begin with students' own experiences (Dewey, 1916/1966), involve them in analyzing and discovering patterns, support them in reasoning and describing relationships among concepts, and encourage learners to further their epistemic and inquiry levels of understanding (Perkins, 1992). When students can demonstrate the connections among key ideas, their knowledge becomes available for solving newly encountered problems (Dewey, 1916/1966). If the act of learning involves "transformation—the process of manipulating knowledge to make it fit new tasks" (Bruner, 1960, p. 48), we can infer that students understand mathematics.

Genuine mathematical learning occurs through active engagement in explorations that give students the opportunity to recognize how mathematical ideas connect and through activities that promote reflection and communication (NCTM, 2000). Effective teaching occurs whenever students are challenged and supported during their journey to mathematical understanding.

Few mathematics educators would deny the centrality of conceptual understanding and problem solving to their discipline. Yet schools continue to produce new generations of math-phobic students who unashamedly acknowledge that they do not understand the fundamental principles of mathematics (Burns, 1998). Most students complete schooling feeling unsatisfied about their mathematical accomplishments, lacking confidence in their mathematical abilities, and convinced that they are mentally unequipped to understand mathematics.

Both the explanation and the cure for this self-perpetuating cycle lie within the essence of the mathematical domain. How does someone develop a talent in any area? Baseball players, pianists, even chefs build confidence, satisfaction, and mastery only through practice over extended periods of time. For the learner, frequent and active engagement in a challenging environment, diligence, and reflective experiences are necessary ingredients for overcoming the difficulties inherent to developing any new skill or body of knowledge. Mathematics is no exception to this rule.

Students must be continually exposed to carefully selected experiences that motivate, challenge, guide, and support conceptual understanding through problem solving. According to Siegel, Borasi, and Fonzi (1998), inquiry incorporates social experiences such as collaboration and communication. But inquiry also incorporates problem-solving experiences such as understanding a problem, devising a plan for attacking the problem, carrying out the plan, reflecting on the solution, and expanding the problem definition (Polya, 1945/1973; Schoenfeld, 1985). Teaching through inquiry requires that all partners be actively involved in the search for mathematical meaning, a search that we refer to as the process of mathematical inquiry.

Our belief in the goals for mathematics education, our analyses of educational and cognitive psychology research findings, and our own teaching experience underlie our comprehensive definition of mathematical inquiry. Inquiry in the mathematics classroom is a cyclical process that consists of the following:

Challenging problem situations—students applying problem-solving strategies, posing and testing hypotheses, reflecting on results, checking, searching for alternative solutions, generalizing, and extending

Instructional support and guidance—teachers asking questions and providing appropriate hints; probing for conceptual and procedural understanding; demanding explanations, reasoning, and proof; developing students' mathematical metacognitive skills

Communication and reasoning—writing and verbally exchanging ideas among teachers and peers; sharing questions, predictions, and findings; formulating new questions and problems

Forming investigative habits—problem-solving skills and flexibility in thinking; the ability to work independently and in groups; the inclination to listen, consider, and respect one another's reasoning; the development of character traits such as persistence, curiosity, accuracy, and positive mathematical dispositions

Guiding Students' Learning Through Mathematical Inquiry: Role of the Teacher

The task of the teacher in an inquiry-based classroom is multifaceted. As the primary initiator of inquiry, he or she must target mathematical concepts and select investigations that are appropriate to students' ages, interests, levels of readiness, and preparedness for independent or team investigations. The teacher leads by motivating, supporting, and challenging students throughout the process of inquiry. As the evaluator, the teacher monitors student performance, assesses understanding, anticipates difficulties, makes necessary curriculum adjustments, and summarizes results to foster learning.

Selecting Tools for Inquiry

Instructional Materials

Inquiry is a way of thinking about mathematics that presupposes the availability of rich mathematical content that encourages students to problem solve, investigate, make connections, test hypotheses, and infer. Inquiry does not provide the foundation for special types of textbooks or particular resource materials per se.

Often, classrooms are supplied with instructional materials that are not truly supportive of inquiry. What is the teacher to do in such a situation? For students to make connections and inferences, and to persist in their mathematical endeavors, it is critically important for teachers to skillfully select and/or appropriately modify the curriculum and student learning materials.

Challenges associated with choosing appropriate instructional materials for inquiry-based instruction are rooted in the teacher's depth of mathematics content knowledge, the teacher's attitude and beliefs about students' learning abilities, and the students' dispositions and readiness to conduct the selected inquiries. Teachers often underestimate students' readiness for challenging activities (Bruner, 1960). Our own research revealed that students in Grades 1 through 6 could successfully investigate and solve algebraic problems with two unknowns (Dobrynina, 2001; Tsankova, 2003). Preservice and inservice teachers, who may themselves experience difficulty with algebraic content, sometimes make a priori assumptions about students' ability to solve certain problems and therefore avoid engaging their students in algebraic inquiry. Thus a teacher's limited knowledge of mathematics may hinder a student's willingness and ability to explore challenging problems. Teachers must become problem solvers and investigators themselves in order to appreciate the importance of inquiry and take risks in engaging their students' minds (Schoenfeld, 1992).

Choosing Problems

An inquiry-based mathematics environment is anchored in challenging problems and worthwhile questions for student investigation. Selecting problems with the correct degree of difficulty and attainable levels of success is the most difficult part in planning inquiry lessons. Questions must be answerable given suitable amounts of personal effort and support from the teacher and peers. Problems need to hinge on key mathematical ideas, bridge prior knowledge with new concepts to be mastered, allow for student reflection, and connect with similar problems and applications. Only through a process of wrestling with ideas does inquiry become transformed into a personal process of discovery and meaning making.

In Japan, teachers believe that finding the right problem or question is the key element of an effective mathematics lesson (Hashimoto

& Becker, 1999). Solving problems becomes a conceptual exploration for students in which alternative solution possibilities are shared before any computations are attempted. Investigations in Japanese classrooms are differentiated according to individual students' learning styles and readiness. Once a problem is posed, students reason independently for 3 minutes. This gives all students the opportunity to think about a problem without the quick assistance of a more capable or convincing peer. Then, students are given the choice of discussing the problem in pairs, small groups, or reading hint cards independently. In this way, every student is encouraged to reach a solution in the most personally fitting manner. This process also enables the teacher to overhear discussions, informally assess students' work, and select students to demonstrate different problem-solving approaches. At this point, the teacher summarizes the process of inquiry and reviews the key mathematical principles. In the final stage, a second problem is posed that focuses on application and connections. Thus exploration, inference, reflection, and authentic assessment are naturally embedded in an inquiry-based classroom.

Choosing problems that can be solved in a variety of ways enhances students' abilities to consider other students' solution methods, enrich their problem-solving toolboxes, and grow in their flexibility in reasoning and approaching problem-solving situations. Investigating problems that have numerous solutions or no solution promotes students' curiosity and ability to reason and justify results. Even in early grades, students can reason about a frame equation of the type (square + triangle = 10) and find all natural numbers that satisfy the equation. Later, the students themselves can extend such investigations. They create their own new problems or modify the existing problem to achieve multiple correct solutions or no solution. These types of inquiries take students' reasoning to a level of understanding where the students are asking the questions and meeting the goals for the investigation.

Manipulative and Technology Tools

Another key component in successfully setting up an inquiry-based classroom is creatively implementing the use of manipulative and technology tools that support effective mathematics instruction. Such materials appeal to students and provide the concrete, hands-on experiences many students need as a transition to understanding more abstract ideas (Baroody, 1989; Fuson & Briars, 1990; Ginsburg, 1982). However, incorporating manipulatives does not ensure that students are engaged in the process of inquiry (Ma, 1999). Many researchers argue that using such tools without careful consideration of their special value or the specific goals of the investigation fail to help students make connections and inferences between concrete and symbolic representations (Baroody, 1989; Clements & McMillen, 1996; Thompson, 1994). In an inquiry-based mathematics classroom, teachers should reflect regularly on the practice of using various tools, understand the levels of thinking and reasoning students must apply when working with tools, and assess how students increase their ability to investigate with the help of mathematical learning tools.

Motivating and Supervising Students During Inquiry-Based Learning

Step 1: Initiating Inquiry

Inquiry-based activities need to be aligned with key mathematical ideas and standards. They should build on students' prior knowledge, that is, previously introduced concepts that need to be reinforced or assessed. Inquiry lessons should never be initiated for the simple purpose of having students perform explorations. All learning activities should fit tightly within the sequence of developing students' understanding and be a natural component of the mathematics curriculum. For example, when middle school students compare the base 10 with other number systems, teachers may lead them through an inquiry activity of constructing/inventing another number system using any number of symbols. For instance, using three symbols (e.g., circle, triangle, and square), students may express numbers 1 through 20 and show how to write and perform addition and subtraction operations. Initiating such an inquiry requires students to apply knowledge and understanding about place value and algorithms for addition and subtraction. This investigation provides an excellent foundation for reflecting and summarizing key mathematical ideas about the specificity of the base 10 system. It also serves as a springboard for an extension inquiry such as investigating divisibility rules, the mathematics underlying the rules, and whether these rules apply equally to other number bases.

Motivating students is of equal importance to the mathematical principles involved. An element of puzzlement (Kennedy & Tipps, 1994); a connection to popular books, shows, or events; or the addition of a personal element to a problem situation heightens interest. In the base 10 example described above, the teacher could assign a project in which students are given the opportunity to select an activity, time themselves performing the activity, and then represent in scientific notation using powers of 10 the total amount of time needed to repeat this process a million times. Such an approach promotes the students' personal interest and eagerness to discover how much time it would take to eat a million pieces of pizza, listen to a million CDs, walk to school a million times, drink a million cans of soda, and so on. Students become personally motivated to answer mathematical questions, and the computations and representations are the means for achieving the desired outcome.

Step 2: Coaching During an Inquiry

Coaching is the delicate art of balancing the students' freedom to explore with the likelihood that the desired outcomes and direction taken by the investigation can be achieved successfully. A key aspect of effective coaching is careful planning. The planning includes solving and exploring the same problem situations to be required of students, considering alternative solutions, and identifying potential student difficulties. Although it remains true that one can never anticipate everything that might happen during inquiry, the more one is prepared, the easier it is to predict directions of students' reasoning, ask the right questions, provide appropriate hints, and manage the classroom effectively and efficiently.

The amount of time devoted to an inquiry is important to all participants and to the process itself. Adequate time must be allocated for students to fully analyze and understand the problem, decide how to approach an investigation, and summarize and reflect on the results. Unsuccessful strategies and dead ends may lead to fruitful discussions about the mathematical reasons for these false starts. However, repeated frustration may cause students to lose self-confidence and interest in the investigation. Teachers must take students' difficulties into account and provide the necessary support system.

Overcoming difficulties builds self-confidence. An essential ingredient of effective inquiry teaching is creating support for students when they are wrestling intellectually with challenging ideas. Confronting demanding problem situations requires functioning at the zone of proximal development. Vygotsky created this expression to describe the "distance between the actual development level as determined by independent problem solving and the level of potential development as determined through problem solving under adult guidance or in collaboration with more capable peers" (Vygotsky, 1978, pp. 85–86). As Vygotsky pointed out, what children can do with assistance today, they can do by themselves tomorrow. Therefore, teachers need to decide when and how to provide guidance and strike a subtle balance between giving too much information and providing too little assistance. In their effort to facilitate students' reasoning and prevent frustration, teachers generally offer more support than is actually needed. Students grow accustomed to having the teacher provide answers and solutions. Their first inclination is to inquire about how to solve a problem before any attempt to reason independently. When asked for help, teachers should start with general hints or probing questions instead of offering concrete suggestions. Questions such as "What is given? What did you try to find? How did you try to find the answer?" provide insights into students' thinking and help students to reflect on where they are in the inquiry process. Reflection and verbalization help students to decide whether to progress along the same path or abandon the initial strategy. This approach also leaves the students with the understanding that it was their efforts and not the teacher's that enabled them to solve the problem.

Organizing feedback and communication during inquiry activities is a complex task. Monitoring discussions among students should allow the teacher to orchestrate students' work in small groups and assess their individual performances. Communication in an inquiry-based classroom moves along multiple pathways. Information flow is pictured in Figure 5.1.

Teachers must organize opinion sharing, coordinate questions among students in small groups, and facilitate discussions of whole-class findings. For communication to be effective, teachers have to model questioning, respect other people's mathematical ideas, and practice listening without interruption.

The process of inquiry is incomplete without student reflection. Schön (1983) described two types of reflection. Reflection in action occurs when a person thinks about what is going on and decides what to do. Follow-up reflection occurs when he or she ponders what was learned and how this knowledge can be generalized to other situations. Both forms of reflection are significant for successful problem solving and should be fostered by teachers. Krulik and Rudnick

Figure 5.1   Information Flow

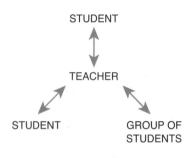

(1993) viewed the postreflection after a problem is solved as a compound activity. When reflecting on the answer, students have to test its reasonableness, write a summary paragraph explaining the method used to derive the solution and the reason it was chosen, propose other solutions, change the conditions of the problem and identify the consequences of the change, extend the problem, and generalize the results. Testing whether the answer makes sense in the context of the problem forces students to switch back from the mathematical model to the concrete problem situation. Writing a summary paragraph demands students' awareness of their thought processes, reflection on their ideas, and reasoning about the strategies employed. Teachers need to focus on developing students' metacognitive skills and use them as a source for uncovering students' misconceptions or for discussion topics, or as feedback for planning further instruction.

When probing for students' understanding, teachers must encourage students to explain and justify their answers, and find out whether the answer makes sense and under what conditions (Schoenfeld, 1992). The "what if" approach causes students to examine cause-and-effect relationships that exist between the given conditions and the results. Changing some of the initial conditions of the problem and determining how this affects the new outcome helps students to better understand the structure of the problem (i.e., what is known and unknown, and the role of constraints).

Step 3: Assessing Inquiry-Based Learning

Assessment of inquiry-based learning should be informed and driven by the meaning and contents of the inquiry process. Assessment of inquiry must include ongoing, embedded checkpoints during the inquiry, careful examination of end reflections, and measurements of student work in terms of learning expectations. As an integral part of the learning process, assessment should provide feedback to all participants and help to improve the quality of ongoing inquiry (Kulm, 1990; Lester & Lambdin-Kroll, 1990).

Inquiry-based assessment begins with selecting an inquiry activity and formulating student expectations that are communicated clearly at the onset of the lesson. Formative assessment by the teacher and student self-assessment should be embedded throughout the inquiry activity. Teachers observe the investigations, listen to student conversation, monitor progress, ask clarifying questions, and push for explanations. Students need to learn how to monitor their own reasoning process (think aloud or write down) and know when and how to change the course of an inquiry. Monitoring and modifying is similar to the process described by Polya (1945/1973) and Schoenfeld (1992). Students start by questioning: "Do I understand what is given and what is required in the inquiry? How can I start and proceed? If I do this, what happens?" Monitoring, modifying, and reflecting on the learning process is a learning process in itself.

Summative assessment of students' learning often occurs through presentations and reports. Teachers must ensure that presentations are accompanied by questions, discussion, and feedback from peers. Interactive presentations that involve all participants are especially powerful. Reports are likely to include self-assessments focused on growth in students' learning. Teachers should provide assessment feedback and allow students to redo and improve the reports.

In assessing the process of inquiry, teachers compare the demonstrated learning outcomes with the original expectations. Knowing how successfully students conducted an inquiry provides valuable information for the teacher to improve the inquiry, focus on particular problem-solving strategies through instruction, modify presentations of mathematical ideas, and determine the next steps in developing students' mathematical understanding.

FROM INQUIRY TO PERSONAL CREATIVITY

To be effective, inquiry-based instruction should become a fundamental practice across a school's mathematics program. Conducting mathematical inquiry is not an unrealistic vision, but implementation does require dedication and persistence. Collaboration among teachers is the key to making inquiry-based teaching and learning a school- or districtwide orientation. Only through mutual support in planning, selecting problem situations, sharing difficulties, modifying assessments, and reflecting about the everyday work can such an innovation become part of the school's culture.

The need for collaboration among teachers and students arises from the fact that as students progress through the grades, they develop certain expectations of what a mathematics class should look like. Unless they frequently encounter the unique challenges of an inquiry-based approach to learning mathematics, they may be reluctant to actively explore problem situations. When opportunities for inquiry are presented across the K–12 spectrum on a regular basis, students consistently enter mathematics classrooms where they are challenged and enthusiastically supported in their mathematical investigations.

Conducting mathematical inquiry should not be an occasional activity that is simply superimposed on an already packed mathematics block. Neither should it be the problem-solving component, problem of the day, or the semester math project. Inquiry is a distinct approach to teaching and learning in which teachers and students are challenged to explore problem-solving situations and communicate and share solution strategies, and in which the flexibility to change a solution is regarded as a step toward understanding. Inquiry forges connections among prior knowledge, formation of new skills, and new conceptual understanding. Inquiry is a habit of critical analysis aimed at creating a balanced cycle of schoolwork, homework, and summer work to support and extend understanding of mathematical ideas.

The ability to successfully engage in inquiry develops over time and with experience. Younger students need more guidance and support, whereas older students are generally more sophisticated problem solvers. They are more capable of guiding discussions, posing their own questions, considering cases of solutions, and even creating their own problem situations. The ability to conduct mathematical investigation should be consistently nurtured and supported throughout all grades in order for students to develop the habits of mind shared by all active inquirers. It is through our teaching that we develop curious minds, minds searching for meaning and nonstandard solutions, risk takers, investigators, and problem solvers. When we ask kindergarten children to create and pose their own addition and subtraction story problems, we plant the seed of inquiry that hopefully will blossom into mathematical creativity.

IDEAS FROM THE FIELD

Four Examples of Mathematical Inquiry

These inquiry-based lessons cut across the entire K–12 grade spectrum. To develop investigation habits and become experienced investigators, students need to grapple with demanding problems, reflect on each solved problem, and compare solution strategies. Inquiry-based activities have implications that extend beyond solving isolated problems. When learners investigate families of similar problems, they gain insights into the underlying mathematics and can transfer their problem-solving strategies and conjectures.

When selecting activities for student inquiry, teachers should select explorations that provide learning experiences for the current topic as well as those forming the basis for future learning. These four examples of inquiry-based problem situations illustrate the depth of mathematical understanding expected from students and model instructional approaches for achieving this end. The activities illustrate developmental aspects because they include different levels of inquiry.

Example 1: Solving Systems of Equations Using Hints (Grades 1–5)

The following problems and the instructional methodologies were pilot-tested successfully with students in Grades 1–3. Students are asked to solve systems of equations with two variables, where letters represent variables. A predetermined set of questions facilitates student reasoning. The hints are of three types: (a) *Look*—focuses students on key information, (b) *Record*—requests students to record given problem information, and (c) *Solve*—leads students to discover the algorithm for solving the problems.

$$\text{Problem 1: } a + b = 12$$
$$a = 8$$
$$b = \underline{\quad}$$

Look at these letters. Tell me what you see. Point to the letter a. The letter a stands for the number 8. What do you have to figure out (the number for the letter b)? How did you figure out the answer? What did you do first? Second? Third?

Hint: Look again.

Point to the first equation. Do you know the number for *a* (yes)? What is the number for *a* (8)? How much are *a* and *b* together (12)? How can you figure out the number for *b*?

Hint: Record what's known.

Point to the letter *a* in the second equation. Write the number for *a* here. Can you tell how much *b* is? How did you figure it out?

Hint: Solve the problem.

The letter *a* is 8. Together, *a* and *b* make 12. So, 8 plus how much more makes 12? How much is *b*?

$$\text{Problem 2: } c + c = 10$$
$$c + c + h = 12$$
$$h = \underline{\quad}$$
$$c = \underline{\quad}$$

Look at these letters. Tell me what you see. What do you have to figure out (how much *c* is and how much *h* is)? How did you figure out the numbers? What did you do first? Second? Third?

Hint: Look again.

Look at the two rows. How are they different? Point to the first equation. How much are *c* and *c* together (10)? Point to the second equation. How much are *c* and *c* together here (10)? Can this help you figure out how much *h* is? How much is *h*? How did you figure this out?

Hint: Record what's known from the first equation in the second equation.

Point to the second equation. How much are *c* and *c* together here (10)? Draw a ring around *c* and *c*. Write the total number in the ring. Now can you figure out the number for *h*? How much is *h*? How did you figure it out?

Hint: Solve for *h* in the second equation.

Point to the second equation. Together, *c* and *c* are 10. So, 10 plus how much more makes 12? How much is *h*? How much is *c*? How did you figure this out?

Hint: Solve for *c* in the first equation.

If *c* + *c* is 10, then *c* must be half of 10. How much is *c*?

$$\text{Problem 3: } m + y = 7$$
$$m + y + y = 11$$
$$y = \underline{\quad}$$
$$m = \underline{\quad}$$

Look at these letters. Tell me what you see. What do you have to do to figure out how much *m* is and how much *y* is? How did you figure out the numbers? What did you do first? Second? Third?

Hint: Look again.

Look at the two rows. How are they different? Point to the first equation. How much are *m* and *y* together (7)? Point to the second equation. How much are *m* and *y* together here? Can this help you figure out how much *y* is? How much is *m*? How did you figure this out?

Hint: Record what's known from the first equation in the second equation.

Point to the second equation. Draw a ring around *m* and *y*. Write the total number for *m* and *y* in this circle. Point to the second letter *y* in the second equation. Now can you figure out the number for *y*? How much is *m*? How did you figure it out?

Hint: Solve for *y* in the second equation.

Point to the second equation. You know that *m* and *y* are 7. So, 7 plus how much more makes 11? How much is *y*? How much is *m*? How did you figure this out?

Hint: Record what's known from the second equation in the first equation.

Point to the first equation. You know that *y* is 4. Write the number for *y*. So, *m* and *y* make 7. How much is *m*? How did you figure this out?

Hint: Solve for *m* in the first equation.

So, *y* is 4. Then 4 plus how much more makes 7? How much is *m*?

Every time, the computations are incorrect.

Hint: Let's check. Write the numbers for the letters. Do the numbers make sense? How can you fix your answer?

Note that the hints progress from general suggestions for observations to concrete pointers in which students are offered methods to solve the problems. When the above problems were tried in the field, only 5% of Grade 1 students (and fewer in the upper grades) needed the last type of hint. This illustrates that students need time and experience in focusing on key information to successfully solve challenging problems and not necessarily step-by-step modeling of algorithms.

Example 2: Explorations With Tiles (Grades 5–8)

To facilitate students' reasoning, teachers may suggest that students use square tiles, draw pictures, or construct data tables.

Tile Problem 1

The towers below are made of tiles.

Figure 5.2   Unnumbered Squares for Example 2

Tile Problem One

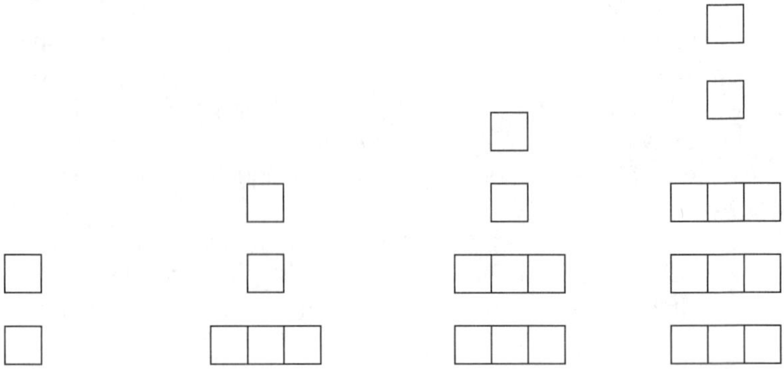

First tower   Second tower   Third tower   Fourth tower

2 tiles   5 tiles   8 tiles   ? tiles

What patterns can you see?

How many tiles would it take to make the fifth tower? The tenth tower?

How many tiles would it take to make the 20th tower?

How many tiles would it take to make the *n*th tower?

Which tower is made of 110 tiles?

Which tower is made of 90 tiles?

Students should discuss patterns that they identify. For example, for the first problem, some students may notice that the number of tiles increases by three for each consecutive tower, and all towers have two tiles on the top. Other students may rearrange the tiles and move the two tiles from the top to make a new row. In this case, students will observe that each tower is made of rows of three tiles with a missing tile.

Both observations provide information for making generalizations and answering the question "How many tiles would it take to make the *n*th tower?" Note that the first observation produces a formula $T(n) = 3(n - 1) + 2$, where $T(n)$ is a number of tiles and *n* is a tower number, whereas the second observation leads to the formula $T(n) = 3n - 1$, where $T(n)$ is a number of tiles and *n* is a tower number.

Figure 5.3   Unnumbered Squares That Follow This Line of Type

Observe that each tower is made of rows of three tiles with a missing tile:

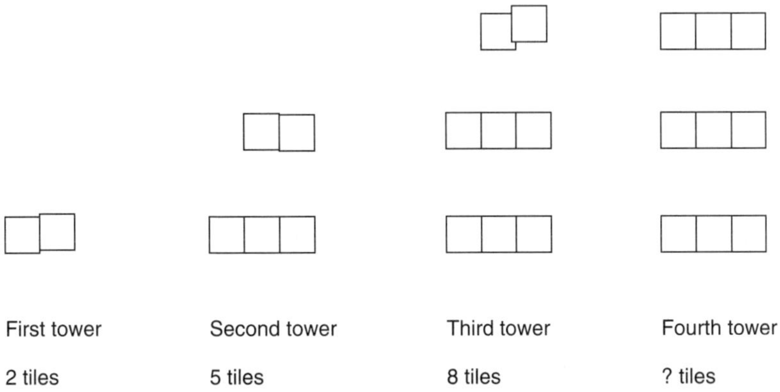

First tower	Second tower	Third tower	Fourth tower
2 tiles	5 tiles	8 tiles	? tiles

If students are familiar with algebraic representations of equations, they can prove that the above formulas are equivalent. Younger students may generalize the pattern without algebraic notation. For example, they may say, "To find a number of tiles needed for the 20th tower, one needs to multiply 20 by 3 and subtract 1." Either way, in this problem, students are to reason and argue why the noted patterns and generalizations are valid. Teachers should provide students with opportunities to communicate their ideas and reasoning. Teachers also must ensure that the investigation reaches its goal and students make connections between their findings and the topic of study.

Tile Problem 2

The towers below are made of tiles. Note that each column contains two more tiles than the preceding column.

What patterns do you see?

How many tiles would it take to make a tower with 5 columns?

How many tiles would it take to make a tower with 10 columns?

How many tiles would it take to make a tower with 50 columns?

How many tiles would it take to make a tower with n columns?

How many columns are in a tower made out of 156 tiles?

How many columns are in a tower made out of 199 tiles?

Figure 5.4   Unnumbered Squares for Tile Problem 2

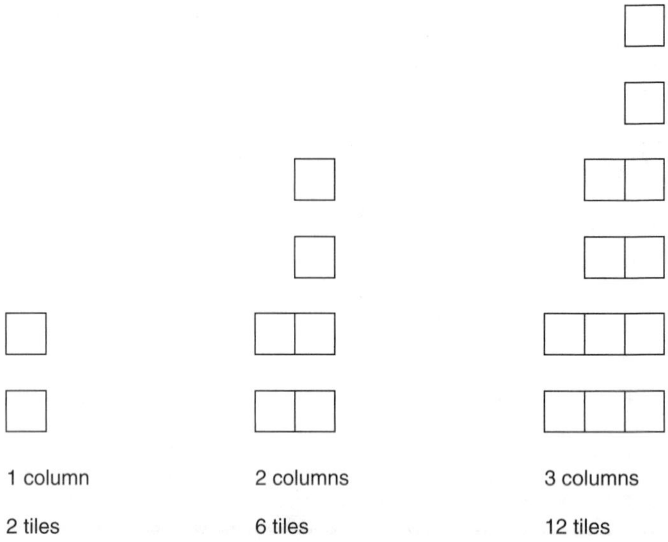

1 column	2 columns	3 columns
2 tiles	6 tiles	12 tiles

Initially, the second tile problem looks similar to the first one. Yet mathematically, these two problems are different because the growth of tiles in the first problem goes by 3 (a constant), whereas the number of tiles in the second pattern grows by consecutive even numbers starting from 4. The difference in growth leads to a completely different generalization.

To facilitate students' reasoning, teachers may encourage students to compare the two problems to identify similarities and differences. Then, after the pattern in the second problem is generalized, students need to compare the formulas. Later, students may be directed to pose similar problems to their classmates. Not all students may be able to generalize a pattern at first. However, it is important that all students understand the meaning of the generalization and how it was formed. Following with similar problems and with opportunities for creating their own problems will provide students with opportunities to apply their understanding and generalize patterns on their own.

Example 3: Classification of Quadrilaterals (Grades 6–9)

The goals of the following investigation focus on reviewing, strengthening, and extending students' understanding about how quadrilaterals are

Figure 5.5   Group 1

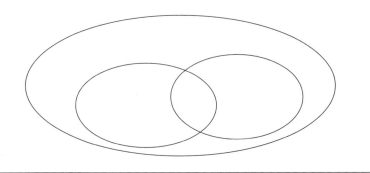

defined and how they are related. Because students may be at different levels of understanding, this activity can also serve as a preassessment.

> Group 1: Place the following quadrilaterals in the Venn diagram—parallelogram, trapezoid, square, rectangle, and rhombus.

> Group 2: Draw a diagram (e.g., Venn diagram, flow chart) showing the classification scheme for the following quadrilaterals—square, rectangle, rhombus, parallelogram, and trapezoid.

> Group 3: If the definition of a trapezoid is "a quadrilateral with at least two parallel sides," and not "a quadrilateral with exactly two parallel sides," what would that mean for the classification of the following quadrilaterals—square, rectangle, rhombus, parallelogram, and trapezoid?

For the purpose of this activity, you may want to have students form three groups. Explain to students that if they need to refresh their memories about the concept of quadrilaterals, they may join the first group that is working with the Venn diagram. Students who feel comfortable with the concept of quadrilaterals may wish to join Group 2. Students who feel they are experts and ready for a more challenging question may join Group 3. Remind students that groups are flexible, and they can move from group to group if they find that they may be better off in another group. Once the groups are formed, give the questions to Groups 2 and 3 and focus on Group 1.

Group 1 is provided with an envelope containing the names of the following quadrilaterals—parallelogram, trapezoid, square, rectangle, and rhombus—on sheets of paper that can be moved around. Set up the Venn diagram as shown below. You may wish to explain the diagram in the following way: "Pretend that the big outer oval represents apples. What will we place outside of the Venn diagram (other fruits)? One of the small ovals inside represents yellow apples. Are all the yellow apples, apples (yes)? Are all apples yellow (no)? The other small oval represents red apples. Then the intersection of the small ovals may be apples that are yellow with red spots."

Following that line of reasoning, ask students to discuss the quadrilaterals and come up with some informal definitions of the quadrilaterals. Then, they need to place one sheet in each oval, one in the intersection of the small ovals, and one outside of the diagram. To facilitate students' reasoning, you may demonstrate objects or pictures of the quadrilaterals. Check with the group from time to time to make sure they have formulated the right definitions.

After Group 1 has completed its task, ask students to define each quadrilateral and answer the following questions:

1. Is the rectangle a parallelogram? Why? Is the parallelogram a rectangle? Why?
2. Is the square a rectangle? Why? Is the rectangle a square? Why?
3. Is the square a rhombus? Why? Is the rhombus a square? Why?

Have each group choose a speaker who will present to the whole group the task and the results. Ask all three groups to present their results in order starting from Groups 1 to 3. Point out the similarities and differences among the tasks. Refer back to the definitions and results derived by Group 1 to clarify the work of the other groups. When Group 3 presents, note that both definitions for trapezoid are correct. You may wish to give examples from non-Euclidian geometry (e.g., spherical geometry, taxicab geometry) to point out the importance of defining terms. Finally, have all students answer the questions posed to Group 1 to further ensure that all students have understood the relationships among quadrilaterals.

Example 4: Growing Fir Trees (Grades 8–10)

A new plan is under design for a farm growing fir trees for the holiday season. There are 2,000 trees growing on the farm today. According to the plan, each year, 1/4 of the trees will be harvested, and 500 new trees will be planted. Investigate a situation over a sufficient period of time. Graph how the number of trees changes from year to year.

Explore the situation further by choosing different initial numbers of trees in the farm (1,000; 4,000), fractions (1/3; 3/4) of harvested trees, and numbers of trees (200; 1,000) planted each year. Keep in mind that to find the influence of each variable (factor), you have to change one variable at a time. For each situation, build a graph describing how the number of trees changes over the years.

This activity is targeted at older students, but a version of it may be used in earlier grades. The activity may take more than one class period. Students may do the first part of the investigation in groups. But for further explorations, teachers may assign parts of the investigation to different groups of students: One group may explore an input of initial numbers of trees on the total number of trees, while another group may find the input of a number of harvested trees on the total number of trees, and so on. Upon completion, students present their findings to the large group. Because each group will look at a different part of the problems, it is important that all students actively participate in the presentations, ask questions to clarify understanding, and take notes. To ensure that all students understand all facets of the investigation, students should write individual reports of the results with reflections and explanations.

REFERENCES

Baroody, A. (1989). One point of view: Manipulatives do not come with guarantees. *Arithmetic Teacher, 37*(2), 4–5.

Bruner, J. (1960). *The process of education.* Cambridge, MA: Harvard University Press.

Burns, M. (1998). *Math: Facing an American phobia.* Sausalito, CA: Math Solutions.

Clements, D. H., & McMillen, S. (1996). Rethinking "concrete manipulatives." *Teaching Children Mathematics, 2*(5), 270–279.

Dewey, J. (1966). *Democracy and education: An introduction to the philosophy of education.* New York: Free Press. (Original work published 1916)

Dobrynina, G. (2001). *Reasoning processes of grade 4–6 students solving two- and three-variable problems.* Unpublished doctoral dissertation, Boston University.

Fuson, K., & Briars, D. (1990). Using a base-ten blocks learning/teaching approach for first- and second-grade place value and multi-digit addition and subtraction. *Journal for Research in Mathematics Education, 21*, 180–206.

Ginsburg, H. P. (1982). *Children's arithmetic: How they learn it and how you teach it.* Austin, TX: Pro Ed.

Hashimoto, Y., & Becker, J. (1999). The open approach to teaching mathematics: Creating a culture of mathematics in the classroom: Japan. In L. J. Sheffield (Ed.), *Developing mathematically promising students* (pp. 101–119). Reston, VA: National Council of Teachers of Mathematics.

Kennedy, L., & Tipps, S. (1994). *Guiding children's learning of mathematics.* Belmont, CA: Wadsworth.

Krulik, S., & Rudnick, J. (1993). *Reasoning and problem solving: A handbook for elementary school teachers.* Boston: Allyn & Bacon.

Kulm, G. (1990). New directions for mathematical assessment. In G. Kulm (Ed.), *Assessing higher order thinking in mathematics.* Washington, DC: American Association for the Advancement of Science.

Lester, F. K. J., & Lambdin-Kroll, D. (1990). Assessing student growth in mathematical problem solving. In G. Kulm (Ed.), *Assessing higher order thinking in mathematics* (pp. 53–70). Washington, DC: American Association for the Advancement of Science.

Ma, L. (1999). *Knowing and teaching elementary mathematics.* Mahwah, NJ: Lawrence Erlbaum Associates.

National Assessment of Educational Progress. (1970). *The First National Assessment of Mathematics.* Denver, CO: Education Commission of the States.

National Center for Education Statistics. (2003). *Teaching mathematics in seven countries: Results from the TIMSS 1999 video study.* Washington, DC: U.S. Department of Education, Institute of Education Sciences.

National Commission on Excellence in Education. (1983). *A nation at risk: The imperative for educational reform.* Washington, DC: U.S. Department of Education.

National Council of Teachers of Mathematics. (1980). *Agenda for action.* Reston, VA: Author.

National Council of Teachers of Mathematics. (2000). *Principles and standards for school mathematics.* Reston, VA: Author.

National Council of Teachers of Mathematics. Commission on Standards for School Mathematics. (1989). *Curriculum and evaluation standards for school mathematics.* Reston, VA: Author.

National Research Council. (1990). *Reshaping school mathematics.* Washington, DC: National Academy Press.

Perkins, D. (1992). *Smart schools: From training memories to educating minds.* New York: Free Press.

Polya, G. (1973). *How to solve it.* Princeton, NJ: Princeton University Press. (Original work published 1945)

Robitaille, D. F., & Travers, K. J. (1992). International studies of achievement in mathematics. In D. A. Grouws (Ed.), *Handbook of research on mathematics teaching and learning* (pp. 687–709). New York: Macmillan.

Schoenfeld, A. H. (1985). *Mathematical problem solving.* New York: Academic Press.

Schoenfeld, A. H. (1992). Learning to think mathematically: Problem solving, metacognition, and sense making in mathematics. In D. A. Grouws

(Ed.), *Handbook of research on mathematics teaching and learning* (pp. 334–370). New York: Macmillan.

Schön, D. (1983). *The reflective practitioner.* New York: Basic Books.

Siegel, M., Borasi, R., & Fonzi, J. (1998). Supporting students' mathematical inquiries through reading. *Journal for Research in Mathematics Education, 29*(4), 378–413.

Thompson, P. (1994). Concrete materials and teaching for mathematical understanding. In D. Chambers (Ed.), *Putting research into practice in the elementary grades: Readings from journals of the National Council of Teachers of Mathematics* (pp. 246–249). Reston, VA: National Council of Teachers of Mathematics.

TIMSS. (1996). *Mathematics achievement in the middle school years: IEA's Third International Mathematics and Science Study.* Chestnut Hill, MA: Boston College, TIMSS International Study Center.

Tsankova, E. (2003). *Algebraic reasoning of first through third grade students solving systems of two linear equations with two variables.* Unpublished doctoral dissertation, Boston University.

Vygotsky, L. S. (1978). *Mind in society: The development of higher psychological processes* (M. Cole, V. John-Steiner, S. Scribner, & E. Souberman, eds.). Cambridge, MA: Harvard University Press.

CHAPTER SIX

Language Arts

Explore, Create, Discover Through Inquiry

Jane S. Townsend

The thing is, when you talk in a group and you discuss things in a group, sometimes you see one thing, and, you know, it's kind of hard to get out of seeing that one thing, but if everybody gives all these different ideas, then you kind of see it from a different perspective and kind of get a wider view of everything.

—Stephanie (pseudonym), an 11th grader

What does inquiry look like in the language arts? What does it *sound* like? Inquiry's many different shapes reflect diverse students' interests and intellects. We are probably most likely to hear "the sounds that inquiry makes" (Lindfors, 1999, p. 245) during classroom discussions of literature. As an act of language, inquiry is born in dialogue. And the dialogue of real discussion supports the reading, writing, thinking, listening, and speaking that meet the National Standards for the English Language Arts (National Council of Teachers of English & International Reading Association

[NCTE/IRA], 1996). Opportunities for such dialogue cross the curriculum, but they come to special fruition in talk about literary characters' plights and possibilities. When students are collectively engaged in imaginative wonderings about issues of compelling human interest, the resulting dialogue supports their intellectual and social development in powerful ways.

From research conducted with children, Vygotsky (1986) suggested that our problem-solving abilities draw from our experiences talking with others. Diverse perspectives enlarge our understanding, enabling us to consider the world from various viewpoints. Making sense of the complicated motives and problematic behaviors of literary characters requires, then, both communicative and textual competence. In Bakhtin's (1986) view, our reading, writing, speaking, and listening form part of a dialogic chain that connects us while we exchange our views, our understandings, and our inquiries. The question and response rhythm of that chain creates the beating heart of inquiry in the language arts. To see inquiry as an act of language is to see it as a kind of dance: Inquirers turn to others, asking for help in moving beyond their present understandings. They shift from the edges of what they know to pull another into their space of confusion, perplexity, or wondering. In language, inquiry is an act of *interaction*. The dance is in the dialogue.

If teachers are to support this turning toward others for understanding, then patterns of discourse among members of a classroom community merit careful attention. Bakhtin (1986) believed that when the question dropped out of conversation, the dialogue collapsed. Vygotsky (1986) wrote that intellectual growth depends on "mastering the social means of thought" (p. 94) and saw the learner's development moving from the language used in social contexts to egocentric, problem-solving speech, and later to "inner speech," or the interpreting, conceptualizing, and synthesizing of mature thought. As Moll (1990) notes, Vygotsky believed that "children internalize and transform the help they receive from others and eventually use these same means of guidance to direct their subsequent problem-solving behaviors" (p. 11).

In a classroom, others from whom we seek help may be sitting in the next seat, standing in the front of the room, residing in written texts in books or online, or waiting for us in memory. It makes sense that one's ability to solve complicated, ambiguous, abstract puzzles develops most fully from experiences interacting with other people's perspectives and frames of reference. The very language that we have available to explore a problem comes from our previous social engagements with others. Experiences considering multiple perspectives and sign systems provide the means and material for independent problem solving, allowing a thinker to draw on myriad ways of construing and expressing the problematic issues that fuel inquiry. Because this kind of thinking supports academic achievement, such skills are crucial for those who struggle in our schools. One great challenge for teachers is to be skillful at hearing inquiry, especially when it is expressed in culturally or linguistically unfamiliar ways.

One feature that makes the practice of classroom inquiry particularly difficult is the struggle to manage the imposition of such an act in a polite and inviting way (Lindfors, 1999). When we direct an inquiry to someone, we pull on that person. We ask him or her to think about what we are interested in, to spend time at our behest, to help us learn what we want to learn. For most students, that kind of exchange does not form the normal pattern of classroom interaction. Typically, teachers control the issues for discussion as well as assign particular texts for reading and topics for writing. Teachers rarely ask genuine questions of real, personal uncertainty (Albritton, 1992; Feldman & Wertsch, 1976). Indeed, findings from studies of oral classroom discourse confirm that most students are restricted in their language functions to responding to teachers' initiating questions that have preconceived correct answers (Marshall, Smagorinsky, & Smith, 1995; Mehan, 1979; Nystrand, 1997).

When students seek help in understanding, the polite way to make such a request is culturally bound and can lead to misunderstandings and misjudgments in the classroom. Sometimes, such requests can create antagonism between a teacher and students from different backgrounds (Delpit, 2002; Heath, 1983). When students do not understand, for example, that a polite request is really a command ("Don't you want to get started on your project?"), and when a teacher thinks students are unprepared—or worse, unable—because they fail to participate in a group discussion (drawing attention to oneself publicly is frowned upon by many non-Western cultures), opportunities for teaching and learning may be thwarted.

What opportunities, then, do students have to express and explore their inquiries in a language arts class? Authentic classroom discussions where students engage actively and ask substantive questions of personal interest are possible, and talk about literature seems to offer a particularly inviting context for such wondering (Almasi, O'Flahavan, & Arya, 2001; Hadjioannou, 2003; Townsend, 1998). In responding to and interpreting the multilayered meanings of literary conundrums and conflicts, students and teachers can entertain new views and build their understanding of compelling human concerns. And because, as Bruner (1986) asserted, the study of literature should be "trafficking in human possibilities rather than in settled certainties" (p. 26), discourse about literature that is dialogic—that invites multiple perspectives and multiple possibilities—can help students open their minds and think deeply.

A Classroom Example

In the following exchange from a study of wondering discourse (Townsend, 1991), a group of high school juniors and their teacher were engaged in a dialogic interaction, trying to untangle perhaps one of literature's most famous puzzles: Was Hamlet sane? In their first class discussion of *Hamlet,* the teacher, Ms. Hale, planned to focus students' attention on the array of characters in the play. However, Fidel initiated the topic of Hamlet's odd behavior in the following exchange (students chose their own pseudonyms):

Fidel: Is Hamlet, is acting crazy part of his revenge?

Silca: Is Polonius the one who's making up this, who, who wants Hamlet to seem like he's crazy?

Students (unidentifiable): Yeah. Yeah. Yeah.

Ms. Hale: He's, yes, he's saying to the king that he's crazy because of his love for Ophelia.

Rex: Yeah, didn't he, didn't he say something like that when, when what's her face, when the girl came and told him that Hamlet was looking pretty bad?

Ms. Hale: Uh huh. That's Polonius, right. Fidel?

Fidel: Um, is Hamlet using, like, the thing with Ophelia as part of his revenge, or anything? Is it, is it true love? I don't know. I can't really tell.

Ms. Hale: No. I can't really tell either.

Sam: It's true love.

Katia: Well, he was living, he was living with her before she, he saw the ghost, wasn't he?

Ms. Hale: That's the impression we get, right? Because, um, in scene, if you remember in scene 3, when Laertes and, and Polonious are, um, admonishing Ophelia to beware of Hamlet, to stay away from him and that he's trying to take advantage of her. I think we get the impression that Hamlet's really been in touch with her for quite a long time. Remember she said that . . .

Flenoy: Yeah.

Ms. Hale: . . . he's offered many tenders of his affection. And, so you sort of assume that this had been going on for a while. Um, I, I kind of think you have to make up your mind as you go along whether, you know, whether you think that he's, he's been true in his affection. I'm not sure that his dealings with Ophelia are as affected, I mean that he uses her because of the revenge that he has to seek.

Fidel: I was, 'cause we know, I mean, that he's not mad 'cause of Ophelia.

Ms. Hale: Right. I mean that, that seems to be what we know and what Gertrude suspects, what his mother suspects, right?

First, notice that participation was widespread. In this 11th-grade literature class, students responded not only to the teacher but also to the questions and comments of their classmates. Indeed, a number of students were inquiring and expressing uncertainty in this exchange, using markers such as "I don't know," "I can't really tell," "I kind of think," and "I'm not sure." Silca, Fidel, Rex, and Katia all asked questions seeking clarification and information; Flenoy and Sam freely chimed in with their ideas. Fidel initiated the topic of Hamlet's motivation for acting crazy, and he adopted a wondering stance, playing-with-possibilities, not-seeking-closure way of thinking and talking.

Ms. Hale thought little of Fidel's question during the discussion, responding with a perfunctory though agreeable "No. I can't really tell either." When she talked about that particular interchange during an interview, she mused: "I think if I had attended to it properly, it would have been fruitful." Even so, we can see in this excerpt the students and teacher working together to make sense of a literary issue—what kind of person was Hamlet?—in a way that was congenial, collaborative, and welcoming of different views. The possibilities they generated shed light on issues of human relationship and motivation. The invitation and the inquiry sound clear.

That same kind of invitation can extend to other kinds of discourse, such as engaging students in creative drama, language exploration projects, character and author studies, and personal experience stories. In inquiry-supporting language arts classrooms, students will speak, listen, read, and write about multiple texts, topics, and genres. What may be most important for classroom inquiry is that the students be made the active party in the process and gain a sense of agency. A teacher's most important role, then, is helping students find and shape topics that make connections to what they themselves know and wonder about. A sample lesson provides an example of this strategy.

Nothing is harder than writing about someone else's topic, especially when we have little knowledge or personal interest in the matter. Nothing is more boring than being forced to read about something about which we care little. Teachers should reevaluate their sense of responsibility for maintaining complete control over classroom topics. Students need help with the difficult task of choosing books and other textual materials, and selecting fruitful topics about which to write. Indeed, making such selections in a thoughtful way may be one of the most important abilities teachers can help students to develop. To be engaged in productive reading and writing, students must make these kinds of choices with a careful and critical eye.

Encouraging students to reflect upon, identify, and express their inquiries informs and broadens what they already know. Choosing one's own topics and focus is not simple; it may be a writer's greatest challenge, and a reader's, too. However, teachers neither apprentice students in the process of learning (Rogoff, 1990) nor support their spirit of inquiry when the teacher makes all the choices. Instead, teachers can build classroom communities that provide forums for exchanging ideas and strategies, for modeling the kinds of thinking they wish to foster, for motivating reluctant students to discover the joy of learning (Gallas, 1995; Paley, 1981; Whitin, 1999). Teachers can provide the scaffolding that will give students the assorted nudges and boosts they need to make good choices, and teachers can highlight the benchmarks required to meet standards of excellence.

National Standards

The National Council of Teachers of English and the International Reading Association (NCTE/IRA) collaboratively developed the National Standards for the English Language Arts (1996). This 4-year project involved thousands of teachers, researchers, parents, and policy makers in writing, reviewing, and revising successive drafts of the document that lists and describes the standards. In essence, the standards remind teachers that they must help students to develop communicative and textual competence—their abilities to communicate across a range of situations with a variety of people and to read and write in multiple genres. Inquiry itself is intertwined in the various meaning-making processes of interpretation and expression, of composition and comprehension, and is an essential skill for developing such abilities.

Although I present the standards here in the following list of four sets for ease of discussion, the NCTE/IRA commission underscores that these standards are interrelated, not "distinct and separable," and also emphasizes that they not be "prescriptions for particular curricula or instructional approaches" (p. 2). To consider them separately enables us to consider their many different facets. Examining the rationale for inquiry in terms of the standards helps us see the many roles that inquiry can play in students' language and learning.

Set 1

Standard 1:   Students read a wide range of print and nonprint texts to build an understanding of texts, of themselves, and of the cultures of the United States and the world; to acquire new information; to respond to the needs and demands of society and the workplace; and for personal fulfillment. Among these texts are fiction and nonfiction, classic and contemporary works.

Standard 2:   Students read a wide range of literature from many periods in many genres to build an understanding of the many dimensions (e.g., philosophical, ethical, aesthetic) of human experience.

Standard 3:   Students apply a wide range of strategies to comprehend, interpret, evaluate, and appreciate texts. They draw on their prior experience, their interactions with other readers and writers, their knowledge of word meaning and of other texts, their word identification strategies, and their understanding of textual features (e.g., sound-letter correspondence, sentence structure, context, graphics).

In the transcript above of high school juniors and their teacher discussing Hamlet's sanity, we find one example of the kind of textual work that can be accomplished when student inquiry finds room for expression in a classroom. Teachers can learn a great deal about students' reading comprehension from the nature of their inquiries. For example, in the discussion of *Hamlet,* in an exchange before the one excerpted above, Rex asked what Ophelia's relationship was to Polonius (indeed, she was his daughter), a question with a definite and clear answer. In the excerpt above, Fidel was wondering about the reasons for Hamlet's erratic behavior with Ophelia, a question open to many possible interpretations. Both understandings (Ophelia's relationship to Polonius; Hamlet's assorted motives) combined in this community of inquirers to weave a particular, mutually constructed understanding of the play *Hamlet,* of the characters and their interactions, and of the students' own thinking about these matters.

Students' and teachers' honest questions are unique because they reflect individual knowledge structures. Each of us knows our world in personally distinctive ways that come from interweaving all of our experiences. We alone can identify and fill in the gaps of our own particular knowledge maps. That is why, in helping students meet the three standards of textual competence listed above and in assessing their progress, teachers profit by attending to students' inquiries about what they are reading as well as the *way* they are reading. Concentrating on the processes of students' reading and interpretation allows teachers to place texts in context—historically, culturally, socially— and gives important notice to questions of power and politics. Helping students become critically literate, as the standards direct, means helping them become conscious of the social forces that place all of us in the world. Reading multicultural literature, critiquing media sources, inviting multiple perspectives, and creating multilayered visions of the world all promote inquiry and critical literacy.

Set 2

Standard 4:   Students adjust their use of spoken, written, and visual language (e.g., conventions, style, vocabulary) to communicate effectively with a variety of audiences and for different purposes.

Standard 5:   Students employ a wide range of strategies as they write and use different writing process elements appropriately to communicate with different audiences for a variety of purposes.

Standard 6:   Students apply knowledge of language structure, language conventions (e.g., spelling and punctuation), media techniques, figurative language, and genre to create, critique, and discuss print and nonprint texts.

This second set of standards asks that students learn the nuances of purpose and audience in the texts they themselves create, developing their communicative competence. Students may be writing critical essays about their reading, or they may be creating imaginative scenarios of their ideas and interpretations. They may be analyzing other people's words and expressing cogent understandings of complicated literary issues (e.g., Is Hamlet crazy?). They may be inventing one-act plays or composing short stories. In the active, complicated process of original composition, students can learn to ask themselves questions that fuel revision: a reseeing, rethinking, reconceptualizing that helps students learn to write well. Because writing is an act of creative construction—an act of imagination— inquiry can play a major role in developing students' writing and composition abilities.

Both reading and writing involve numerous, largely unconscious subprocesses, most of which cannot be labeled discretely but involve activating appropriate background knowledge, drawing information from memory, making connections across conceptual categories, and building relevant, contextual information—all to weave a complex tapestry of meaning. For a student to become fluent in either reading or writing, these mental subroutines must become automatic, leaving room for critical interpretations as well as imaginative envisioning of other realities, other worlds (Bruner, 1986). Inquiry forces students to think about their own thinking and, in the process, gain some control of their own learning.

Students can do that kind of work in collaboration with others, as we saw in the excerpt of the *Hamlet* discussion, constructing the "spoken, written, and visual language" for which the standards call. Students can also write stories from their personal experiences or compose persuasive letters to real people. They can draw pictures to illustrate their poetry or select music to frame their ideas and images. They can take on the roles of fictional characters, bringing literary worlds to life in dramatic scenarios (written) and improvisations (on the spot). And in all these activities, they can stop occasionally and step back to reflect upon and assess their own process and progress.

Set 3

Standard 7: Students conduct research on issues and interests by generating ideas and questions and by posing problems. They gather, evaluate, and synthesize data from a variety of sources (e.g., print and non-print texts, artifacts, people) to communicate their discoveries in ways that suit their purpose and audience.

Standard 8: Students use a variety of technological and information resources (e.g., libraries, databases, computer networks, video) to gather and synthesize information and to create and communicate knowledge.

Standard 9: Students develop an understanding of and respect for diversity in language use, patterns, and dialects across cultures, ethnic groups, geographic regions, and social roles.

Using language to explore the things we find curious is natural to human beings. Throughout a lifetime, learning is fueled by what we find salient and compelling. This third set of national standards advises that a language arts curriculum include activities for students such as undertaking language exploration projects, constructing oral histories, mapping information sources, and weighing issues of social justice. When students are given opportunities to investigate their own questions, conduct different kinds of research projects, choose topics for their attention, draw on different resources for information, and express their findings in distinctive ways, they are engaged in the multiple discourses that the standards recommend. And in those various processes, inquiry can be, and often is, the motive.

Of course, to suggest that students might fruitfully choose their own topics for study conflicts with prevailing pressures on teachers. When standardized test taking shapes the curriculum, a prescribed course of materials holds sway. What scripted programs cannot offer, however, is the depth and breadth of inquiry for students. Many teachers know that students who have choices and can follow the stirrings of their own intellectual hearts become intrinsically motivated to learn. How can we help policy makers and administrators understand that if students engaged their full capacities for exploring issues of personal interest and expressing their developing understandings, their learning would grow in powerful ways?

Set 4

Standard 10: Students whose first language is not English make use of their first language to develop competency in the English language arts and to develop understanding of content across the curriculum.

Standard 11: Students participate as knowledgeable, reflective, creative, and critical members of a variety of literacy communities.

Standard 12: Students use spoken, written, and visual language to accomplish their own purposes (e.g., for learning, enjoyment, persuasion, and the exchange of information).

This fourth set of standards may be the most overarching of the group and perhaps the most important. If students see themselves as active agents in the process of learning, if they come to understand something about the social forces of power and position, then they may also take responsibility for their work and find real purpose for their writing and their reading. If we can help students recognize the diverse ways that different communities use language, if we can help them understand the many ways there are to express the multiplicity of ideas, students will come to believe that our classrooms welcome their views. If we are careless, cultural differences can become barriers. For example, an 11th-grade Laotian refugee, Paw, was perplexed by the classroom interactions in her new American school (Townsend & Fu, 2001). As she explained, "When the students have a big argument, especially when they talk back to the teacher, I don't know what I should do. I am not used to that. I can only be quiet" (p. 2). Quiet students may be doing important mental work (Townsend, 1998), and perhaps Paw, who enjoyed reading and writing, could have found other avenues besides classroom talk to express her ideas and broaden her understanding.

Students at all levels may find cultural mismatches with the way their families and neighbors use language and their school's "ways with words" (Heath, 1982). Heath reports on the comments from a young mother in a Black working-class community about her son's elementary school teacher: "Miss Davis, she complain 'bout Ned not answering back. He say she asks dumb questions she already know 'bout" (p. 42). If seen as a resource, the cultural and linguistic diversity natural to most public school classrooms enhances all students' developing communicative and textual competence. Drawing on their differences—indeed, making them explicit—allows students to explore what they each find salient and worth pursuing and provides a forum for sharing experiences and opening minds.

To develop a critical eye for the many social and political forces that shape their possibilities in school and life, students must question their own position in the world. It is important for them to recognize that social status and school achievement are not always fairly awarded. Although those privileged by wealth and strong family support are often at an advantage in school, success can be achieved by those not so well favored. Furthermore, to work toward equity means identifying and understanding issues of race, class, and other markers of diversity. In its reliance on interaction and its benefits from multiple views, inquiry can nurture that kind of thinking among members of a classroom community in many mutually enriching ways. Opening students' minds to the many experiences and possibilities that humans can create is to help them develop the kind of critical literacy and self-efficacy called for in the national standards. However, shifting students from what they are accustomed to in a traditional classroom, where they often play a passive role, to a stance of active inquiry requires an array of tools and strategies.

CREATING CONTEXTS FOR INQUIRY: TOOLS AND STRATEGIES

In my own almost 30 years of teaching at different levels and in different contexts, I have worked to encourage students' inquiry. From my first year of teaching, in a high school with mostly poor Black and Hispanic students whose culture was unfamiliar to me, I wanted to know what my students were wondering. I wanted to know what they were curious about, what they wanted to learn. I asked for their questions because I thought their inquiries would help me plan lessons that would build on what they already knew and be fueled by what they wanted to know. I remember vividly what happened when I asked my students to tell me their questions. They looked at me with consternation and panic. "Miss, you the one s'posed to be asking the questions!" The response was resounding. And for the rest of that first year, I worked to provide activities and experiences that would change that belief.

I also began to develop a toolbox of classroom strategies to which I have added over the ensuing years. Organizing classroom discussion, encouraging students' creative expressions, supporting language exploration projects, and making many opportunities for students' self-assessments are primary strategies I have employed to support students' inquiry. There are undoubtedly many other ways to encourage students to express their wonderings and to help them identify and pursue questions of compelling personal interest, but developing students' abilities to investigate their own inquiries, for me, should be the overarching goal of education in the language arts.

Classroom Discussion

In the classroom example presented earlier from the discussion of *Hamlet,* we read the collaborative dialogue between a teacher and her students as they struggled to solve a rather sophisticated literary puzzle. However, reading and discussing a piece of classic literature with a group of academically able students is not the only route to fruitful classroom discussion. Indeed, in a sharply contrasting classroom context, we can see the value of a student's inquiry during a discussion in a first-grade classroom with a group of at-risk students trying to make sense of their beginning reader (Townsend, 1987a).

The school was in an upper-middle-class White neighborhood, and the students were bused from the poorer side of town. Most of the students in the class were African American or Hispanic. One child was Anglo. The teacher had successfully taught kindergarten for more than 30 years and had been recruited to teach this class of first graders in an effort to provide special enrichment to the kids who had tested lowest on entry exams. Over the course of the year, other students who were having difficulty were sent to her.

I had been conducting an exploratory study of the first graders' expressions of curiosity when I taped a student's inquiry during a discussion in the lowest-level reading group. What makes this example interesting is that the student, Damon, expressed his wondering nested within supportive comments from the teacher, his classmates, and the principal of the school, who just happened to be visiting that day. The teacher, Ms. Bell, had begun the lesson by exclaiming to the principal the exciting news that the four children in this group had just started reading!

The words in the text selection were basic sight words that the students were learning. Ms. Bell drew attention to an illustration in the text of a cow standing on top of a barn, by asking, "What's happening in this picture?" According to the text, a girl was trying to find the cow and was having little luck. When students did not respond, Ms. Bell tried again. "I wonder why she won't look up there." Instead of trying to answer her question, Damon said, "I wonder how the cow got on top." And the teacher replied eagerly, "I wonder that same thing. Do you think she thinks that a cow is going to get on top of a barn? I don't know how it got up there. Do you, Damon? How *do* you think that cow got up there?"

Damon thought that perhaps the cow had jumped up or piled rocks to climb. Ms. Bell complimented his thinking while another student waved her hand for attention. Sylvia said that maybe the cow had glue on its hoofs. The principal supported this idea by suggesting the use of Super Glue. Another student, Thomas, wondered if the cow had used a ladder. The principal chimed in with the idea that a helicopter might have been involved. A good-humored exchange between the teacher and the principal about the feasibility of that mode of transport for the cow continued for several turns. Throughout this episode, the children in this reading group learned that there could be many interpretations of a story, that a student can direct the group discussion, that it is fun and fruitful to imagine possibilities, and that their thoughts are worth attention. By asking questions and playing with possible answers, these young readers were discovering how to read with active attention. Through inviting them to share their wonderings, through repeatedly affirming their ideas, and through encouraging numerous responses, Ms. Bell created an environment that supported her students' expressions of inquiry.

As discussed previously, supporting real discussion in a class can be quite challenging. Many factors are clearly at work in the complicated context of any classroom, but certain features that support discussion are embedded in a sense of community that crosses grade levels and text types.

- Face-to-face interaction so that students and teacher can read the body language and faces of their classmates helps everyone respond in an honest way.
- Framing topics in open-ended ways invites multiple perspectives; participants' use of linguistic uncertainty markers, such as "I'm not sure," "I don't know," and "maybe," supports open-minded exchanges.
- Students have a special interest in their own questions, and student-initiated topics typically generate lively interchanges.
- Preparatory reading and writing helps students ponder, formulate, and express their inquiries.
- Talk in small groups or in pairs supports students' participation in subsequent whole-group exchanges.
- Explicit attention to patterns of interaction encourages widespread involvement and a welcoming of multiple views.
- Regular and routine opportunities for discussion create expectations for interaction and encourage thoughtful contributions.
- Giving students time to think and write about their ideas deepens everyone's responses.

Clearly, more is involved in creating inquiry-supporting contexts, in building classroom communities that welcome diverse views, than simply making time for classroom discussion. However, the circle of voices in a classroom can nurture expressions of inquiry in many special ways. In modeling the way we think and talk about matters that are open to interpretation, we help students learn to think in open-minded ways about language and literacy. We help them attend to the nuances of reading comprehension and writing composition. We equip them for communicating in a variety of forms for multiple purposes and audiences.

Creative Expressions

Students' creativity sometimes gets short shrift in classrooms. Perhaps standardized testing, in demanding singular answers to pre-conceived questions, leaves teachers little time to nurture divergent thinking. However, humans generate special energy and interest when they engage their creative capacities in imagining multiple responses to enigmatic matters. From the use of various colors, paints, music, or lyrics to illustrate the emotions or themes in great fiction and poetry to the movements of dance and drama, students can creatively construct their understandings of literature and life. They can draw on their sense making and imagination to express their ideas and investigate their questions. In the arts, people choose their own focus of study, they learn to observe the details that surround them, and they engage their creativity and curiosity.

One useful strategy for helping students to imagine literary plights and possibilities is to ask them to use their full kinesthetic capacities through creative drama, enacting the themes about which they read and write. The very nature of dramatic play encourages a wondering frame of mind. In its emphasis on process, its interest in individual imaginings, and its reliance on original thinking, creative drama can provide a unique support for inquiry (Townsend, 1987b).

In classrooms, creative drama is improvisational and not focused on performance. It usually involves some kind of cooperative inter-action among group members. As children explore what it feels like to be in another place or body, they develop a full-bodied under-standing of others' positions and situations. Creative drama is a tool for students to discover possible answers to the "what ifs" of life. In acting out a role and inventing improvisations, students bring stories, images, and emotions into their blood and bones.

For example, one year I organized groups of students improvising major scenes from *Julius Caesar.* In one case, we used rolled-up newspapers as swords to depict the assassination of Caesar. What otherwise might have remained entirely academic—and to this group of at-risk students, entirely irrelevant to their daily lives—was energized and brought to life.

In dramatic play, students make what they read and write palpable. In drama, they can entertain someone else's views and enlarge their own perspective and understanding. Because dramatic play is concerned with possibilities instead of right and wrong answers, it provides a powerful support for students of differing abilities, with special needs, and from diverse linguistic and cultural backgrounds. For speakers of English as a second language, creative drama can be especially helpful because it draws on so many kinds of nonlinguistic cues to express ideas, providing imagined contexts and characters for making sense of the new language. As Way (1967) asserts, "There is not a child born anywhere in the world, in any physical or intellectual circumstances or conditions, who cannot do drama" (p. 3).

In encouraging an exchange of perspectives, creative drama is also a useful tool for building classroom community. However, to benefit most fully from drama, participants must learn some basic concepts. As delineated by Siks (1983), the elements of creative drama include movement, concentration, character, language, imagination, and sensory awareness.

- Movement includes body awareness, degree of effort, size of gesture, shape of motion, and orientation to others. Giving students opportunities to move expressively through space to enact an emotion, embody an image, or construct a character helps them learn to use drama to express and communicate their ideas.
- Concentration includes focusing on a goal, building trust in self and others, relaxing muscular tension in the body, and using the imagination to enter alternative circumstances with empathy and careful attention. Concentration is essential for developing any of the elements that support dramatic activity.
- Creating a character requires attention to an imagined person's physical appearance, mood, emotion, action, and motives. As a major component in any story, characters impel the plots and inhabit the settings. In expressing the outward signs and attributes of characters by pulling from physical, emotional, and

intellectual resources, students can come to understand psychological complexity in a personal, interior way.

- Effective use of language includes nonverbal and verbal communication and is a major tool for expression and communication in drama activity and interaction. The timbre and power of voice (both vocally and in writing) imbue students' words with particular meanings and paint explicit pictures. Nonlinguistic cues of body language add depth and credibility to a depiction or presentation.

- Imagination is the foundation for all creative expressions and is the moving force behind drama activity and great literature. Imagining that circumstances are other than they appear requires a wondering frame of mind, inviting a playing with ideas and images.

- Using the five senses stimulates imagination, concentration, and focus, which support all of the elements of drama. Helping students observe the sensations of sight, touch, taste, hearing, and smell improves their sensory recall. And students can use their insights to improvise actions, give reality to imagined environments and objects, and speak and write with the details that bring imaginary worlds to life.

Drama is a useful tool for learning through inquiry, but students need practice to develop proficiency with the tools of dramatic play itself before they use this skill to successfully support their work in other subject areas. If students lack understanding and awareness of body movements, for example, they will lack the confidence and ability to move expressively. Without a full range of voice, students have little control of expressive utterance. Likewise, concentration and focus are essential for drama activity about any topic to proceed in depth. Language arts teachers can provide practice opportunities as an expected form of response to the literature students read.

The process of wondering—asking ourselves questions that don't have definitive answers, playing with possibilities, imagining alternative views—may be integral to dramatic thought and play. Hence creative drama, along with other creative expressions, should provide unique and powerful support for inquiry in the language arts. Indeed, in using multiple sign systems, individual styles, and unique creative energies, the arts in the broadest sense of the term are an enormous resource for giving students and teachers an active role in a learning process where they can open their minds and stretch their capacities.

Language Exploration

Drawing on students' wondering in their reading and writing assignments is another strategy for developing students' communicative and textual competence. Opportunities for students to generate their own topics for writing and select their own materials for reading may be quite limited in the scripted, prepackaged curricula that seem to be burgeoning in the current standardized testing climate found in most schools. To engender inquiry and independent problem solving, teachers can provide time for students to identify questions worth pursuing and topics rich enough for engaging their full efforts in multiple expressive means.

To explore the world of language is to open all kinds of unforeseen doors and windows in students' thinking. As they develop their ability to reflect consciously on their own language use, students gain increased control of the many language tools at their disposal. They begin to realize that we modify the way we speak and write depending on our purpose and audience, and they begin to attend to the often subtle and myriad ways we signal our intentions and form our messages. To engage students in language exploration is to help them design and undertake projects of compelling personal interest.

As in the example provided in the sample lesson for helping students generate topics for writing, teachers can speak aloud to demonstrate their own mental processes for choosing a focus of study. Encouraging students to brainstorm possibilities before making a selection can make the process manageable and create genuine choice for the students. The following are some overlapping guidelines for developing this kind of project.

- Start with an individual student's personal set of interests. Just about everything in the world incorporates some aspect of language, even if it only involves the way we interpret a phenomenon, such as our response to a soccer game or a rap tune. We use language to describe our reactions and discover what we know. We accomplish this either through dialogue or in writing for a larger audience. In both cases, we are most motivated to formulate our thinking when we are exploring a topic of personal interest.

- Projects can be structured as a case study of a particular language user, for example, of a favorite author, a storyteller who is remarkably engaging, a songwriter a student admires, or even a classmate. In that kind of project, students collect samples of the person's language use, either in writing or in transcripts from tape recordings. They can conduct interviews to delve more deeply into issues that spark their curiosity.

- Another learning structure is to have students develop a task or design an experience and document participants' responses. In projects of this type, students develop an open-ended, written questionnaire to survey people about their experiences and opinions on a particular topic (e.g., e-mail, slang, poetry); organize a gathering of people to watch video clips and discuss their responses; or engage a group of friends in recounting and recording their stories, possibly prompted by photographs or wordless picture books.

- Another kind of project could involve selecting, observing, and recording specific, naturally occurring events, usually by audio- or videotape; transcribing the records; and then analyzing the transcripts for features of special interest. For example, students could record dinner-table conversations, small-group discussions in a classroom, or even do a study of communicative competence by taping interactions between a volunteer and people in a variety of personal relationships such as a good friend, a younger brother or sister, and perhaps a boss or a more familiar adult.

In helping students to design and implement language exploration projects, teachers support their inquiries in a particularly distinctive way. When students increase their awareness of the structure and effects of language, they gain proficiency in the use of language. When students study what they are interested in, they simultaneously acquire the tools of learning. When asked to reflect on their work, they gain insights and understandings for use in future endeavors.

Self-Assessment

Revision is at the heart of learning to write well, and self-assessment is at the heart of learning how to learn. To become independent in our reading, writing, thinking, speaking, and listening, to become proficient in all the language arts, requires the ability to step back and assess the ideas we express and the processes used to express them. Too often in school, it is the teacher, the teacher's edition, or a test's answer key that does all of the assessing. Students are left feeling powerless in the matter, buffeted by forces beyond their control and comprehension.

Generally, students who make A's keep making A's, and students who make C's continue making C's. How can we help students get *better*? One possibility is to require that they give careful attention to the details of their work, estimating the effects of their words on real purposes and audiences by stepping back to re-see and re-view with fresh eyes. We can encourage deep revision, the type of self-assessment that demands an ability to take a new look. And here we come full circle to the idea that students benefit from their experiences interacting with a range of people and texts, drawing on their social and textual exchanges as resources for their own intellectual development. We help students see the value of multiple perspectives in an authentic way when we ask them to assess their work and set goals for improvement.

In almost every assignment I make, I ask students to engage in some form of self-assessment, whether it be in the self-evaluative preface they compose for their writing portfolios, in the multiple drafts they undertake for major writing assignments, or in the in-process thinking they record in class. Sometimes, simply asking them to write their current questions, wonderings, and perplexities gives them a chance to stop and think about what they are thinking. When they listen to classmates' inquiries, they also gain the opportunity to hear the beating heart of their own.

Assessment can feel like an assault, especially for students who struggle in school, who live on the margins of our classrooms, or who are lost in a maze of confusion and consternation (Townsend, Fu, & Lamme, 1997). Students with special needs, whose second language is English, or whose culture or dialect is out of the mainstream frequently fail in our schools. To create classrooms that support their inquiries, that welcome their diverse viewpoints, that encourage their creativity, and that guide them in personal explorations is to meet national standards and help all students develop all the language arts.

IDEAS FROM THE FIELD

TOPIC GENERATION FOR A PERSUASIVE LETTER

This inquiry-based lesson helps students to select topics for writing a persuasive letter to a real person for an authentic purpose. The instructional sequence targets the NCTE/IRA standard that "students employ a wide range of strategies as they write and use different writing process elements appropriately to communicate with different audiences for a variety of purposes."

Lesson Overview

To help students develop topics for writing a persuasive letter to a real person for a real purpose, teachers will speak aloud to describe their own mental processes when engaged in this topic generation. Students then individually generate four possible topics for letters they might want to write, talk about their reasons for each with classmates, decide on a topic, and begin writing.

Standards

Students employ a wide range of strategies as they write and use different writing process elements appropriately to communicate with different audiences for a variety of purposes (NCTE/IRA, 1996).

Instructional Goal

The student will be able to choose fruitful topics for writing.

Assessment

Students will write down their ideas, discuss them with classmates, and begin writing. Each step in the process can be checked for completion by the teacher to provide formative assessment data. Pieces of writing with appended drafts will show the full fruition of their efforts. Students will complete a culminating self-assessment of the process and the product. In an earlier lesson, students collected examples and brainstormed characteristics of effective persuasive writing to collaboratively develop a list of assessment criteria for persuasive letters.

Lesson Organization

Opening the Lesson (10 minutes)

The teacher uses a think-aloud strategy to model how two possible topics about which letters will be written and to whom they will be sent were selected. Social or political issues, a report on a favorite or failed product, or a personal appeal are all fruitful possibilities.

Developing the Lesson (20 minutes)

Students are asked to write down two possible topics each of them might choose. They then do their thinking aloud in front of the class, to select two more choices. Students write down two more possibilities for themselves for a total of four.

Closing the Lesson (20 minutes)

The students break into pairs to talk about their possible choices, finally picking one and beginning to write a rough draft of their persuasive letter for whatever time remains in the period. The teacher circulates around the room to assist anyone who needs help.

Teaching Resources

Teachers generate four ideas for a persuasive letter that they might want to write and have a detailed explanation for why they choose each idea.

Enrichment Activity

Follow-up activities include completing a first draft of a letter, obtaining feedback from a classmate, deciding whether to stick with this topic or try another idea, and then writing a final draft that can be edited. When students choose fruitful topics for letters and polish final drafts, the letters can be mailed to real people with the idea that they will receive real responses. Future writing assignments can draw on this topic-generating process.

Accommodations for Special Learners

Given the flexible time configuration and a workshop environment that allows for attention to individual students, this lesson can accommodate the needs of all students.

REFERENCES

Albritton, T. (1992). Honest questions and the teaching of English. *English Education, 24,* 91–100.

Almasi, J. F., O'Flahavan, J. F., & Arya, P. (2001). A comparative analysis of student and teacher development in more and less proficient discussions of literature. *Reading Research Quarterly, 36,* 96–120.

Bakhtin, M. M. (1986). *Speech genres and other late essays.* Austin: University of Texas Press.

Bruner, J. (1986). *Actual minds, possible worlds.* Cambridge, MA: Harvard University Press.

Delpit, L. (2002). No kinda sense. In L. Delpit & J. K. Dowdy (Eds.), *The skin that we speak: Thoughts on language and culture in the classroom* (pp. 31–48). New York: New Press.

Feldman, C. F., & Wertsch, J. V. (1976). Context dependent properties of teachers' speech. *Youth & Society, 7,* 227–257.

Gallas, K. (1995). *Talking their way into science.* New York: Teachers College Press.

Hadjioannou, X. (2003). *An exploration of authentic discussion in the booktalks of a fifth-grade class.* Unpublished doctoral dissertation, University of Florida, Gainesville.

Heath, S. B. (1982). Questioning at home and at school: A comparative study. In G. Spindler (Ed.), *Doing the ethnography of schooling: Educational anthropology in action* (pp. 104–131). New York: Holt, Rinehart & Winston.

Heath, S. B. (1983). *Ways with words: Language, life, and work in communities and classrooms.* Cambridge, UK: Cambridge University Press.

Lindfors, J. W. (1999). *Children's inquiry: Using language to make sense of the world.* New York: Teachers College Press.

Marshall, J. D., Smagorinsky, P., & Smith, M. W. (1995). *The language of interpretation: Patterns of discourse in discussions of literature.* Urbana, IL: National Council of Teachers of English.

Mehan, H. (1979). *Learning lessons: Social organization in the classroom.* Cambridge, MA: Harvard University Press.

Moll, L. (1990). Introduction. In L. Moll (Ed.), *Vygotsky and education: Instructional implications and applications of sociohistorical psychology* (pp. 1–27). Cambridge, UK: Cambridge University Press.

National Council of Teachers of English & International Reading Association. (1996). *Standards for the English language arts.* Urbana, IL, and Newark, DE: Author.

Nystrand, M. (1997). *Opening dialogue: Understanding the dynamics of language and learning in the English classroom.* New York: Teachers College Press.

Paley, V. (1981). *Wally's stories.* Cambridge, MA: Harvard University Press.

Rogoff, B. (1990). *Apprenticeship in thinking: Cognitive development in social context.* New York: Oxford University Press.

Siks, G. B. (1983). *Drama with children.* New York: Harper & Row.

Townsend, J. (1987a). *Speculations and wonderings: Student curiosity in the first grade.* Unpublished manuscript.

Townsend, J. (1987b). Wondering questions in creative drama. *Youth Theatre Journal, 2*(1), 14–18.

Townsend, J. S. (1991). *A study of wondering discourse in three literature class discussions.* Unpublished doctoral dissertation, University of Texas, Austin.

Townsend, J. S. (1998). Silent voices: What happens to quiet students during classroom discussion? *English Journal, 87*(2), 72–80.

Townsend, J. S., & Fu, D. (2001). Paw's story: A Laotian refugee's lonely entry into American literacy. *Journal of Adolescent and Adult Literacy, 45,* 2–12.

Townsend, J. S., Fu, D., & Lamme, L. L. (1997). Writing assessment: Multiple perspectives, multiple purposes. *Preventing School Failure, 41,* 71–76.

Vygotsky, L. (1986). *Thought and language.* Cambridge: MIT Press.

Way, B. (1967). *Development through drama.* Fremont, CA: Humanities Press.

Whitin, P. (1999). Fueled by surprise. In J. W. Lindfors & J. S. Townsend (Eds.), *Teaching language arts: Learning through dialogue.* Urbana, IL: National Council of Teachers of English.

CHAPTER SEVEN

Curriculum Integration

Capitalizing on Student Inquiry

Richard H. Audet

You can tell whether a man is clever by his answers. You can tell whether a man is wise by his questions.

—Naguib Mahfouz

H ere are two examples that illustrate the powerful potential of integrative thinking to solve problems. One case is drawn from a recent novel, and the other describes an elementary school classroom assignment.

Patricia Cornwell, one of America's most popular novelists, recently pooled her considerable writing and investigative skills to produce the nonfiction best-seller *Portrait of a Killer: Jack the Ripper Case Closed* (2003). Without revealing the ending, what I found fascinating about this book was how Cornwell combined her interpretations of the data with a set of first-rate communication and literary skills, and suddenly a book emerged. This oversimplifies her work, but nevertheless, integrating data from a variety of divergent sources gave Cornwell a fresh frame of reference for looking at the evidence and caused her to reach unique conclusions. Some say that she finally unraveled one of the world's greatest unsolved crimes.

Here is another example of integration introduced through a classroom assessment: You are a student at George W. Bush Elementary School. The Mulberry Books company is sponsoring a local classroom competition to see who can create a "Galimoto" that most closely resembles the object invented by the main character, Kondi, in their popular children's book *Galimoto* (Williams, 1990). You'll be provided with a broad range of everyday materials from which you can select to build your object. The only actual clues for creating your model come from hearing the story of Kondi's life. The rest is up to your imagination. Good luck and listen carefully!

This learning assignment, adapted from the work of Welch (2000), engages young children in a straightforward task that requires them to apply language arts skills, the science of design, and the creative arts. Completing the task taps into the multiple intelligences, requires active listening, supports creativity and higher-order thinking, and incorporates a multicultural ingredient.

The procedures that these children and Cornwell applied to complete the task have much in common. The fundamental similarity is that both problem-solving quests began with answerable questions: "What does Galimoto's invention look like?" and "Who was the real Jack the Ripper?" Almost every inquiry-based activity is anchored in generating, exploring, and answering questions (Krajcik, Czerniak, & Berger, 1999). Questions with the most enduring impact on learning are those that follow data trails that crisscross disciplines naturally and take the problem solver along paths that meander into unexpected, unanticipated, thought-provoking, and often uncharted domains of learning.

This chapter describes how curriculum integration provides a conceptual framework for structuring the learning environment. Two of the most noteworthy integration models are case studies and problem- or project-based learning (PBL). They share so many similarities that, generally, what can be said of one method applies equally to the other. Herreid (2003) contends that PBL is actually a variety of the case study method. Both approaches to curriculum integration incorporate the essential features of inquiry described in earlier chapters. They employ practices that help students learn a body of core information, develop the ability to solve problem situations, and successfully apply their understanding in future situations (Delisle, 1997). What distinguishes these instructional approaches is that they are *intentionally* designed to foster interdisciplinary connections and provide opportunities for students to simultaneously meet standards across multiple content areas. These situated learning approaches tend to mirror the way that learning and action occur beyond the restrictive, artificial boundaries of the classroom.

THE CASE STUDY METHOD

During the mid-1800s, the legal profession began turning toward original source documents to extract information and provide perspectives to establish legal principles. This strategy is now referred to as the case study method. Applications of case studies have spread widely through business colleges and medical schools and occupy an important niche in a number of K–12 classrooms. For example, Harvard Business School (n.d.) describes its learning model in this way:

> The case method forces students to grapple with exactly the kinds of decisions and dilemmas managers confront every day. In doing so, it redefines the traditional educational dynamic in which the professor dispenses knowledge and students passively receive it. The case method creates a classroom in which students succeed not by simply absorbing facts and theories, but also by *exercising* the skills of leadership and teamwork in the face of real problems. Under the skillful guidance of a faculty member, they work together to analyze and synthesize conflicting data and points of view, to define and prioritize goals, to persuade and inspire others who think differently, to make tough decisions with uncertain information, and to seize opportunity in the face of doubt.

Successful completion of a case study assimilates the central understandings and abilities needed to conduct inquiry. The National Center for Case Study Teaching in Science (n.d.) describes cases as stories with an educational message. A case study framework for student investigation begins with a richly worded, teacher-created narrative, original source document, or visual description of an event (Fogarty, 1997). Ethical paradoxes or moral dilemmas are often embedded in the storyline. Case studies depicted through scenarios, vignettes, excerpts from original source materials, recordings, video-clips, and so on establish a rich context for instruction, collaboration among peers, research, and understanding (Koballa & Tippins, 2004).

Students involved in this learning model typically follow prescribed steps as they review and react to the case description: paraphrase facts, identify assumptions, isolate key issues, and explore possible solutions. After participating in small-group and teacher-led discussions, students state their proposed solutions to the central problem and carefully describe the thought processes underlying their decisions or projected courses of action. The product of a case study investigation is typically an evidence-based presentation at a final debriefing session in front of a larger peer group.

Teachers can find numerous examples of case studies on the Internet that range from selecting the site of the next Olympic games to defining the ethical issues associated with stem cell research. An award-winning Web site maintained by the National Center for Case Study Teaching in Science at the University of Buffalo (http://ublib .buffalo.edu/libraries/projects/cases/case.html) contains an extensive library of field-tested case studies.

THE PROBLEM-BASED LEARNING METHOD

Barell (1998) described problem-based learning as "an inquiry process that resolves questions, curiosities, doubts, and uncertainties about complex phenomena in life" and defined a problem as "any doubt, difficulty or certainty that needs some kind of resolution" (p. 7). Instruction anchored in a problem is aimed at developing transferable investigative strategies and learner dispositions and generating new knowledge bases that cut across disciplines. PBL is an effective way to organize classroom learning for three main reasons: It enhances student learning, motivates students, and prepares students for real-life decision making and smooth school-to-career transitions.

Learning

There is a growing consensus in today's educational community about what constitutes a quality learning experience. These beliefs are founded on the idea that learning is

- An active process in which students connect new ideas with prior understandings

- Optimized by student-to-student dialogue in cooperative settings
- Most motivating and interesting to students when situated in real-world, discovery-oriented contexts
- Supported by student-centered contexts in which participants are given the opportunity to make decisions about their own learning
- Requiring students to reflect and be able to explain what they have learned to convince others
- Lifelong, making it essential for continued growth that students learn how to learn
- Motivation

PBL is fun for students and teachers. This brand of classwork is exciting, engaging, and active. Traditionally, instruction is organized around a set of hierarchical experiences in which students are first provided with an information base and skill set before progressing to more sophisticated and advanced learning, such as problem solving and decision making. As a consequence, students have been subjected frequently to dull and boring tasks that emphasize basic skills and fact acquisition as the intended precursor to more complex and engaging work. Too often, any inherent interest in a topic is lost during this initial preparation phase.

Teachers who use PBL in their classrooms believe that students learn basic facts and how to apply skills best in genuine contexts and on a need-to-know basis. With PBL, knowledge and skills emerge through attempts to solve problems or answer questions. Many students find this a more natural, relaxed, and comfortable way to learn. They participate more fully because they are the ones who make decisions about what resources to use, how to solve problems, and the most effective way to present their findings. Students and teachers have clear expectations about final products and outcomes because the assessment criteria are predetermined and communicated in advance. All of these factors combine to make PBL a motivational context for learning.

School-to-Career Transitions

PBL helps students acquire skills for the workplace because they require working collaboratively in small groups, the ability to apply strategies for solving real-world problems, and effective communication skills.

What Does PBL Look Like?

PBL is an instructional technique for organizing an integrated curriculum. Expectations for what is to be learned are embedded in the problem statement. Problems frame, focus, organize, and stimulate learning. Teachers or their students can create or encounter authentic problems that are typically fuzzy or ill-structured; that is, PBL scenarios seldom offer sufficient clues about what prior knowledge must be applied to the problem and always lack essential pieces of information needed to complete the puzzle. Students, working alone or in small groups, investigate these problems using a variety of research tools and technologies. A typical model for implementing PBL in a classroom setting involves four stages that flow seamlessly from one to the next. For example, here is a PBL scenario for an aquaculture class:

1. Your small aquaculture company has been relatively success-ful during its first year of operation. You have made a small profit, and restaurants are lining up to buy all the tilapia you can produce. The problem is that the company has become a 24/7 business with never any time off. Even though you love what you're doing, this is a killer pace. What you desperately need is an aquaculture operator's manual so that you can hire and train an assistant to properly supervise the operation in your absence. You hire a writer to produce the handbook and give her two simple instructions: Keep it simple, clear, and comprehensive enough so that a new worker can reference this document and easily find the information needed to maintain a smooth operation. What will the manual look like?

2. Students prepare lists of what they know about the problem and generate ideas about additional information they might need to address the problem.

3. Students select the specific aspect of the problem they want to investigate, identify the resources needed to complete their investigation, create a project time line, and decide on the products they will generate.

4. In the final stage, students communicate and analyze results and share their products. Teachers sometimes organize this final stage as a culminating event at which parents and community members observe student presentations (Audet & Bednarz, 2001).

Lave lamented that "students appear to occupy a peripheral role as objects or clients on whom services are to be performed. . . . Students are not viewed as powerfully influential on teacher, subject, pedagogy, or the learning that transpires in the classroom" (Polman, 2000, p. 29). I am confident that Lave's concerns would be allayed if he were to visit classrooms in which problem-based and case study learning were the dominant approaches to student learning. The NASA-supported Classrooms of the Future project at Jesuit College in Wheeling, West Virginia, maintains an excellent Web site with a library of PBL units (http://www.cotf.edu/ ete/teacher/teacher.html).

Topics for Curriculum Integration

When developing integrated units, themes such as catastrophic events, 20th-century poetry, or politics in America—instead of easily recognizable bodies of knowledge—often provide the curriculum focus. In other instances, teams of teachers plan multidisciplinary units such as the Roaring Twenties, Watersheds, or the Battle for Civil Rights in which a single broad topic or issue is examined from various content area perspectives. A fully integrated approach is open-ended, incorporates some aspects of problem solving, and encourages high levels of student autonomy. For example, students in a social studies class might be asked to compose an editorial on a local referendum aimed at regulating pesticide spraying for the West Nile virus. In educational settings where curriculum integration is a strongly held value, students have significant latitude in making decisions that channel their own learning. As Silberman maintained,

> Learning is likely to be more effective if it grows out of what interests the learner rather than what interests the teachers. To suggest that learning evolve from the child's interest is not to propose an abdication of adult authority; only a change in how it is exercised. (Katz & Chard, 1994, pp. 8–9)

Ronis (2002) used terms such as *contextualized, relevant, messy,* and *student-centered* to describe the characteristics of topics suitable for open-ended investigation. Other recommendations about the salient features of quality case studies, questions, and problems found in the literature on this subject are that they

- Be developmentally appropriate (Delisle, 1997)
- Accommodate a range of student ability levels and learning preferences (Delisle, 1997; Glasgow, 1997)

- Align with standards (Fogarty, 2002)
- Grow out of student interest and experience (Katz & Chard, 1994)
- Be ill-structured and ambiguous, and promote cognitive conflict (Delisle, 1997; Torp & Sage, 1998)
- Possess intellectual rigor in the complexity of the problem and the measures needed to resolve the issue (Glasgow, 1997)
- Are scaled in terms of context, connectedness, and relevance from global to local (Glasgow, 1997)
- Include value-laden dilemmas and paradoxes (Glasgow, 1997)
- Apply genuine cognitive tasks, demands, and challenges (Krajcik et al., 1999; Torp & Sage, 1998)
- Require active engagement and promote student ownership of the task (Krajcik et al., 1999)
- Use primary information sources (Torp & Sage, 1998)
- Incorporate contexts whose complexity continues to emerge while they are being investigated (Stepien & Gallagher, 1993)
- Generate conclusions supported by evidence, but that are tentative, emergent, and negotiable (Katz & Chard, 1994)
- Situate reflection and resolution of cognitive conflict in social contexts (Howe & Nichols, 2001; Krajcik et al., 1999)
- Are designed for evaluation by a broader audience than a single teacher (Glasgow, 1997)
- Prepare students for later life (Katz & Chard, 1994)

This extensive list illustrates the importance of properly framing the problem or case. The broad scope of considerations also suggests that developing effective case studies and problem-solving scenarios may initially pose significant challenges for the teacher who is a newcomer to this instructional approach.

Principles of Integrated Instruction and Assessment

Most schools have fallen into a pattern of giving kids exercises and drills that result in their getting answers on tests that look like understanding. It's what I call the "correct answer compromise": students read a text, they take a test, and everybody agrees that if they say a certain thing, it'll be counted as understanding. (Gardner, in Fogarty, 1998, p. 26)

Savery and Duffy (1995) summarized the key instructional principles associated with planning, managing, and delivering integrated curriculum models such as case studies and PBL as follows:

1. Anchor all learning activities in a larger task or problem.

2. Support the learner in developing ownership for the overall problem or task.

3. Design an authentic task.

4. Design the task and the learning environment to reflect the complexity of the environment that students should be able to function in at the end of learning.

5. Give the learner ownership of the process used to develop a solution.

6. Design the learning environment to support and challenge the learner's thinking.

7. Encourage testing ideas against alternative views and alternative contexts. (pp. 33, 34)

The major responsibilities for the teacher who implements an integrated approach to curriculum are that of designer, guide, and evaluator (Delisle, 1997). Thier (2001) referred to teachers as "academic executives" (p. 13) who are responsible for implementing a plan that is consistent with both local educational resources and the community's goals for education. The designing role encompasses all of the elements of effective planning listed in the previous section. Among the tasks of the teacher as guide are to direct learning by careful prompts at strategic times, help identify information sources, provide encouragement, and monitor student and group performance.

The role of evaluator is a tricky one. As Herreid (2001) remarked, "The thing I most dislike about teaching is assigning grades. . . . Evaluation is an odious affair." Anyone having experience in an integrated classroom setting is well aware of the assessment issues peculiar to this instructional delivery system. Nontraditional methods of instruction demand nontraditional forms of assessment. Does a multiple-choice, true/false exam properly assess what a student knows or is able to do after having completed a case study or problem-based assignment? Krajcik et al. (1999) offer a comprehensive overview of authentic strategies appropriate for assessing student work in both inquiry and integrated learning environments. Their recommendations include the use of observations and discussions for gathering anecdotal evidence, performance checklists, interviews, and, of course, products that can be scored with well-designed scoring guides.

Real-world tasks and problem-based inquiry are best suited for some form of performance-based assessment. Individual or team products and performances provide the evidence to assess progress in gaining content knowledge and associated problem-solving skills. In a PBL or case study activity, scoring guides with clear expectations for students are critical and send messages about the standards and valued outcomes to which learners must aspire. In addition to final product evaluation, teachers may develop a sequence of embedded assessment tools to ensure that students remain attentive and motivated. Formative assessments can include a daily grade based on observations, task completion, progress reports, logbooks, student group-teacher conferences, or journal records that help students stay on task and enable the teacher to monitor both the project and student progress. Peer and self-evaluations are also integral features of project-based work.

Debriefing and reflection are critical events that follow completion of the project. How do students assess their own performance in this activity? What learning strategies and responsibilities were most useful? This stage is very important because it cements learning by making students acutely aware of their accomplishments and the cognitive strategies they applied to reach the desired outcome of their case study or problem-based learning project.

Polman (2000) and Delisle (1997) offered important cautions about teaching and learning through an integrated curriculum. They noted that students might feel uncomfortable in the new role as active, self-directed inquirers and suffer from having underdeveloped time management skills. Topics that are interesting and relevant to some may be unappealing to others. Conflicts may arise because of student beliefs about what constitutes effective teaching. Ambiguity over grades can produce high levels of student anxiety. Time, content coverage, and the availability of adequate materials and equipment are the constraints most frequently cited by teachers who experiment with both inquiry-based teaching and an integrated curriculum.

IDEAS FROM THE FIELD

HOUSTON, WE'VE GOT A PROBLEM HERE!

This case study incorporates many of the ideas reviewed in this chapter. The topic explores the distinction between precision and accuracy. Accuracy refers to the degree to which a particular measurement or calculation represents the actual value. Precision is the degree of consistency within a set of individual measurements or results. Figure 7.1 identifies the compendium of standards targeted by this project.

Figure 7.1   Connections With the National Standards

SCIENCE	NSES: Science as Inquiry - Understandings About Scientific Inquiry • Accuracy and precision of the data and therefore the quality of the investigation depends on the technology used: 9–12, 3, p. 176. NSES: Science as Inquiry - Abilities to Do Scientific Inquiry • Think critically and logically to make the relationship between evidence and explanations: 6–8, 5, p. 145. NSES: Science and Technology - Abilities of Technological Design • Choose suitable tools and work with appropriate measurement methods to assure adequate accuracy: 6–8, 3, p. 165. Benchmarks for Science Literacy: Nature of Technology • The value of any given technology may be different at different points in time: 3B 9–12b, p. 52.
LANGUAGE ARTS	Standard 7: Students conduct research on issues and interests by generating ideas and questions and by posing problems. Standard 8: Students use a variety of technological and information resources to gather and synthesize information and to create and communicate knowledge.
MATHEMATICS	Measurement: 9–12, Apply appropriate techniques and tools for determining measurements. Measurement: 9–12, Understand measurable attributes of objects and the units, systems, and processes of measurement. Number and Operations: 9–12, Compute fluently and make reasonable estimates.

"Houston, we've got a problem here."

On April 11, 1970, the world's attention was riveted on a dramatic set of events unfolding in space. Three American astronauts on the Apollo 13 mission relayed a message back to the Command Center in Houston, Texas, describing failures in their space vehicle that jeopardized their safe return to Earth. The following is a transcript of that famous transmission (National Aeronautics and Space Administration [NASA], 1970).

SPACECRAFT (SC)—"Hey, we've got a problem here."

Thus, calmly, Command Module Pilot Jack Swigert gave the first intimation of serious trouble for Apollo 13—200,000 miles from Earth.

CAPSULE COMMUNICATOR (CAPCOM)—"This is Houston; say again, please."

SC—"Houston, we've had a problem. We've had a Main B bus undervolt."

By "undervolt," Swigert meant a drop in power in one of the Command/Service Module's two main electrical circuits. His report to the ground began the most gripping episode in humankind's venture into space. One newspaper reporter called it the most public emergency and the most dramatic rescue in the history of exploration.

SC—"And we had a pretty large bang associated with the caution and warning here."

Lunar Module Pilot Fred Haise was now on the voice channel from the spacecraft to the Mission Control Center at NASA's Manned Spacecraft Center in Texas. Commander Jim Lovell would shortly be heard, then again Swigert—the backup crewman who had been thrust onto the first team only 2 days before launch when doctors feared that Tom Mattingly of the primary crew might come down with German measles.

Equally cool, the men in Mission Control acknowledged the report and began the emergency procedures that grew into an effort by hundreds of ground controllers and thousands of technicians and scientists in NASA contractor plants and on university campuses to solve the most complex and urgent problem yet encountered in space flight.

SC—"We've got a Main B bus undervolt, now, too. . . . Main B is reading zip [zero] right now."

CAPCOM—"We'd like you to attempt to reconnect fuel cell 1 to Main A and fuel cell 3 to Main B."

SC—"Okay, Houston. . . . I tried to reset, and fuel cells 1 and 3 are both showing zip on the flows."

CAPCOM—"We copy."

SC—"Houston, are you still reading 1, 3?"

CAPCOM—"That's affirmative. We're still reading you. We're still trying to come up with some good ideas here for you."

SC—"Let me give you some readings. . . . Our O2 [oxygen] cryo number 2 tank is reading zero—did you get that?"

CAPCOM—"O2 quantity number 2 is zero."

After peaking briefly just before the bang, pressure in one of the two cryogenic (supercold) oxygen tanks, back in the service module, dropped to zero in 8 seconds. These oxygen tanks, with the companion cryogenic hydrogen tanks, fed the three fuel cells that generated the spacecraft's electrical current, provided breathing oxygen, and produced water.

Precision Versus Accuracy
Case Study Scenario

You just finished seeing the IMAX showing of *Apollo 13*. It was really awesome on that huge screen! The whole theater shook during liftoff! When you returned home, you went to your computer to learn more about the events surrounding this famous space voyage. During your Internet search, you ran across a comic strip (http://vesuvius.jsc.nasa. gov/er/seh/) that illustrates Apollo 13's sequence of events. As you read the comic, you realized that an awful lot of what happened on that historic Apollo 13 mission was connected with topics that you'd been studying in physics and math. There's even material here that you recall from studying Greek mythology.

When you mentioned this to Mrs. Rodriguez, your physics teacher, the next day, she asked, "What about this comic strip reminded you of this class? Can you give me some examples?" You replied, "Well, it's got all this stuff in it about precision and accuracy like we've been talking about." The following day Mrs. Rodriguez said to the class, "You've given me an idea. Let's use this comic strip about the Apollo 13 mission to assess your understanding of what we've been studying. Here's my challenge to the class. Study the comic strip carefully. It contains three distinct references to how issues surrounding accuracy and precision were connected with the successful outcome of the Apollo 13 voyage.

Figure 7.2   Precision Versus Accuracy

INTRODUCTION	"If you have only one watch, you always know exactly what time it is. If you have two watches, you are never quite sure . . . " The fact is, when we take a single reading, whether from a thermometer, a wristwatch, or a fancy laboratory instrument, we tend to accept the readout without really thinking about its validity. People seem to do this even when they know the reading is inaccurate. Your fancy digital watch is probably off by a minute or two right now! Try as you might, with the most expensive instruments, under the most ideal conditions, every measurement is subject to errors and inaccuracies. But worse still, modern digital instruments convey such an aura of accuracy and reliability that we forget this basic rule . . . *there is no such thing as a perfect measurement!* As a consequence of this fact, it is important for all measurements to include an estimate of the accuracy and precision offered by a particular instrument or experimental procedure.
TASK	A dartboard consisting of concentric circles is a powerful model for illustrating the relationship between precision and accuracy. After completing your Internet research, you should draw a diagram showing four dart targets. Label them as follows: Precise but not Accurate, Accurate but not Precise, Neither Accurate nor Precise, and Both Accurate and Precise. On each of the dart targets, place six arrows that illustrate each of the four categories listed above.
PROCESS	With a partner, conduct Internet research to establish a clear meaning for the terms *accuracy* and *precision* and an understanding of the distinction between the two concepts. Draw your labeled dartboards with the correct placement of the darts.
RESOURCES	• Essay: www.ee.unb.ca/tervo/ee2791/intro.htm • Figure: www.chemistrycoach.com/math_skills_for_chemistry_tutori.htm#Accuracy%20and%20 Precision

Before you begin, please complete the activity found in Figure 7.2." (See also Figure 7.3.)

Assessment

Your task is to investigate the topics of precision and accuracy and prepare a report based on the Apollo 13 mission that

Figure 7.3   Precision Versus Accuracy

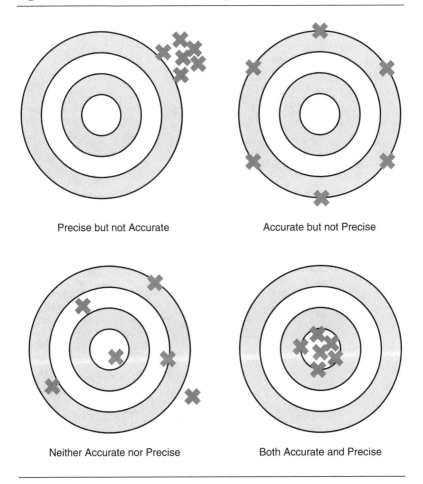

Precise but not Accurate

Accurate but not Precise

Neither Accurate nor Precise

Both Accurate and Precise

- Identifies the three scenarios mentioned in the comic book that involved issues associated with precision and accuracy
- Relates these scenarios directly to the concepts of precision and accuracy
- Provides sufficient support and reasoning to establish a parallel between accuracy and/or precision and each Apollo 13 scenario

Refer to the Apollo 13 Scoring Rubric (Figure 7.4) for a detailed description of how your work will be graded.

Figure 7.4   Apollo 13 Scoring Rubric

	4	3	2	1
IDENTIFICATION OF SCENARIOS	• Three scenarios identified.	• Two scenarios identified.	• One scenario identified.	• No scenarios identified.
CONTENT KNOWLEDGE	• Correct explanations are used to define the term *accuracy* and/or *precision* for each scenario.	• Correct explanations are used to define the term *accuracy* and/or *precision* for two scenarios.	• Correct explanations are used to define the term *accuracy* and/or *precision* for one scenario.	• Explanations are not provided.
CLEAR PARALLEL	• Clear parallel is established between accuracy and/or precision and all Apollo 13 scenarios. • Scenarios include sufficient reasoning.	• Clear parallel is established between accuracy and/or precision and two Apollo 13 scenarios. • Reasoning may or may not be sufficient.	• Clear parallel is established between accuracy and/or precision and one Apollo 13 scenario. • Scenario lacks sufficient reasoning.	• No parallels are established between accuracy and/or precision and any Apollo 13 scenarios.

REFERENCES

Audet, R. H., & Bednarz, S. W. (2001). Problem-based learning and aquaculture. In *RASCALs* (pp. 2–5). Boston: New England Board of Higher Education.

Barell, J. (1998). *Problem based learning: An inquiry approach.* Arlington Heights, IL: SkyLight Professional Development.

Cornwell, P. (2003). *Portrait of a killer: Jack the Ripper case closed.* New York: Putnam.

Delisle, R. (1997). *How to use problem-based learning in the classroom.* Alexandria, VA: Association for Supervision and Curriculum Development.

Fogarty, R. (1997). *Problem-based learning and other curriculum models for the multiple intelligence classroom.* Arlington Heights, IL: SkyLight Professional Development.

Fogarty, R. (1998). *Problem based learning: A collection of articles.* Arlington Heights, IL: SkyLight Professional Development.

Fogarty, R. (2002). *How to integrate the curricula.* Arlington Heights, IL: SkyLight Professional Development.

Glasgow, N. A. (1997). *New curriculum for new times: A guide to student-centered learning.* Thousand Oaks, CA: Corwin.

Harvard Business School. (n.d.). The case study method. Retrieved January 18, 2005, from http://www.hbs.edu/case/

Herreid, C. F. (2001). When justice peeks: Evaluating students in case method teaching. *Journal of College Science Teaching, 30*(7), 430–433.

Herreid, C. F. (2003). The death of problem-based learning. *Journal of College Science Teaching, 32*(6), 364–366.

Howe, A. C., & Nichols, S. E. (2001). *Case studies in elementary science.* Upper Saddle River, NJ: Merrill Prentice Hall.

Katz, L. C., & Chard, S. C. (1994). *Engaging children's minds: The project approach.* Norwood, NJ: Ablex.

Koballa, T. R., & Tippins, D. J. (2004). *Cases in middle and secondary science education.* Upper Saddle River, NJ: Pearson.

Krajcik, J., Czerniak, C., & Berger, C. (1999). *Teaching children science: A project based approach.* Boston: McGraw-Hill.

National Aeronautics and Space Administration, Office of Public Affairs. (1970). *Apollo 13: "Houston, we've got a problem"* (EP-76). Washington, DC: U.S. Government Printing Office.

National Center for Case Study Teaching in Science. (n.d.). Available: http://ublibd.buffalo.edu/libraries/projects/cases/teaching/teaching.html

Polman, J. L. (2000). *Designing project-based science: Connecting learners through guided inquiry.* New York: Teachers College Press.

Ronis, D. (2002). *Clustering standards in integrated units.* Arlington Heights, IL: SkyLight Professional Development.

Savery, J. R., & Duffy, T. M. (1995, September–October). Problem based learning: An instructional model and its constructivist framework. *Educational Technology,* pp. 31–38.

Stepien, W. J., & Gallagher, S. (1993). Problem-based learning: As authentic as it gets. *Educational Leadership, 50*(7), 25–28.

Thier, H. D. (2001). *Developing inquiry-based science materials.* New York: Teachers College Press.

Torp, L., & Sage, S. (1998). *Problems as possibilities.* Alexandria, VA: Association of Supervision and Curriculum Development.

Welch, D. (2000). Galimoto's inventions. In A. McCormack & C. Mason (Eds.), *Project Vista: Visual/spatial thinking activities* (pp. 1–4). San Diego, CA: University of San Diego Press.

Williams, K. L. (1990). *Galimoto.* New York: Lothrop, Lee, & Shepard.

PART II

Creating Conditions for Successful Student Inquiry

Two of the most profound educational changes that have occurred during the past two decades are reflected in this second section. One issue pertains to our rapidly changing assessment climate; the other deals with matters of equity and access to opportunity. Both are fundamental elements of successful student inquiry.

No single issue has galvanized—some might say, polarized—education more than the topic of assessment. The term itself has such a multiplicity of meanings that range from the Friday vocabulary quiz to the rigorous performance task to the annual norm- or criterion-referenced standardized test. Some earlier chapters expressed concern over the apparent divide between teaching and learning in an inquiry-based environment and the impact of state and federally mandated testing. For the purposes of this book, we assume that classroom inquiry is happening and that to obtain an accurate picture of student work, one must rely on data generated by nontraditional measures of student performance. The chapter on assessment identifies types of evaluation tools that students can use to self-assess prior knowledge, monitor ongoing performance, and draw summative conclusions about their work. The Vermont Expectations for Inquiry provide benchmarking tools that link ideas about inquiry with learning expectations for students.

The chapters on special education and English language learners are powerful and provocative. They present strong advocacy positions for shaping the inquiry-based learning environment so that it is inclusive of all learners. Both describe specific accommodations to make inquiry equally accessible to every student regardless of his or her native language, culture, physical ability, or emotional status. The authors point out that this is the morally correct thing to do and also every teacher's legal obligation.

A recent supplement to the journal *Science Education* (2004) was devoted exclusively to museum learning research. Museum people are interested in knowing more about how visitors interact with museum displays and exhibits, and how the nature of the context shapes the learning experience. The final chapter concerns the important role that museums can play in supporting inquiry in schools. It provides a vivid description of the Exploratorium's vast influence on teaching science as inquiry via its many professional development initiatives.

CHAPTER EIGHT

Assessment in the Inquiry Classroom

Asking the Right Questions

David White
Patricia Fitzsimmons

The conceptions of learning represented by theories and learning and cognition appear strikingly different from those implied in current educational assessment and measurement practice.

—Delandshere (2004)

When I (White) was growing up, I remember my father's creative touch to just about everything. I could always be sure that no one else in the Maine campgrounds where we spent our summer vacations would be sleeping in a 200-square-foot portable screen house with retractable canvas covering! My father was a tinkerer; someone who constantly explored, invented, constructed, or made minor adjustments. I recall wishing that we could simply go to the store and buy already-made things like other people.

From an adult perspective, I now realize and appreciate that my father was very much a scientist, historian, inventor, and engineer, even though he held none of these actual titles in his professional career. What he possessed in all aspects of his life was the inclination to ask questions and a driving desire to explore these questions through organized, purposeful inquiry.

Whether one is a child or an adult, asking the right question can be the starting point for a wonderful odyssey into the world of discovery. Asking the right question is also the essence of quality assessment. When student questioning and inquiry combine with teacher questioning and inquiry in the classroom, a powerful and dynamic relationship develops. The synergy that emerges from this condition enables teachers to help students acquire the skills and dispositions needed to become lifelong inquirers. For some, that path might eventually lead to a diverse array of everyday applications, such as in the case of my father. For others, it can support intense, focused research on a single topic. For all, possessing the inclination to inquire manifests itself in the self-fulfillment and sheer joy that comes from solving problems and understanding the unknown. Physicist Richard Feynman labels this "the pleasure of finding things out" (Robbins, 1999, p. xiv).

In this chapter, we share a developmental framework for assessing student inquiry, the Vermont Grade Expectations for Inquiry. These guidelines have direct implications for any classroom, regardless of the discipline, in which students are engaged in inquiry. The framework is based on three guiding principles.

Humans possess an innate curiosity that motivates us to inquire about our world. However, asking the right questions and engaging in purposeful inquiry to answer such questions require knowledge, skills, and dispositions that must be learned. To borrow from the thinking of Forman and Kuschner (1983),

> Biology gives us the competence to make inferences while culture gives us guides regarding what inferences have been useful to those who have come before us. Intelligent behavior results from integration between the natural operations of the mind and the accumulated knowledge of the culture. (p. 6)

The knowledge, skills, and dispositions of inquiry are learned according to a conceptual continuum that develops from birth through adulthood.

The process of purposeful student inquiry closely parallels the action research that teachers employ as they facilitate and assess student inquiry in the classroom.

The chapter first presents a brief review of the research base that underlies these guiding principles. The next section provides examples of the developmental framework and offers information about its development. The final section examines specific examples where the developmental framework is being used to guide assessment and teaching in classrooms.

Action Research and Teaching and Learning Through Inquiry

Teachers who express a genuine commitment to teaching through inquiry are often misguided or underinformed about employing strategies that support a developmentally appropriate instructional sequence. One extreme belief is that simply providing students with access to hands-on materials and the opportunity to explore will enable them to successfully develop the skills and understandings of inquiry. The other end of the spectrum is exemplified by learning experiences that, although referred to as student inquiry, are driven by prescriptive procedures, require continuous teacher guidance, and have predetermined outcomes. Neither practice offers the opportunity for students to develop the reasoning and problem-solving skills that purposeful inquiry requires. Both extremes falsely assume that inquiry focuses on skills that are not critically intertwined with the knowledge that we expect students to develop. A rich, inquiry-based curriculum provides learners with the opportunity to construct understanding as they seek evidence from data and observations, patterns and models from evidence, and explanation from patterns and models (Coffey & Atkin, 2003).

The National Science Education Standards (National Research Council, 2000) gives a comprehensive illustration of inquiry teaching and learning. The approach they recommend scaffolds inquiry teaching over time from stages marked by significant teacher guidance to those that are essentially student directed. Instructional decisions about appropriate levels of student autonomy are derived through data from the teacher's ongoing assessment of students' content knowledge and their ability to conduct inquiry.

The ultimate purpose for introducing students to the complex tasks, abilities, and elements of inquiry is to enable them to gather evidence, build models, clarify concepts and explanations, and successfully apply their new understandings in novel situations (Atkin, Black, & Coffey, 2001). To achieve this end, teachers need an instructional plan supported by the assessment evidence that they collect and interpret as teacher researchers. For any discipline, teaching inquiry through this approach becomes a dynamic process that is fueled by teacher research but always focused on developing deep student understanding of concepts.

Action research is "systematic self-reflective scientific inquiry by practitioners to improve practice" (McKernan, 1991, p. 5). As with all attempts at understanding, action research begins with what the individual already knows, and then builds on that knowledge base to explore and formulate higher levels of awareness and appreciation. By investigating their own questions, teachers who engage in action research reflect on evidence that informs their continuous efforts to improve student performance. Practice-based professional inquiry stems from the belief that practical reasoning and problem solving—when used to examine the direct interactions between teachers and students—provide valuable feedback for improving instruction (Loucks-Horsley, Love, Stiles, Mundry, & Hewson, 2003).

Duschl (in Coffey & Atkin, 2003) suggests that to help students appreciate how scientists gain their scientific knowledge and believe in this knowledge over other competing claims, teachers must create conditions that enable the teacher to listen actively while students engage in inquiry. To successfully study classroom inquiry through action research, teachers must understand that the skills of purposeful inquiry must be learned, and they must be able to implement a systematic process for examining evidence of such learning. The developmental framework for inquiry described in this chapter helps teachers identify current levels of student ability and understanding while focusing on a clear picture of what steps come next. Figure 8.1 illustrates the striking parallel between the cycle of classroom inquiry and the cycle of action research.

Classroom Assessment and the National Science Education Standards (National Research Council, 2001) identifies three guiding questions for the teacher and the student as they practice ongoing assessment:

1. Where are you trying to go?

2. Where are you now?

3. How can you get there?

Figure 8.1   Comparing Classroom inquiry to Teacher-Driven Action Research

ESSENTIAL FEATURES OF CLASSROOM INQUIRY	CONDUCTING ACTION RESEARCH
• Learners are engaged by scientifically oriented questions. • Learners give priority to evidence. • Learners formulate explanations. • Learners evaluate their explanations. • Learners communicate and justify their proposed explanations.	• Teachers reflect and focus. • Teachers clarify questions. • Teachers collect data. • Teachers analyze data. • Teachers take informed action. • Teachers report results.
Source: National Research Council (NRC). 2000. *Inquiry and the National Science Education Standards*. Washington, DC: National Academy Press, p. 35.	Source: Action Research With Impact. *Focus, 10* (1), January 2003. Columbus, OH: Eisenhower National Clearinghouse for Mathematics and Science Education, p. 36.

The essential idea is that assessment (second question) linked to clear learning goals (first question) and action (third question) results in effective formative assessment.

Through conversations, observations, writing, performance tasks, and other forms of assessment, teachers can probe for these demonstrations of student understanding. In the example described below, teacher questioning is guided by the inquiry expectations as the core target of student learning. Strategies for appropriate scaffolding can be developed when teachers identify a student's current performance position along the inquiry continuum. Then, true facilitation of student learning can proceed.

Vermont Expectations for Inquiry

Cognitive research provides valuable insights into the way that knowledge is represented, organized, and processed by the brain (Gazzaniga, Ivry, & Mangun, 2002). Educators can take advantage of these findings to monitor and assess the developing skills and knowledge of students and plan an instructional program that supports their progress over time.

Although national and state standards documents describe learning goals for inquiry, these statements generally lack the level of detail needed for diagnostic analysis and assessment. A developmental continuum that captures in words and examples what it means to progress or improve in an area of learning can be extremely helpful for guiding instruction. In Vermont, developmental descriptions of inquiry are incorporated in the state's grade expectations (http://www.vermontinstitutes.org). These inquiry expectations represent a research-based developmental continuum of learning. They describe the evidence teachers can search for as they assess their students' current level of understanding and illustrate the skills and dispositions students will display when they reach the next learning plateau. The expectations incorporate a cognitive demand based on a student's prior experience with the concept. Cognitive demand within the inquiry continuum begins with the basic level of "recall" and progresses to the level of "skills and concepts" followed by "strategic thinking" and finally "extended thinking" (Webb, 1997). With this type of developmental framework as a guide, teachers can truly operationalize the content of the standards when they assess student understanding and plan instruction.

The Vermont Department of Education assembled a team of educators, content experts, and assessment specialists to address the need for helping teachers assess the skills, knowledge, and dispositions of inquiry. The group's challenge was to construct a research-based developmental framework for assessing inquiry. The product of that work, *Vermont's Grade Expectations for Inquiry* (GE) (White et al., 2004), synthesizes educational research findings, the wisdom of nationally and internationally renowned experts, and the craft knowledge of experienced classroom practitioners. The GEs inform the design and development of an instructional pathway that follows a continuum of learning from grades PreK to 12. Milestones of understanding along this course are clearly identified. As student and teacher researchers progress through a cycle from questioning and hypothesizing to research design, data collection, analysis, and application, this developmental framework can guide both assessment and instruction.

Organized into grade clusters, students are expected to know or be able to do everything that came before as well as having developed the new skills and concepts at the targeted range. As an example, for the concept of Questioning, students in Grades 3 and 4 would be expected to know or be able to do everything described in the Pre-K & Kindergarten and the Grade 1–2 clusters. Figure 8.2 shows the K–12 continuum for questioning from the scientific inquiry grade expectations.

In the Grade 1–2 cluster for Questioning in science, 6- and 7-year-old students demonstrate their understanding of scientific questioning by posing observational questions that compare things in terms of number, shape, texture, size, weight, color, motion, and so on (e.g., How fast does a ladybug move compared to a bess beetle?); and by investigating and completing questions to identify a variable that can be changed (e.g., What will happen if . . . ? Or, I wonder if I change . . . ?).

With these first- and second-grade questioning expectations as a guide, a first-grade teacher can plan instructional activities that provide opportunities for students to pose questions regarding the comparative properties of objects. The teacher investigates the students' ability to identify variables by listening for questions such as "What will happen if . . . ?" and observes the student behaviors that follow. As a teacher researcher, the data derived from this type of ongoing assessment inform the next instructional steps for the class as well as for individual students.

Suppose, for example, that in this class, some students appeared to be engaged in purposeful inquiry, but their focus was strictly on doing their work and not communicating ideas and generating questions with peers. By referencing the developmental framework, the teacher notices that students in pre-kindergarten and kindergarten were expected to demonstrate a "questioning mind" through extended, intentional (purposeful) interactions with materials or people; experiment with possibilities; and develop questions by completing the prompt "I wonder . . . ?" Clearly, these students are demonstrating a questioning mind as they interact with materials. A question starter from the teacher, along with encouragement to share their thinking with peers, could provide the necessary intervention to move them toward the 1–2 grade cluster expectation. In this case, clear and explicit learning expectations, careful observation on the part of the teacher, and specific direction for next steps illustrate how a teacher can effectively conduct and apply formative assessment data.

The teacher might also notice that some students in the class are going beyond simply wondering to identifying potential effects of an action. Identifying at least one variable that affects a system and using the variable to generate an experimental question that includes

Figure 8.2 Continuum for Scientific Inquiry (Questioning)

Enduring Knowledge (Scientific Questioning): Students raise scientifically oriented questions that can be answered through observations, experimentation, and/or research. At early stages, students learn how to develop investigatable questions that guide their work. At later stages, students connect their questions to scientific ideas, concepts, and quantitative relationships that inform investigations. *Vermont's Framework 7.1 Evidence a 2.1 Evidence a, b, c, d, e*

PreK–K	1–2	3–4	5–6	7–8	9–12
GCE 1: Evidence of Understanding: Students demonstrate their understanding of SCIENTIFIC QUESTIONING by demonstrating a "questioning mind" through extended, intentional (purposeful) interactions with materials or people; experiments with possibilities; and by developing a question by completing the prompt "I wonder . . . ?"	**GCE 1: Evidence of Understanding:** Students demonstrate their understanding of SCIENTIFIC QUESTIONING by posing observational questions that compare things in terms of number, shape, texture, size, weight, color, motion, etc. (How fast does a ladybug move compared to a bess beetle?); and by investigating and completing questions to identify a variable that can be changed (What will happen if . . . ? Or, I wonder if I change . . . ?); and by generating new questions that could be explored at the end of an investigation.	**GCE 1: Evidence of Understanding:** Students demonstrate their understanding of SCIENTIFIC QUESTIONING by identifying at least one variable that affects a system and use the variable to generate an experimental question that includes a cause-and-effect relationship.	**GCE 1: Evidence of Understanding:** Students demonstrate their understanding of SCIENTIFIC QUESTIONING by distinguishing between observational, experimental, and research questions, a. (observational) How does a cricket chirp? b. (experimental) Does the amount of light affect how a cricket chirps? c. (research) Do all crickets chirp? Why do crickets chirp? and by identifying multiple variables that affect a system and using the variables to generate experimental questions that include cause-and-effect relationships.	**GCE 1: Evidence of Understanding:** Students demonstrate their understanding of SCIENTIFIC QUESTIONING by developing questions that reflect prior knowledge; and by refining and focusing broad ill-defined questions.	**GCE 1: Evidence of Understanding:** Students demonstrate their understanding of SCIENTIFIC QUESTIONING by framing testable questions showing evidence of observations and prior knowledge to illustrate cause and effect, and by developing a testable question appropriate to the scientific domain being investigated.

164

a cause-and-effect relationship is a questioning expectation for Grades 3 and 4. The teacher can confidently structure students' learning to conduct more sophisticated inquiry. The developmental continuum provides a clear looking glass into student performance.

A similar strategy can be applied in social studies and historical contexts in which 6- and 7-year-olds ask questions based on what they have seen, what they have read, what they have listened to, and what they have researched as a class. Figure 8.3 illustrates the K–12 continuum for social and historical questioning. Although the context for assessing inquiry through the social sciences will be different from that for other subject areas, the fundamental expectations for students remain the same. In Grades 1 and 2, students are generating comparative questions from personal observation and experience. The cross-disciplinary nature of the inquiry continuum enables teachers to assess student learning across a wide range of subjects.

It is important to recognize that the grade expectations for inquiry were designed as an assessment framework to guide teachers as they investigate their students' thinking, skills, and understandings. It is a tool aimed at improving practice, not a lockstep taxonomy that describes reasoning definitively across age groups. As the description of the first-grade classroom above illustrates, children of the same age inevitably vary in their level of ability. By providing the evidence that teachers look for in determining current and future levels of student achievement, the expectations for inquiry help teachers provide appropriate learning opportunities for all students.

Simultaneously, a teacher's action research enables him or her to monitor the effectiveness of the learning opportunities and guide the learning sequences for individual students.

Illustrations of Inquiry

One of the authors (Fitzsimmons) recalls one teacher's story as she used the inquiry expectations to guide instruction and assessment for her third-grade class: "We found it! Look! Look! This is our caterpillar." A group of third-grade students enthusiastically shares its discovery with the class. "We found a swallowtail caterpillar! Here it is in the book. It looks just like the one we saw in the garden. See our picture. They're the same." Students are referring to their notes and comparing similarities between their drawings and the photographs in the butterfly book *See How They Grow: Butterfly* (Ling, 1992).

Figure 8.3 Continuum for Social and Historical Inquiry (Questioning)

Social & Historical Questioning

PreK–K	1–2	3–4	5–6	7–8	9–10	11–12
H&SSPK-K:1 Students develop investigatable questions by developing a question by completing the prompts such as "I wonder . . . ?", "Why . . . ?", "How is this like . . . ?"	**H&SS1-2:1** Students develop investigatable questions by asking questions based on what they have seen, what they have read, what they have listened to, and what they have researched as a class. (e.g., How are their lives different from others' lives?)	**H&SS3-4:1** Students develop investigatable questions by asking relevant, focusing questions for independent research based on what they have seen, what they have read, what they have listened to, and what they have researched. (e.g., Why was the soda machine taken out of the school? Why are family farms in Vermont disappearing?)	**H&SS5-6:1** Students develop investigatable questions by asking relevant, researchable questions based on what they have seen, what they have read, what they have listened to, and what they have researched. (e.g., How will global warming affect me and my community? Is there intolerance in my school and community?)	**H&SS7-8:1** Students develop investigatable questions by asking relevant, probing, researchable questions based on what they have seen, what they have read, what they have listened to, and what they have researched. (e.g., How will recent changes in the global economy affect me and my community? Does my purchasing behavior affect child labor practices in the developing world?)	**H&SS9-10:1** Students develop investigatable questions by asking significant, probing, researchable questions that incorporate ideas and concepts of personal, community, or global relevance. (e.g., What are the effects of China's admission to the World Trade Organization?)	**H&SS11-12:1** Students develop investigatable questions by asking significant, probing, researchable questions that incorporate ideas and concepts of personal, community, or global relevance leading to answers that allow students to become participants in solutions.

PreK–K	1–2	3–4	5–6	7–8	9–10	11–12
		AND BY Asking questions about what makes a historical era unique and/or what defines a historical era. (e.g., How were the lives of children in colonial America different from the lives of children today?)	AND BY Asking questions that lead to an analysis of a historical era through primary source materials.	AND BY Asking questions that lead to an analysis of a historical era and primary source materials and ways they connect to the present. (e.g., How does a 19th-century Vermont diary show different roles and responsibilities for women compared to today?)	AND BY Asking questions that lead to an analysis of a historical era and primary source materials and ways they connect to the present. (e.g., How does a 19th-century Vermont diary show different roles and responsibilities for women compared to today?)	AND BY Asking questions that lead to an analysis of a historical era and primary source materials and ways they connect to the present and the implications for the future. (e.g., How does a 19th-century Vermont diary show different roles and responsibilities for women compared to today? How will these change in the future?)

The caterpillar discovery is part of a third-grade inquiry investigation that takes place in our community's Butterfly Garden. The program begins by establishing clear expectations for outdoor science explorations through an activity called the *Unnature Trail* (Almeras & Heath, 2001). Unnatural objects—hence the title, the *Unnature Trail*—are hidden throughout the Butterfly Garden. The goal is for students to look carefully and find as many of the hidden items as possible.

A scientists' meeting sets the stage for our work. We discuss how we can act as scientists would in the Butterfly Garden. Children create the ground rules: We will move slowly, look carefully, and work quietly. We were ready to begin!

Working individually, students walked through the garden and recorded their observations. At the end of the path, each child proudly whispered the number of found objects into my ear. After listening carefully to tallies, I announced that not even the teacher had found everything. More items remained to be discovered. "Would you like to try again?" I asked softly. Students were eager for another chance. The pace was slower now, and observations were more thoughtful. The second attempt along the path revealed objects that at first seemed invisible. Finally, a third search with a partner gave them a firsthand opportunity to experience the benefits of working cooperatively with a classmate.

Additional insights and ideas about science work outdoors emerged during a second scientists' meeting. Students argued that looking once was not sufficient to gather all the information. They reasoned that "the more you look, the more you see. We saw things the second time that we couldn't see the first time." The benefits of collaborating with a partner became obvious. Everyone agreed that four eyes were better than two. Some of the challenges of science work were identified. Each time we moved through the garden, we had to work harder to find new information. Even though we looked and looked and looked, some objects still remained undiscovered.

After developing our outdoor guidelines and new appreciations about fieldwork, we continued to explore the garden by capturing small animals in bug boxes. Small groups of students were given two bug boxes and assigned to designated areas of the garden. Groups were expected to discuss and agree on which animals to study. The magnifiers on the boxes allowed students to examine the garden inhabitants carefully and notice their detailed features. Although we had previously practiced drawing scientifically in the classroom, the excitement of the outdoors, along with the capture of interesting

Figure 8.4   Inquiry Self-Assessment Rubric

	NEEDS WORK	GOT IT
SHAPES	• The shapes I drew don't really match the object or organism.	• I drew the shapes that I observed.
DETAILS	• I forgot to include details inside or outside of the shapes.	• I included a variety of details inside or outside of the shapes.
ORGANIZATION	• I had trouble putting the parts in the right places.	• I drew all of the parts in the right places.
PROPORTION	• I drew some parts too big or too small.	• I drew parts that are the right size compared to each other.
LABELS	• I did not include a title for the drawing.	• I wrote a title for my drawing.
	• I did not label the parts of my drawing.	• I labeled important parts of my drawing.

small animals, challenged students' ability to record details through drawings.

When we later returned to our drawings in the classroom, students used a scientific drawing self-assessment to analyze their work (Figure 8.4).

We discussed possible ways of improving the scientific drawings, and then students were given the opportunity to include additional details. Because we no longer had the small animals, students searched through books to learn more about their type of animal and used information from pictures and photographs to add details to their scientific drawings.

In retrospect, holding on to the animals until the following day would have enabled students to revisit and change their initial drawings. Drawing in the classroom can reduce many of the distractions that influenced student work in the garden. However, nothing fully replaces the value of outdoor drawing. As students sat surrounded by the lush, colorful vegetation of the garden, talking about the small animals in their habitat fostered a dawning appreciation for the interdependence of living things. Drawing was a learning strategy that encouraged students to look closely and pay attention to details that otherwise might have been overlooked. Outdoor conversations among students confirmed that drawing accomplished this goal.

Still eager to learn more about the animals in our garden, we returned to search for animals that lived in soil and under plants. Armed with shovels, groups were given only *one* box to fill with *one* animal. Critical decisions had to be made. When students selected their study animal, groups appeared to be focused more intently on recording information. Perhaps a growing familiarity with the animals in the garden and practice with scientific drawing enabled students to use this skill more purposefully. By day's end, when students reported their discoveries to the class, everyone had begun to develop an appreciation for the diversity of living things within our garden (Figure 8.5).

After getting to know the garden and its inhabitants, students wrote questions, their wonderings about the garden. We discussed these questions and talked about how we might investigate different kinds of questions. Would observation, experimentation, or research be our next step? We agreed that observation is an essential part of all good science work, and that research helps us to compare our thinking with other scientists, but different types of questions influence how we proceed.

Because this investigation took place at the beginning of the school year, I selected one question for third graders as the focus for our future investigation: "What will happen to the plants and animals in the garden after a frost?" As the class brainstormed about how we would answer this question, we recorded ideas on the blackboard. We then ordered them stepwise to develop our plan and listed necessary materials for the study. We looked at digital pictures of the garden and discussed how the garden might change as a result of a frost. Students wrote predictions and explained their thinking. Mother Nature cooperated with a hard frost the next day! Everyone was ready and eager to return to the garden.

Equipped with our plan and clipboards and paper for recording observations, we ventured back to the garden in search of answers to our question. First, we observed and drew the plants. Next, we searched for animals and recorded observations. Finally, we tallied

Figure 8.5   Inquiry Self-Assessment Rubric

Types of Scientific Questions

- **Experimental** (E): Questions with a cause and an effect that can be answered by doing an experiment.
- **Observational** (O): Questions that can be answered by looking closely.
- **Research** (R): Questions that can be answered by reading information or talking with an expert.

QUESTIONS	TYPE OF QUESTION (E, O, OR R)
How many butterflies visit the garden in a day?	
What kind of caterpillar did I find?	
What food do grasshoppers like to eat the best?	
What will happen to the plants and animals after a frost?	
Can grasshoppers fly?	
What do worms do to the soil?	
Where do butterflies live in the winter?	
Are there any snakes in the garden?	

the number of animals that we could find in 2 minutes. Another year, I would have students do a 2-minute tally before the frost so that we could compare data. Teaching is a process of continual learning for my students and me! Our plan had guided our work. Observations, both pictures and words, were recorded throughout the investigation. We referred back to these observations to help answer our initial question. Students used evidence from their observations to draw conclusions and shared their discoveries with the class.

Integration of expectations, instruction, and ongoing assessment guided by the grade expectations for inquiry was an essential component of this investigation. Students recorded questions that focused primarily on research and observation. The need for additional opportunities for students to become familiar with experimental questions became clear. Students seemed comfortable making predictions, but they needed encouragement to propose explanations that supported or negated these original ideas. The experimental design, a challenge for young third graders, was developed with the class so that a model for future use could be constructed. Students recorded observations through drawings and analyzed their work with a scoring guide based on the third- and fourth-grade expectations for conducting an investigation. Conclusions were expected to reflect observations and provide an interpretation of patterns observed over time. Students then compared findings to their original predictions. I wondered if they could resist the temptation to erase a prediction that wasn't supported by the evidence. New questions about the butterfly garden were identified, and additional information about students' ability to raise questions was gathered.

Inquiry, as described through this Butterfly Garden investigation, is a way of student knowing that demands active engagement in a multisensory process over time. Students are engaged in a cycle of questioning, gathering evidence, sharing ideas, reading research, communicating findings, and developing new questions (NRC, 2000). Science process skills, essential habits of mind, and content knowledge are woven together through meaningful interactions with the natural world.

SUMMARY

Purposeful inquiry is a way of knowing that spans all disciplines and human endeavors. Student and teacher researchers have a unique opportunity to practice inquiry in the classroom and beyond. Achieving the deep conceptual learning offered by purposeful inquiry requires ongoing reflective assessment on the part of both students and teachers. The skills, concepts, and dispositions of purposeful inquiry are complex. Even the best teachers can benefit from a framework to guide their assessment, instruction, and professional practice. The inquiry assessment framework described in this chapter offers a promising tool for any educator who believes that "inquiry has its roots in the inherent restlessness of the human mind" (Dow, 1991, p. 5).

References

Almeras, B., & Heath, D. (2001). *Access nature.* Washington, DC: National Wildlife Federation.

Atkin, J. M., Black, P., & Coffey, J. (2001). *Classroom assessment and the national science education standards.* Washington, DC: National Academy Press.

Coffey, J., & Atkin, M. (2003). *Everyday assessment in the science classroom.* Arlington, VA: NSTA Press.

Delandshere, G. (2004). *Assessment as inquiry.* Retrieved June 9, 2004, from http://tcrecord.org/printContent.asp?contented=10992.

Dow, P. (1999). Why inquiry? A historical and philosophical commentary. In *Foundations: Inquiry. Thoughts, views, and strategies for the K–5 classroom* (pp. 5–8). Arlington, VA: National Science Foundation.

Forman, G., & Kuschner, D. (1983). *The child's construction of knowledge: Piaget for teaching children.* Washington, DC: National Association for the Education of Young Children.

Gazzaniga, M., Ivry, R., & Mangun, G. (2002). *Cognitive neuroscience.* New York: Norton.

Ling, M. (1992). *See how they grow: Butterfly.* New York: Dorling Kindersley.

Loucks-Horsley, S., Love, N., Stiles, K. E., Mundry, S., & Hewson, P. W. (2003). *Designing professional development for teachers of science and mathematics.* Thousand Oaks, CA: Corwin.

McKernan, J. (1991). *Curriculum action research.* New York: St. Martin's.

National Research Council. (2000). *Inquiry and the National Science Education Standards: A guide for teaching and learning.* Washington, DC: National Academy Press.

National Research Council. (2001). *Classroom assessment and the National Science Education Standards.* Washington, DC: National Academy Press.

Robbins, J. (1999). *The pleasure of finding things out.* Cambridge, MA: Perseus.

Webb, N. (1997). *Determining alignment of expectations and assessments in mathematics and science education.* Madison, WI: National Center for Improving Science Education.

White, D., et al. (2004). *Vermont expectations for scientific inquiry.* Montpelier: Vermont Department of Education.

CHAPTER NINE

Inquiry Learning and Special Education Students

Rejecting Instruction That Disables

Bruce Marlowe
Marilyn Page

> *It is, in fact, nothing short of a miracle that the modern methods of instruction have not yet entirely strangled the holy curiosity of inquiry; for this delicate little plant, aside from stimulation, stands mainly in need of freedom; without this it goes to wreck and ruin without fail.*
>
> —Einstein (1949)

In 1997, when her world was still fresh and ripe with possibility, my (Marlowe's) 6-year-old daughter Rachel ran off the school bus one windy October afternoon waving a single sheet of paper high over her head. "I have homework! I have homework!" she shouted excitedly. Now, 7 years later, her delight in school learning has been replaced with ennui, languor, and a precocious world-weariness about formal education. Rachel's school narrative lumbers forward, plodding predictably to its tedious, anticlimactic finish. But she will survive. Unfortunately, for students with disabilities, their school stories are considerably less sanguine, even for the fewer than half who finish high school. And what of students who are gifted and talented? Or those who feel marginalized by curricula insensitive to their histories or experience because of racial and ethnic differences?

If you have read this far into the book, you are probably feeling as if you need no further justification for building instruction around inquiry. In this chapter, my coauthor and I will try to convince you otherwise. Although all students benefit from inquiry-based approaches, those who do not fit the mold, for whatever reasons, need good teachers who understand that the *questions students ask* are what is most central to knowledge construction and active engagement. You already know that teachers who simply deliver information, or introduce teacher-created "discrepant events" for student analysis, or provide all of the questions without ever turning to student-developed inquiries (even if the teacher-created questions are interesting), will invariably face students who are unmotivated, disengaged, and perhaps even hostile. For students with disabilities and other learning differences, though, the stakes are even higher, the need more urgent.

Spirited arguments for a student-centered, inquiry-based instruction may have been introduced first by Rousseau (1762/1957) and Pestalozzi (1801/1898). Dewey (1938/1972) and Piaget (1941/ 1995), as well as more contemporary theorists (e.g., see Bruner, 1961; Freire, 1974; Suchman, 1966; von Glasersfeld, 1996; Wigginton, 1985), have all maintained that traditional education, in one form or another, is "guaranteed to rot your brain" (Commager, 1980, p. 34). Inquiry, on the other hand,

- Leads to greater ownership of content
- Promotes more elaborate knowledge construction
- Encourages more empowered, informed, and independent thinking
- Fosters deeper understanding of concepts

And yet, inquiry-based instruction is remarkably hard to come by. Some might find this extraordinary given the substantial number of books and teacher workshops with words and phrases such as "inquiry," "constructivism," "hands-on," and "active engagement" in their titles. In fact, there is a virtual cottage industry of professional developers and book publishers committed to producing "progressive" educational manuals, inservice presentations, workbooks, and teaching guides. Then why is such pedagogy so uncommon?

SHAM INQUIRY

> *Teachers create constructivist learning experiences for students based necessarily on what they, the teachers, find salient. But, what is salient to the teacher is not necessarily so to the learner.*

—Winitzky and Kauchak (1997)

In spite of the avalanche of both anecdotal and empirical reports (Capraro, 2001; Cole & McGuire, 2004; Marlowe & Page, 1998; Spinner & Fraser, 2002; Thomason, 2003) concerning the positive results of progressive, inquiry-based learning, passive traditional practices appear firmly entrenched (Apple, 2001; Cuban, 1990, 2001; Goodlad, 1984). In fact, the repertoire of most teachers continues to be limited strictly to the familiar cycle of information transmission and evaluation.

More chillingly, a relatively new trend is emerging in our schools, one that arose, ostensibly, to counter the perception of teacher overreliance on "talk and chalk." And it is this trend that, perhaps more than any other, accounts for the scarcity of real inquiry in our classrooms. For lack of a better expression, I refer to it simply as "sham inquiry"—that is, teaching practices that look like inquiry, sound like inquiry, but on closer inspection, are revealed to be just as unhealthy to student learning as a steady, uniform diet of teacher-directed instruction. In its various guises, sham inquiry gives solace only to the teachers, who, thinking they have reformed their practice, continue to ignore, discount, or put aside the questions *students ask* in favor of those they believe are more valuable.

At the root of sham inquiry is the fundamental misunderstanding that real inquiry is largely about what teachers do, as opposed to what their students do. Making a similar point about constructivist educational practices, Fosnot (1996) reminds us that constructivism, like inquiry, is really "about learning, not a description of teaching. No 'cookbook teaching style' or pat set of instructional techniques can be abstracted from the theory and proposed as a constructivist approach to teaching" (p. 29).

From at least the time of Dewey, progressive educational movements have always been co-opted by a large set of players that, historically, has viewed teachers simply as technicians. In an effort to codify good practice, school administrators, teacher education programs, state licensing agencies, professional developers, and textbook publishers have become overly preoccupied with the "how-to," often producing scripted materials, teacher prompts, protocols, and other programmed forms of instruction—what Ohanian (in Canestrari & Marlowe, 2004) calls "Stir and Serve Recipes for Teaching." Such approaches "are based on the erroneous assumption that all students can learn from the same materials, classroom instructional techniques and modes of evaluation" (Giroux, 1985, in Canestrari & Marlowe, 2004, p. 209).

Nowhere is this sort of sham inquiry more prevalent than in its use with students with disabilities and other learning differences. This appears to be true for two separate but related reasons: first, the predominance of low expectations by teachers of low-achieving students (particularly those who are African American and Latino); and second, a "fix" that is worse than the problem: "Teaching styles that stress drill, practice, and other mind-numbing strategies" based on the mistaken belief that "such children lack ability" (Berliner & Biddle, 1995, quoted in Kohn, 1999, p. 99).

So, there are really two different problems that this chapter will address: the exigency for real inquiry-driven approaches for students whose learning styles and needs are different from their age peers, and a compass to help guide those teachers laboring under the false impression that what they are doing under the name of inquiry is, in reality, often nothing more than what Freire described as the banking model, where teachers (i.e., the bankers) make "deposits" into their students (the passive accounts).

Sham Inquiry in Practice

Inquiry is the way people learn when they're left alone.

—Suchman (1966)

Consider Jonah, a highly gifted fifth-grade student in a mixed-ability classroom. His school story captures the need for real inquiry, as well as the seduction and danger of sham inquiry. Jonah's teacher,

Mr. Stevens—young, energetic, charismatic—began his review of fractions and their relationships one Friday by passing out a variety of materials to each of the cooperative groups he had previously established: poster board, empty egg cartons, calculators, construction paper, markers, scissors. He asked simply, "Using the strategies we have talked about all week, please demonstrate that 3/4 is greater than 2/3." As Mr. Stevens circled the room, checking for understanding and periodically asking probing questions to individual groups about their work, the students attacked the problem with vigor, applying what they had been taught during the past 4 days. They divided the fractions (in order to compare the decimal amounts), filled the egg cartons, drew pie charts, and found common denominators. Mr. Stevens was thrilled that the students seemed to remember everything he had covered, and as he made the rounds, he expressed pride in them with great enthusiasm.

Jonah sat pensively, immobile. While his group was busy pasting their work onto the poster board, he seemed to be just staring at the numbers. And then, 15 minutes after the activity had begun, he said to Mr. Stevens, "I just noticed something. . . . That's *so* cool. Look, Mr. Stevens, if you multiply from the bottom up and across like this,

$$\frac{3}{4} \diagdown\!\!\!\!\diagup \frac{2}{3}$$

you get 9 on the left side and 8 on the right side. That's *really* cool. Is that a way to show that 3/4 is greater than 2/3? I mean, will this always work? I think it will, but I'm not sure I really get it yet. Why does this work? I think I can figure it out. Can I work on this instead? Can I?" Uncertain about where Jonah was going, and nervous about his taking such a divergent path, Mr. Stevens reminded Jonah that he was to use the strategies he had been taught in class during the week. Mr. Stevens pointed out that there was no evidence that Jonah had done any work at all. Besides, Mr. Stevens had no idea if Jonah was on to something or not.

In the span of 15 minutes, Mr. Stevens communicated several potent lessons to Jonah—lessons that distinguish sham inquiry from the "real McCoy" and underscore the need for real inquiry for students with learning differences. Mr. Stevens believes, mistakenly, that the activity he created provides an opportunity for *all* students to engage in genuine inquiry. But here is what Jonah really learned:

1. It is more important that I answer my teacher's questions than my own.

2. Independent thinking and problem solving are not to be pursued unless my teacher understands the problem and/or it conforms to teacher-approved methods and strategies.

3. It is very important that I move at the same pace, and produce the same products, as my peers.

4. My understanding can be demonstrated only by repeating back what has been transmitted and nothing more.

There is another, subtler message often embedded in practices that masquerade as inquiry, a message to which Mr. Stevens probably does not ascribe. The message, delivered inadvertently but powerfully through his words and actions, is that memorization is more important than deep understanding; that activity, simply for the sake of activity, leads to greater comprehension than deep reflection and inquiry. To wit, teacher-directed activities often sabotage real inquiry. As Sewall (2000) has noted, "Activity based learning is vain. . . . At rock bottom, projects and activities provide mere entertainment. Teachers . . . seek to fill dead time in the classroom. Projects and activities keep kids occupied and unmutinous" (p. 2).

Clearly, Jonah is a remarkably bright and unusually perceptive student. Yet there is something all too familiar about his developing school story, a story that most of us remember from our own school experiences, or see in our children, or worse, watch unfold on the faces of our students. Here is what one high school student had to say after years of experiences just like Jonah's:

"I don't do a lot in school. . . . I don't like any of the high school classes really. You just sit there and they tell you something and they give you a test and you tell it right back to them. Everybody has the same answer on the test if you do it right. (Clark in Page, 1992, p. 37)

But that may be as far as the comparison goes, because Jonah is so unlike most of his age peers. Many students, like Marlowe's daughter Rachel and the high school student quoted above, are essentially teacherproof; they will survive years of bad schooling relatively unscathed. Students like Jonah, however, and those with a myriad of other learning differences often get trampled in school. As noted above, although inquiry-driven educational practices clearly benefit all students, their implementation is considerably more urgent for our students who learn differently from their peers. That is, although the implications of poor instruction for most students' learning are relatively benign, the relationship between such traditional notions of teaching and learning and the outcomes for students with exceptions is much more dire. And because special education law now requires that students with disabilities be educated with their nondisabled peers to the maximum extent appropriate (i.e., in the least restrictive environment), all teachers, regardless of their politics about inclusion, must assume responsibility for the learning of all students.

A LOOK AT TODAY'S CLASSROOMS

On average, public school districts formally identify between 10%–12% of their students with disabilities, about 2%–5% of their students as gifted and talented if IQ scores are used as the sole criterion, and 15%–20% if a talent pool model is employed (Renzulli, 1999; Turnbull, Turnbull, Shank, & Smith, 2004). Figure 9.1 provides an overview of who these students are at the national level and how their learning differences may manifest themselves in today's classrooms.

If you teach in a public school, the data in Figure 9.1 indicate that a gifted student, or a student with one of the four most prevalent disabilities, will invariably find his or her way into your classroom. This is true regardless of the grade level you teach, the tracking policies of your district, or your school's philosophical orientation about mainstreaming. Both the law and social policy make it certain that students with quite dramatic learning differences will be your students. But despite the progressive nature of special education legislation, individuals with identified disabilities, as a group, continue to fare quite poorly both in our schools and in their transition to adulthood. Here is what can be said about the situation in the United States:

- About half of all students with disabilities spend 80% or more of the day in a regular education classroom.

Figure 9.1   Categories of Disabilities

TERM	DEFINITIONS	% OF ALL STUDENTS WITH DISABILITIES
Specific Learning Disabilities	Students of average intellectual ability or higher with significant difficulty in one or more academic domains (e.g., reading).	50.5
Speech or Language Impairment	Students with significant difficulty in either producing language (e.g., articulation difficulty) or understanding language (e.g., following directions).	19
Mental Retardation	Students with significantly below-average measured intellectual ability *and* age-appropriate social skills (e.g., communication, independent living, etc.).	10.8
Emotional Disabilities	Students with chronic emotional, behavioral, or interpersonal difficulties extreme enough to interfere with learning.	8.2
Other Health Impairments	Students with chronic conditions that limit strength, vitality, alertness (e.g., epilepsy, arthritis, asthma).	4.5
Multiple Disabilities	Students with more than one disability.	2
Orthopedic Impairments	Students who have limited functional use of legs, feet, arms, hands, or other body parts.	1.3
Hearing Impairments	Students with significant hearing loss in one or both ears.	1.3
Visual Impairments	Students with low vision, even when corrected.	0.46
Traumatic Brain Injury	Students who have had brain injury as the result of external force (e.g., car accident) or internal occurrence (e.g., stroke).	0.24
Deaf-Blindness	Students with both significant hearing loss and low vision.	0.03
Giftedness	(% of total population)	15–20

Source: U.S. Department of Education. (1999). *To assure the free appropriate public education of all children with disabilities: 21st annual report to Congress on the implementation of the Individuals with Disabilities Education Act* (p. A-2). Washington, DC: Author.

- Whereas the overall national graduation rate is approximately 88%, only about 27% of all students with disabilities leave high school with a diploma.
- The employment rates of people with disabilities is only about 32%, compared to an 81% employment rate for people without disabilities; the employment rate—either full- or part-time—for individuals with severe disabilities is only 19%.
- Approximately two thirds of individuals without disabilities report that they are "very satisfied" with life; only one third of individuals with disabilities report the same level of satisfaction.
- One in five school-age children is estimated to have reading disabilities. Eighty percent of these students who fail to make significant reading progress by the age of 9 will continue to be unskilled readers in the 12th grade, if they even stay in school that long.
- Juel (1988) found that about 40% of unskilled readers in the fourth grade would prefer cleaning their rooms to reading.
- Among the prison population, 75%–80% are estimated to have specific learning disabilities and/or serious emotional disturbance.

Although clearly beyond the scope of this chapter, the most recent data on independent living, wage earning, and rates of incarceration are equally bleak for individuals with disabilities. Why is the dropout rate so high for students with disabilities? Why is academic underachievement so prevalent? Why have behavioral problems increased so dramatically? Why do students prefer cleaning their rooms to reading? The answers to these questions are complex and multifaceted, but we must ask, To what extent do teaching approaches that focus on the transmission of information contribute to student failure, disengagement, and disenfranchisement? Is it plausible in all (or even most) cases of student failure that students and/or their families are to blame for weak academic skills and/or behavioral problems? Goodlad (1984) and Cuban (1990) found that students spend slightly more than 10% of their time in school asking questions, reading, writing, or engaged in some other form of active learning. Is there something wrong with our children, or are schools and teachers contributing to this state of affairs? Can 5,000 reports that show little or no relationship between problems students suffer and shortcomings in school practice be valid? Or, does Carnine's

(1994) question about this finding ring more true: "If 5,000 medical files of patients who failed to respond to treatment were analyzed, would there be an absence of professional shortcomings in all 5,000 cases?" (p. 341).

Disabilities make learning and classrooms more challenging. Some disabilities may even make learning some things impossible. As teachers, we must create opportunities for learning that are more exciting, more enriching, and more rewarding—in short, more appealing than the desire to clean one's room, leave school, get involved in criminal activity, or become a ward of the state. Others have noted that a focus on the ways in which students do not fit into traditional classrooms (in addition to putting system and teacher needs ahead of student needs) also often reflects cultural biases. For example,

> Only when formal education came to the Indian Nations were labels supplied to the differences between children. Public Law 94–142 . . . caused multitudes of children to be labeled mentally retarded or learning disabled who up until that time were not considered handicapped in their cultures. (Locust, in Turnbull, Turnbull, Shank, & Leal, 1995, p. 15)

How do students with disabilities learn? Is it really different from the learning of other students? Perhaps more importantly, we should be asking how we can spark their curiosity, facilitate their learning, and, perhaps most importantly, get out of their way, as Suchman suggests above. These questions are extremely important for students with disabilities as they are at increased risk of school failure and difficult transitions to adulthood. As noted above, the high school dropout rate for students with disabilities is unacceptably high. Because students with disabilities do not have a compelling reason to stay, and they experience little academic success and a great deal of frustration, this should come as no surprise. For many students with disabilities, school is deadly boring; it is irrelevant to their lives, needs, and interests; and for many others, it is extremely punishing as well. But the questions posed at the top of this paragraph are virtually never asked. Instead, teachers blithely assume that students with disabilities are so different, so impaired, and so damaged that it is a waste of time to pursue inquiry with them. As Billy Golfus remarks in *When Billy Broke His Head . . . and Other Tales of Wonder,* many believe individuals with disabilities are just "too gimped out to work" (Simpson & Golfus, 1995).

In fact, such students are in much more urgent need of inquiry-based approaches, but they are far less likely to receive them. The most recent research indicates that students with disabilities spend much of their day on tasks requiring little more cognitive energy than rote memorization. Worse still, many advocate for just this approach. Consider the following statement, which neatly summarizes a very popular view of inclusion, and one of inquiry as well.

> There are several reasons for opposing a policy of full inclusion. One reason is because full inclusion . . . makes direct, systematic instruction nearly impossible. In addition, once full inclusion is implemented, teachers are forced to change their teaching methods to more child-directed, discovery-oriented, project-based learning activities in which every student works at his or her own pace. (Crawford, 2001)

The only shocking thing about Crawford's position is his candor.

INFREQUENTLY ASKED QUESTIONS

Assuming, as we do, that there is nothing wrong, and everything right, with changing one's teaching so that it *is* more child-centered, discovery-oriented, and project-based, how does one begin to develop an inquiry-based learning environment knowing that students with an enormous range of abilities and interests may populate a single classroom? With earlier caveats about following a lockstep, prescribed sequence of instructional activities, we propose here instead a series of *infrequently asked questions,* or *IAQs,* as a point of departure for setting up inquiry-based approaches in mixed-ability classrooms. These IAQs are not designed simply to be provocative; rather, it is our hope that they will lead to careful teacher self-reflection about the importance of inquiry, about the pitfalls of sham inquiry, and about the true conditions necessary for students to get excited about learning.

IAQ 1. How are inquiry-based instruction and standards-based education incompatible for students with learning differences? The short answer to this IAQ is that standards and inquiry may be incompatible in many, many ways, particularly for students with disabilities. Students with disabilities and/or giftedness are, by definition, different academically, emotionally, physically, and/or cognitively from their age peers. In some sense, then, they are the paradigmatic case of how standards and inquiry are often incompatible, in that such students are in a nonstandard place at a nonstandard time and will, by necessity, have questions that may differ from those of their peers. But this raises an even larger question: Does it make sense to assume that there is a standard time and place in which students are ready (to say nothing of eager) for particular kinds of content learning? Despite overwhelming evidence to the contrary, an increasing number of states seem to be making precisely this assumption as an ever-growing number of them prepare to roll out detailed sets of grade-level expectations. But in a recent study (Peterson, Feen, Tamor, & Silagy, 2002), when teachers were asked, "What is the range of abilities of students in your class?" every teacher in the sample stated that students crossed at least five grade levels, with some teachers describing even larger grade-level differences. Clearly, student difference is not merely a special education issue. In a very succinct summary of this problem, Tomlinson (2000) notes,

> Students who are the same age differ in their readiness to learn, their interests, their styles of learning, their experiences, and their life circumstances. The differences in students are significant enough to make a major impact on what students need to learn, the pace at which they need to learn it, and the support they need from teachers and others to learn it well. (p. 6)

As every alert teacher knows, what Tomlinson says is true whether or not one's classroom contains students with disabilities. To some extent, then, all of the ways that the very notion of standards have come to be defined are often inconsistent with inquiry-driven practices for students who are exceptional (i.e., nonstandard) and have, by definition, unique interests, needs, and skills.

The old teaching adage that you must "meet your students where they are" assumes even greater urgency when we consider the abilities and skills of students with learning differences. And because authentic student questions reflect their *current* skills and interests, teachers, at best, can only hope to win a Pyrrhic victory when "meeting standards" is interpreted to mean that all students will learn the same things at the same time in the same way. Again, real inquiry is concerned primarily with the questions that occupy the attention, and reflect the capability, of students *now*. Standards, on the other hand, are forward driven. As Crain (2004) noted, "An intense anxiety about the future has driven the standards movement. . . . When we focus too intently on what children will need for the future, we rob them of the chance to develop their capacities at their current stage" (p. 5).

Crain's observation is especially true for students with disabilities and other learning differences. Standards are forward-looking in the sense that the instruction built around them has a predetermined destination (one chosen, incidentally, by the teacher) already in mind, rather than an attempt to pay attention to what is of current interest and concern to students (to say nothing about an individual student's developmental level). It is in this sense that standards may become another form of sham inquiry. Real inquiry, by contrast, is student driven, and true inquiry-based instruction is built around students' attempts to answer their own questions, not those that necessarily lead to anything prearranged, much less something that someone else identified as a benchmark or goal.

In a similar vein, many educators suggest that teachers should "begin with the end in mind." But the most educationally valuable experiences are often the result of something far less planful. Instead, they often evolve, or erupt suddenly, unexpectedly, in the context of classrooms where teachers have particular dispositions. New research by Sawyer (2004) suggests that *improvisation* is a much more powerful and productive metaphor for teaching than is *performance*. Sawyer notes that learning is a creative, improvisational process, and that skilled teaching involves dispensing with the notion of teacher as performer (i.e., one who follows a script), and instead building instruction from the kind of student questions and issues raised as they actively solve problems, whether or not they are part of the end the teacher has in mind.

For example, Sawyer (2004) describes a study by Lampert, Rittenhouse, and Crumbaugh in which a teacher hoped his students would arrive at an algorithm for generating numbers in sequence. The teacher chose not to lecture or ask known answer questions. But as the students worked collaboratively to determine which number pairs came next in the sequence, 8–4, 4–2, 2–1, 0–0, he noticed a very strong student interest, and fruitful discussion, emerge about variables and fractional relationships, even though the teacher originally hoped they would simply arrive at the rule "divide by two." Wisely, he encouraged their discussion and questions and made value-neutral observations in an attempt to facilitate further inquiry and analysis. Although it is certainly true that teachers, new teachers in particular, need routines, recent research indicates that skilled teaching requires flexibility, variation, and embellishment *improvised* from student questions, responses, and interests (Sawyer, 2004).

IAQ 2. Don't students with learning differences need to learn basic skills before they engage in real inquiry?   To remain interested and engaged in learning, *all* students need opportunities to discover, create, and problem solve. But what if problem-solving skills are precisely what they lack? Many teachers treat students with disabilities as if they have a defect that needs correcting. To fix the disability, some professionals believe that students need high levels of teacher-directed information transmission. At the other extreme, some advocate fostering student strengths wherever they may lie, following the students' lead in learning, and letting students decide whether or not to attempt to improve the academic skill areas in which they are struggling.

Both approaches are at best inadequate. The first often results in temporary memorization of chunks of content knowledge. The second is inappropriate because most students with disabilities demonstrate weak ability to approach tasks strategically and often have difficulty carefully monitoring their own progress. Also, the majority of students with disabilities do not spontaneously initiate problem-solving behaviors. They frequently have difficulty sustaining attention, even in areas of interest, inhibiting impulsive responding, and remaining cognitively flexible. Therefore, many students with disabilities need a bridge to support the transition from traditional special education practices to inquiry-based learning experiences.

Real inquiry is simply impossible until students possess some fundamental skills; however, this does not mean that students need to earn the right to engage in inquiry by demonstrating minimum competencies in reading, writing, or mathematics. The skills referred to above are not academic per se. Rather, they are thinking tools based largely on the work of Meichenbaum's (1977) cognitive-behavioral approach to problem solving. These tools were developed to help students initiate their own learning; sustain attention for complex, multistep tasks; form hypotheses; and evaluate their own performance.

Although many kinds of learning strategy models have grown from this work, perhaps the easiest and most practical of these approaches is Bonnie Camp's Think Aloud Program (1987, 1996). The Think Aloud Program is designed to increase student self-control by the explicit teaching of self-talk strategies for solving a range of problems. Because many students with disabilities lack verbal mediation skills, teaching students to think aloud is a natural step to move them toward self-directed, inquiry-based learning. This practice can also be incorporated easily into whole-class instruction. Camp (1996) suggests that teachers introduce specific questions that students can ask themselves as they set about to learn. They involve

- Problem identification (What am I to do? How can I find out?)
- Choice of a plan or strategy (How can I do it? What are some plans?)
- Self-monitoring (Am I using my plan?)
- Self-evaluation (Is my plan working? How did I do? Do I need a new plan?)

When students use these questions in the context of the curriculum, together with applying a host of problem-solving strategies (such as brainstorming, means/ends analysis, mnemonic memory strategies, etc.), they quickly acquire a wide repertoire of powerful learning tools that can help them succeed with real inquiry.

IAQ 3. Isn't "I differentiate my instruction for students with disabilities" just a more politically palatable way to say "I use tracking within my classroom"?   In practice, this is, unfortunately, almost always the case. As Peterson, Hittie, and Tamor (2002) noted, most of what is referred to as differentiated instruction is "simply a complex form of ability grouping" (p. 11). Even well-intentioned teachers traditionally think of differentiation this way and will often group students by a single, global measure of their perceived ability, require less of students they view as below average, and create more challenging assignments for those who are facile verbally and/or mathematically. What distinguishes true differentiation from such ability grouping is largely dispositional. That is, in classrooms where instruction is truly differentiated so that all learners may engage in real inquiry, teachers believe that all learners have strengths, that a uniform lesson format for the whole class is destined to fail, that flexible grouping strategies (e.g., see the Jigsaw groups in Aronson & Bridgeman, 1979) are critical for every student to succeed, and that the collaborative problem solving of authentic (i.e., student-created) problems is essential to learning. Such teachers believe further that students can obtain information and demonstrate their learning in many ways. Two approaches that exemplify these beliefs are Howard Gardner's (1983) view of multiple intelligences and Sharan and Sharan's (1989) Group Investigation model. Both are particularly well suited for students with learning differences because each requires that group processes be built around individual student strengths and the collaboration of students with differing abilities in heterogeneous, rather than homogeneous, groups.

Gardner (1983, 1993) indicates that there are at least eight, and perhaps more, distinct types of human intelligences. Although he was not the first to theorize that intelligence comes in many forms, Gardner has written extensively on the ways in which an understanding of multiple intelligences (MI) can be applied in educational settings. A few model schools around the country are demonstrating how powerful this approach can be. For example, at the Middle School of the Kennebunks, in Kennebunk, Maine, students work in groups of eight, structured so that each member demonstrates a particular strength in one of Gardner's intelligences. In other schools that have adopted MI approaches, a variety of common administrative and curricular features recommended by Gardner have been instituted. These include having

- assessment specialists, who are responsible for keeping a record of each student's learning and development in each of the intelligences.
- student-curriculum brokers, who seek to match available school resources (course electives, personnel, materials) with student interests and intellectual proclivities.
- school-curriculum brokers, who seek to match community resources with student needs.
- collaborative groups, composed of students who represent each of the intelligences.
- pods, a type of learning group composed of students with similar interests and talents led by a teacher who serves as a mentor in an apprenticeship-like setting (Gardner, 1993).

Any of these features can be adapted and modified to a single classroom, and each goes a long way toward reframing students with disabilities as able. Gardner reminds us that to recognize student talents and interests, to give value to *their questions,* we must look beyond our limited conception that to be intelligent and to learn, one must have strong verbal and/or logical mathematical ability. Indeed, failure to perform well in one of these two ways is how virtually all students with disabilities come to be identified, labeled, and ultimately thought of as not able. When we think of students who are doing poorly in our classrooms, we typically focus on the things they cannot do, or we speculate about the kinds of difficulty we believe may account for their weak school performance. The MI theory allows us to reframe our thinking about student performance. It demands that we consider what our students do well, how they learn, and what they find intrinsically interesting so that we can label their strengths, as opposed to their weaknesses, and validate the types of inquiry they are most likely to pursue successfully.

Sharan and Sharan (1989/1990) proposed a model for inquiry that can be adapted easily to differentiate instruction for real inquiry. Their approach focuses on academic achievement and the development of higher-level thinking skills. In this project format, students work in small groups to gather, analyze, and evaluate data and draw conclusions on a topic of their choosing. They then prepare reports and demonstrate their learning to the class, which evaluates their work.

Research by Sharan and Sharan (1989/1990) demonstrated that students involved with this approach in both elementary and secondary schools showed a higher level of academic achievement than did students in traditional classes, and they also did better on questions assessing higher-level learning and on measures of social interaction. After the teacher and/or class develop an overarching question or theme, the remaining steps of the model are simple:

1. The group decides on the topics to be explored by brainstorming possible subtopics/subquestions related to the larger theme or question. Questions work the best, but they must be critical questions—how or why questions—that require and promote substantial investigation.

2. Students sort the subtopics/subquestions into categories.

3. Students form groups by subtopics. If the investigation occurs at the beginning of the year and the teacher does not know the students very well, a random group selection probably is best. Otherwise, groups can be organized according to their

likelihood for success. The very brave teacher, who has experience working with groups in this way, might allow students to select their own group members.

4. Groups plan how they will investigate their subtopics or subquestions. This requires much work on the teacher's part. Students must provide explicit details about how they will conduct their investigation. Students also give specific information about the roles for each student in the group and how their work differs from what others in the group are doing. The teacher is responsible for ensuring that these tasks are possible, productive, and explicit.

5. Students carry out tasks; the teacher monitors the ongoing performance. Students must complete all tasks before moving ahead, and they need to provide detailed descriptions of how they will demonstrate task completion. Students may have to create additional investigation tasks after they complete this initial work.

6. Students plan a class learning experience based on their findings. The details for the presentation must be as explicit as they were for the task descriptions. Who will do what? What is the optimum format for the main experience: a debate, role-playing, a simulation? What will this look like?

7. The students conduct their learning experiences, which should demonstrate their understanding. Peers provide feedback to students.

8. The entire class evaluates the investigation and the contributions of each individual. Although the evaluation is the last step, teachers should decide the form of assessment before the process has begun.

IAQ 4. How can I demonstrate to my students, colleagues, and administrators that having different behavioral and academic expectations is not only necessary but also fair? For most students who are eligible for special education service, disabilities are lifespan issues. The ways in which they approach material, the challenges they face, and the compensatory strategies they use are unlikely to change over time. Many years ago, one of us was involved in a consultation with a 10th-grade chemistry teacher who complained that a hyperactive student in her class continually tapped his pencil on the lab table, disrupting her and other students. Because the student would continue tapping moments after he was asked to stop, the teacher shared with us that most days ended with arguments and an occasional angry exchange. It was unclear to the teacher whether the tapping was a willful attempt to continually disrupt the classroom or a manifestation of a behavior that was out of the boy's control. Either way, from the teacher's perspective, the behavior had to stop.

Thinking about this tapping behavior as something that must be changed (i.e., thinking that the student must be changed) is a mind-set that guarantees teacher frustration and anger, student resentment, and general feelings of inferiority and impotence in both. Another way to frame this dilemma is as follows: The student needs to tap, and the teacher needs a distraction-free environment. Accepting for the moment that both are, in fact, true needs and that the student is not simply trying to be difficult, we ask, are these needs mutually exclusive? Of course not. Readers who already have begun to think about how we can change the environment and not the student already know this. For the rest of you, one solution to this dilemma can be found at the end of the chapter.

Unfortunately, many teachers believe that accommodating an individual student's needs is somehow unfair to other students. As Richard Lavoie (1989) has elegantly pointed out on his well-known video about the F.A.T. city workshop, it is not about the other students! He asks us to consider the teacher who resists making accommodations for a student with a disability because he or she feels it would be unfair to the others. Lavoie points out that a teacher skilled in CPR could apply the same reasoning to refuse resuscitation to a student who collapses because there is not enough time to administer the same treatment to all students. Obviously, not all of the students need CPR. Fairness is about need, not about ensuring that all students receive the same things at the same time. In practical terms, this may mean that some students will need note takers, others will need books on tape, and still others will need extended time to take tests, complete assignments, and so on. Some students will need to demonstrate their learning in writing, whereas others may demonstrate comprehension orally, in song, or through some other form of creative expression. What is important is that we remember our goal: to facilitate real inquiry. For some students, getting out of their way is not enough; they need support.

IAQ 5. Can students with disabilities really engage? Can they teach one another about real inquiry? When I (Marlowe) first started teaching English in a high school for students with learning disabilities in Washington, DC, I certainly did not think this was possible. Like most high school teachers, I was asked to teach from a text handed to me on my first day, and I did. I was expected to assign 30 minutes of homework each night, and I did. I was to test students at the end of each week, and I did. During a unit on propaganda that was clearly outlined in the text I was provided, I tried to teach my students how to analyze an argument and how to weigh evidence. I introduced them to terms like *red herring* and *stereotype,* and I lectured about how governments have historically used objectification and demonization of their enemies to sway the populace. My students were bored out of their skulls. With no background knowledge, little ability to read or write, and nothing from their own experience with which to connect propaganda, they quickly lost interest. I blamed them. After all, they couldn't read or write, they had no academic interests, they were unmotivated and lazy. Didn't they understand how important this material was? My colleagues suggested that I plow ahead. Fortunately, one of my students, perhaps in a moment born out of desperation, wondered aloud why no one used propaganda anymore. This was the straw that broke the proverbial camel's back.

After convincing the principal that I needed to take my entire class to the national Mall, with virtually all of the school's audiovisual equipment in tow, I asked my students to prepare questions, as well as rebuttals to predicted responses, for people with whom they had the strongest political disagreements. A week later, we visited the Mall, and my students engaged a variety of demonstrators stationed in their semipermanent encampments. Students interviewed aspiring politicians, militant animal rights activists, Vietnam veterans, individuals protesting U.S. foreign policy in Central America, and a host of others with strong views and sharp rhetoric. My students came alive in ways I was told, in ways I felt certain, that students with learning disabilities could not. They debated with demonstrators, collaborated to make videotape productions, recorded and analyzed the language and logic of the people they interviewed, and presented their findings to others, first in our class, and later to other classes in the school. Their projects were based on their own questions; the products were of their own design. It was the first time I witnessed the enormous power of real inquiry.

Ironically, one of the most powerful learning approaches for students with disabilities is to ask them to teach others. We observed this dramatically in Jan Carpenter's classroom, a teacher in a multi-age elementary school classroom. Steve, a student with severe attentional and organizational difficulties, typically arrived unprepared for school: He rarely brought books or writing utensils, had difficulty settling down for class work, and often appeared confused after receiving instructions.

Many special educators and proponents of collaborative groups emphasize the importance of pairing students like Steve with academically advanced students who can model appropriate classroom and social behaviors. Jan chose a seemingly counterintuitive approach and paired Steve with a student whose organizational skills were weaker than his own. After a variety of interventions that often resulted in Steve becoming upset and Jan becoming frustrated, she asked Steve if he would help a student with mild autism named Maria to get organized in the morning, keep her materials tidy, and remember to bring her books home for homework assignments. At the end of the first day of Steve's teaching, he approached Maria and asked the following questions: "Maria, what do you need to do to make sure you have everything you need? How can you remember to bring these materials home? What will you do tomorrow morning to remember to bring your homework to school?" Jan's strategy worked brilliantly. Steve began to rehearse verbally the exact strategies and questions he needed to ask himself to become more focused, responsible, and engaged with school assignments. For the first time, Steve felt empowered, as if learning was something within his control. For the first time, Steve saw firsthand the value of *self*-questioning, teaching, and collaborating with another. Finally, Steve became a model for Maria, and slowly she began to learn. Who might she teach next?

CONCLUSION

Although at first glance it seems counterintuitive, the most powerful learning occurs not in what we communicate to our students as teachers, but in the process of what our *students* say and do, usually with one another. In the IAQ discussion above, the real-life story of Steve and Maria personifies one of Meier's (1998) most insightful observations about the teaching-learning process: "Teaching is mostly about listening and learning is mostly about telling" (p. 6), a maxim teachers would do well to remember every time they plan for real inquiry.

Unfortunately, research at the national level indicates that although almost all teachers seek the kind of student outcomes real inquiry promotes, very few are aware of the wide range of instructional options available to them. As a result, the educational system is still stuck where it was 20 years ago, when Goodlad (1984) noted in *A Place Called School* that schools are dominated not by Meier's vision of pedagogy, but by "a lot of teacher talk and a lot of student listening" (p. 242).

We know that to remain interested and engaged in learning, students need opportunities to discover, create, and problem solve, but more importantly, they need opportunities to build the investigation from the ground up, not simply answer questions posed by their teachers. Good instruction is built primarily, then, on real inquiry, that is, *student-created inquiry,* a form of instruction that holds the greatest promise in enabling all learners.

Solution to the Pen-Tapping Dilemma

A rubber pad was placed on the lab table, allowing the student to tap to his heart's content without disturbing his classmates or the teacher.

REFERENCES

Apple, M. W. (2001). Comparing neo-liberal projects and inequality in education. *Comparative Education, 37*(4), 409–423.

Aronson, E., & Bridgeman, D. (1979). Jigsaw groups and the desegregated classroom: In pursuit of common goals. *Personality and Social Psychology Bulletin, 5*(4), 438–466.

Bruner, J. S. (1961). The act of discovery. *Harvard Educational Review, 31*(1), 21–32.

Camp, B. W. (1987). *Think aloud games.* Starkville, MS: Think Aloud Associates.

Camp, B. W. (1996). Think aloud. *Communique: Newspaper of The National Association of School Psychologists,* 1–7.

Canestrari, A., & Marlowe, B. (Eds.). (2004). *Educational foundations: An anthology of critical readings.* Thousand Oaks, CA: Sage.

Capraro, M. M. (2001). *Defining constructivism: Its influence on the problem solving skills of students.* (ERIC Document Reproduction Service No. ED 452204)

Carnine, D. (1994). Introduction to the mini series: Diverse learners and prevailing, emerging, and research-based educational approaches and their tools. *School Psychology Review, 23*(3), 341–350.

Cole, B., & McGuire, M. (2004). *Young children's construction of understanding about families and citizenship using Storypath.* (ERIC Document Reproduction Service No. ED 479143)

Commager, H. S. (1980). *The study and teaching of history.* Columbus, OH: Merrill.

Crain, W. (2004). *Reclaiming childhood: Letting children be children in our achievement-oriented society.* New York: Holt.

Crawford, D. B. (2001). *Full inclusion: One reason for opposition.* Retrieved June 30, 2004, from http://my.execpc.com/~presswis/inclus. html

Cuban, L. (1990). Reforming again, again, and again. *Educational Researcher, 19*(1), 3–13.

Cuban, L. (2001). *Oversold and underused: Computers in the classroom.* Cambridge, MA: Harvard University Press.

Dewey, J. (1972). *Experience and education.* New York: Collier Books. (Original work published 1938)

Einstein, A. (1949). *Autobiographical notes.* New York: Harper & Row.

Fosnot, C. (1996). *Constructivism: Theory, perspectives, and practice.* New York: Teachers College Press.

Freire, P. (1974). *Pedagogy of the oppressed.* New York: Seabury.

Gardner, H. (1983). *Frames of mind: The theory of multiple intelligences.* New York: Basic Books.

Gardner, H. (1993). *Multiple intelligences: The theory in practice.* New York: Basic Books.

Goodlad, J. I. (1984). *A place called school: Prospects for the future.* New York: McGraw-Hill.

Juel, C. (1988). Learning to read and write: A longitudinal study of fifty-four children from first through fourth grade. *Journal of Educational Psychology, 80*(4), 437–447.

Kohn, A. (1999). *The schools our children deserve: Moving beyond traditional classrooms and "tougher standards."* New York: Houghton Mifflin.

Lavoie, R. (1989). *Understanding learning disabilities: Frustration, anxiety, tension: The F.A.T. city workshop* (produced by Peter Rosen for Eagle Hill School Outreach). Alexandria, VA: PBS Video.

Marlowe, B. A., & Page, M. L. (1998). *Creating and sustaining the constructivist classroom.* Thousand Oaks, CA: Corwin.

Meichenbaum, D. (1977). *Cognitive behavior modification.* New York: Plenum.

Meier, D. (1996). *The power of their ideas: Lessons for America from a small school in Harlem.* Boston: Beacon.

Page, M. L. (1992). *National History Day: An ethno-historical case study.* Unpublished doctoral dissertation, University of Massachusetts, Amherst.

Pestalozzi, J. H. (1898). *How Gertrude teaches her children.* (L. E. Holland & F. C. Turner, Trans.). New York: C. E. Bardeen. (Original work published 1801)

Peterson, M., Feen, H., Tamor, L., & Silagy, M. (2002). *Learning well together: Lessons about connecting inclusive education to whole school improvement.* Detroit, MI: Wayne State University, Whole School Consortium.

Peterson, M., Hittie, M., & Tamor, L. (2002). *Authentic, multi-level teaching: Teaching children with diverse academic abilities together well.* Retrieved June 6, 2004, from http://www.coe.wayne.edu/Community Building/WSC.html

Piaget, J. (1995). Essay on the theory of qualitative values in static sociology. In J. Piaget (Ed.), *Sociological studies* (pp. 97–133). New York: Routledge. (Original work published 1941)

Renzulli, J. S. (1999). What is this thing called giftedness, and how do we develop it? A twenty-five year perspective. *Journal for the Education of the Gifted, 23,* 3–54.

Rousseau, J. J. (1957). *Emile* (B. Foxley, Trans.). New York: Dutton. (Original work published 1762)

Sawyer, R. K. (2004). Creative teaching: Collaborative discussion as disciplined improvisation. *Educational Researcher, 33*(2), 12–20.

Sewall, G. T. (2000, Summer). Lost in action: Are time consuming, trivializing activities replacing the cultivation of active minds? *American Educator, 24,* 2, 4–9, 42–43.

Sharan, S., & Sharan, Y. (1989/1990). Group Investigation expands cooperative learning. *Educational Leadership, 47*(4), 17–21.

Simpson, D. E. (Producer/Director), & Golfus, B. (Producer/Director). (1995). *When Billy broke his head . . . and other tales of wonder* [Motion picture]. Boston: Fanlight Productions.

Spinner, H., & Fraser, B. J. (2002). *Evaluation of an innovative mathematics program in terms of classroom environment, student attitudes, and conceptual development.* (ERIC Document Reproduction Service No. ED 464829)

Suchman, J. (1966). *Inquiry development program: Developing inquiry.* Chicago: Science Research Associates.

Thomason, J. E. (2003). *Improving bilingual student learning and thinking skills through the use of constructivist theory.* (ERIC Document Reproduction Service No. ED 479390)

Tomlinson, C. A. (2000). Reconcilable differences? Standards-based teaching and differentiation. *Educational Leadership, 58,* 7–11.

Turnbull, A. P., Turnbull, H. R., Shank, M., & Leal, D. (1995). *Exceptional lives: Special education in today's schools.* Englewood Cliffs, NJ: Prentice Hall.

Turnbull, R., Turnbull, A., Shank, M., & Smith, S. J. (2004). *Exceptional lives: Special education in today's schools.* Upper Saddle River, NJ: Pearson.

von Glasersfeld, E. (1996). Footnotes to the many faces of constructivism. *Educational Researcher, 25*(6), 19.

Wigginton, E. (1985). *Sometimes a shining moment: The Foxfire experience.* New York: Anchor/Doubleday.

Winitzky, N., & Kauchak, D. (1997). Constructivism in teacher education: Applying cognitive theory to teacher learning. In T. V. Richardson (Ed.), *Constructivist teacher education: Building new understandings* (pp. 59–83). London: Falmer.

CHAPTER TEN

Inquiry-Based Instruction for English Language Learners

Ten Essential Elements

Fred Dobb

I am a passionate gardener. In the spring and summer, I parade around my yard tending and enjoying my peonies, roses, and daffodils. From September to June, I roam around my classroom and the corridors of my school making sure that Tiffany, Joe, and Rasheed grow, mature, and bloom to their full potential as students and as citizens. I am a year-round gardener.

—Yearwood (2003)

Quality education must reach an ever-growing segment of the student population classified as English Language Learners (ELLs) or limited English proficient (LEP). Among the many

AUTHORS' NOTE: Material in this chapter was drawn from: Dobb, F. (2004). *Essential Elements of Effective Science Instruction for English Learners* (2nd ed.). Los Angeles: California Science Project.

challenges facing teachers of ELLs at all grade levels are the purposeful development of written and oral discourse, specific forms of academic language, and standards-based understandings. With these skills, ELLs will succeed in the all-English classroom, eventually be reclassified as fluent English proficient (FEP), and graduate from high school prepared for postsecondary study or careers.

This chapter addresses the essential elements of delivering effective inquiry-based instruction for English Language Learners: developing academic language through instruction, affective factors, sheltering instruction, classroom talk, vocabulary development, use of the textbook and teacher's guide, appropriate professional development, and assessment. Examples come from the work of the California Science Project, which has dedicated considerable resources to making the education of ELLs a priority. Lessons learned from science serve as examples for other content areas to examine their approaches for reaching ELLs.

Before addressing activities that affect ELLs and their teachers, it is worth noting key factors that are often lost during national political battles over language minority education. Only by understanding this complex political, social, and economic reality can we establish the necessary foundation for assessing the relative merits of competing pedagogical philosophies and approaches.

Despite abundant evidence that shows our society's past failures in ensuring educational success for all students, our educational system has yet to respond with authenticity and quality implementation. Upgrading services to the ELL population can occur only if the entire educational community becomes personally and professionally committed to guaranteeing only what it would accept for its own children. In light of this, two issues require closer consideration.

First, the U.S. Supreme Court, other federal courts, and voters in various states have identified ELLs as students who require specialized instruction. Ignoring the language proficiency needs of ELLs violates their civil rights and dooms them to academic failure. At a minimum, schools must select and implement appropriate approaches and monitor student progress carefully. Extraordinary means, such as specialized English instruction and use of the primary language, can avoid creating and/or reduce achievement gaps among ELL children.

Some states have foreclosed the possibility of teaching through the primary language by requiring that students be taught and tested only in English. In all subjects, recent standardized testing results reveal that very few ELLs, at any level, score at or above the 50th percentile. Notably, ELLs are generally tested with instruments developed for English-proficient student populations. Such measures fail to distinguish between content knowledge and English proficiency.

Second, teaching demanding content to ELLs is not the same as teaching an English-proficient student. Reaching ELLs requires approaches that go beyond quality instruction. During our professional development sessions on the topic of instructional strategies for ELLs, participants often remark that the ideas we introduce are "just good teaching practices." Such comments fail to acknowledge what the ELLs bring to the pedagogical encounter. Effective teachers view their educational practice within the context of the lives of their ELLs. An approach that may further clarify a concept for other students may be the instructional life raft needed to rescue some ELLs from an otherwise incomprehensible lesson. ELLs are often reluctant to participate actively because they find themselves in an unwelcoming school environment where they are overwhelmed by a language that is not their own. Second-language development is a deeply personal and idiosyncratic journey in which the classroom can provide motivation and opportunities to use English for meaningful communication.

Teachers must commit themselves to brighter academic futures for ELL. This chapter examine the specific role played by inquiry-based instruction in the struggle for educational access and equity for these students.

ESSENTIAL ELEMENT 1:
PLAN INQUIRY-BASED INSTRUCTION

An emerging body of research, particularly in science, has substantiated the benefits of inquiry-based instruction for students who are developing proficiency in English (Amaral, Garrison, & Klentschy, 2002; Bravo & Garcia, 2004; Gibbons, 1993; Valadez, 2002). Most research targets what might be called the English Learner-friendly hallmarks of the inquiry classroom. Among the chief characteristics of inquiry-based instruction are providing shared common experiences for students; hands-on activities; links to prior knowledge; student collaboration; and opportunities to read, listen, talk, and write about events and experiences.

Frequently, ELLs find themselves in the worst-funded schools, facing poorly qualified teachers who lack adequate content knowledge preparation and second-language methodological competence. Without teacher awareness and pedagogical engineering of planned experiences, learning may *not* happen for ELLs in a way that promotes both understanding and growth in English as a second language.

Examples abound of teachers across all content areas who are addressing the challenge of making standards-based instruction comprehensible to ELLs and giving them the opportunity to participate fully in the academic discourse needed to succeed. However, teachers who are rigidly focused on individual standards can lose sight of larger goals for ELLs. What do we mean by larger goals? For second-language learners, it means gradually developing the English proficiency level that approximates that of their English-speaking peers. It means helping them to read, comprehend, and write at a level that meets most academic demands in any discipline and at any grade level. It means being reclassified as FEP using multiple criteria and graduating from high school. For science, the larger goal is for students to be scientifically literate and capable of building connections among science, technology, and society.

When teachers involved with the California Science Program are planning and implementing inquiry-based instruction for ELLs, careful consideration is given to each of the characteristics of inquiry-based instruction described in Figure 10.1. For example, in working with ELLs at the intermediate level of proficiency on a science unit on ecosystems, students are expected to understand the concept of energy flow.

Preparing students to explain concepts in both oral and written form requires lessons that include specific content and second-language instructional features. Before deciding whether it is reasonable to expect students to give presentations or answer essay questions about ecosystems, the precise form of instruction they received should be carefully analyzed. Questions such as the following drive the planning process.

1. Were students able to make connections between the concept of an ecosystem and their own life experiences?

2. Have students been exposed to sufficient information to support their explanations?

3. Do students have command of the patterns of oral and written organization to successfully share what they know?

Figure 10.1   Special Issues for Consideration

Shared common experiences	Is English language sheltered to make information comprehensible? Is primary language used for explanations?
Hands-on activities	Do lab equipment, visuals, and experiments complement and reinforce written information and oral explanations?
Links to prior knowledge	Have there been attempts to probe for student prior experiences and possible misconceptions? Are cross-cultural experiences voiced and validated?
Student collaboration	Are student roles sufficiently structured to provide for significant ELL participation and allow ELLs to demonstrate strengths and talents?
Language opportunities for communication about events and experiences	Are explicit, focused language teaching experiences meaningfully incorporated into the lesson?

4. Have students been given the opportunity to perform the role of teacher or guide with peers or adults?

5. Has corrective feedback been provided before student performance is formally evaluated and graded?

6. Do students feel comfortable as explainers of scientific phenomena?

7. Have classroom activities provided students with an active personal vocabulary specific to describing ecosystems such as food, energy, flow, and interdependence?

Inquiry-based instruction guided by in-depth lesson planning affords collegial groups of teachers the opportunity to improve their practice by purposefully examining the long-range goals for ELLs in both science and English.

ESSENTIAL ELEMENT 2:
DEVELOP ACADEMIC LANGUAGE

Through Content Instruction

Among the many challenges facing teachers of ELLs is the purposeful development of academic language through instruction in both self-contained and departmentalized settings. Most educational organizations dedicate the bulk of their resources to the earliest stages of English language development (ELD), when students' needs are the most obvious. Newcomers and beginning ELD students first learn survival and classroom coping skills. Once oral social language is present, students' need for more demanding academic language can be masked by short answers, smiles, nodding heads, and barely getting by academically. Sometimes, when apparent increases in LEP appear, resources and extra help are shifted to those at lower proficiency levels, or withheld because further attention is deemed unnecessary for continued academic progress.

As a consequence, large numbers of ELLs reach the early intermediate and intermediate levels of English proficiency and stay rooted there. Nationally, these individuals number in the hundreds of thousands; they struggle, but never excel or thrive in the classroom. In some districts, these are known as "the students waiting to be reclassified as FEP." Some leave high school after many years classified as ELLs, with or without a diploma. Their mastery of content is inadequate, leaving them unprepared for higher education or rewarding careers. A linguistic profile of such ELLs reveals that they possess social speaking skills but lack the ability to persuade, debate, or give oral presentations. Decoding skills may mask their inadequate comprehension of complex text. Students can figure out the main idea of a lesson, but fail to notice important technical details or nuances. The specialized scientific meaning of everyday words goes unnoticed.

Support Academic Language Development
Through Investigation and Experimentation

Teachers play a pivotal role in providing a language-rich environment where ELLs can create and express understanding. For ELLs to succeed in the all-English classroom, they need discipline-specific and appropriate language. Inquiry learning helps to develop academic language in two fundamental ways.

1. Inquiry provides shared experiences and an arena where ELLs can experiment with their maturing ideas about phenomena, events, people, or places and use their expanding second-language skills. Only when we express "something" does another language adhere to our lives and becomes part of our identity. Writing a few sentences for a test question is inherently different from completing a lengthy report.

Any content can provide that "something." What is learned through English becomes part of one's understanding of the universe and a step toward growth in a second language. ELLs who plan, plant, observe, and record changes in their garden in English give purpose and significance to both life science and language development.

2. There is a direct correspondence between the steps in the inquiry cycle, with its incremental demands for an expanding vocabulary and literacy skills, and the levels of English language proficiency contained in ELD standards. Throughout the process of inquiry, the students' goal is to use contextually appropriate language that is accurate, precise, and objective. The oral or written descriptions of inquiry activities expose ELLs to a sequence of steps that is different in presentation style from other listening and reading experiences. Language structures expressing causal relationships need to be understood, tried, and eventually incorporated into the linguistic repertoire of every ELL.

There is a growing effort, particularly in science, to define concrete and explicit relationships between instruction and development of academic language. The California Science Project's contribution was its publication *Targeting Academic Language Development for English Learners Through Scientific Investigation and Experimentation*. This document's graphic organizers (Figure 10.2) are designed to be used in professional development programs along with another California Science Project publication, *Essential Elements of Effective Science Instruction for English*. These tools enable teachers to

- Analyze the correspondence between investigation and exploration at all grades in the California Science Standards and the second-language functions required of ELLs at every

Figure 10.2   Graphic Organizer

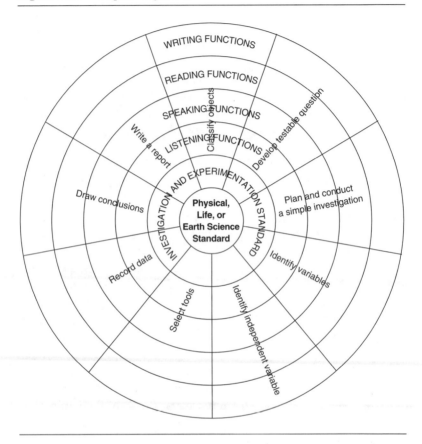

step in the process of learning content and communicating understanding

- Plan ELL instructional units based on the California Science Standards and the California English Language Development Standards (California Department of Education, 1999)
- Examine textbooks, curriculum units, and other instructional materials for their comprehensive treatment of ELL needs in all language skill areas

Although these graphic organizers use California's fifth grade for illustration, they can be adapted to any state or national science or English as a Second Language standards. Information contained in

Chapters 2–7 of this book can provide guidance for modifying these organizers for use across all major subject areas. Every organizer highlights the role of scientific language functions in accomplishing the learning tasks during the investigation and experimentation cycle. The larger figure represents potential interactions between the science standards and the most common scientific language functions for listening, speaking, reading, and writing. The smaller figures support a more focused and detailed examination of the interactions among the same elements, but according to the five proficiency levels articulated in the ELD standards (http://www.cde .ca.gov/re/pn/fd/englangart-stnd-pdf.asp) and the California English Language Development Test (http://www.cde.ca. gov/ta/tg/el/).

The California Science Project continues to evolve as a provider of professional development. We have sharpened our focus on the relationship between inquiry and the academic success of ELLs. This capitalizes on the potential of steps in the inquiry cycle to enhance academic language development at each level of proficiency in listening, speaking, reading, and writing.

ESSENTIAL ELEMENT 3: AFFECTIVE FACTORS

What would happen in today's classrooms to that famous screen beauty and inventor Hedy Lamarr, and other scientists, poets, and historians for whom English was not a first language. Would their talents be recognized and encouraged, or would they be remanded to less demanding courses? Would their lack of academic English skills result in poor grades and discouragement?

When the affective domain is overlooked in considering the positive association between quality inquiry-based teaching and ELLs, neither standards-based content, high-quality materials, nor professional development will have a major impact on ELD. Here are common questions that ELLs ask themselves as they attempt to assimilate, interpret, and explain academic content.

- Does this teacher know who I am?
- Does this teacher care about me?
- Does this teacher want me to succeed?
- Does this teacher realize that I am not intellectually limited, even though I am unable to express myself fully in English?

- Does this teacher understand the fear of ridicule and embarrassment I must overcome whenever I speak, participate in a group, or submit written work?
- Does this teacher see me as a potential contributor to knowledge?

These thought-provoking concerns of students should resonate with all teachers. Teachers must provide constant assurance that they understand the issues underlying these questions and are willing to reach out to each ELL. To successfully connect with ELLs, teachers must communicate that they recognize the struggle to participate, that support is available, and that former ELLs have succeeded in their programs. Effective instructors avoid making false, self-fulfilling assumptions about demanding content knowledge, academic English, and the career goals and futures of ELLs.

Next time you use your cell phone, remember former ELL Hedy Lamarr, whose patent makes wireless communication possible, and think about the other ELLs you see in your classroom. A future important inventor, national political figure, great mathematician, movie star, or award-winning scientist may be sitting before you.

ESSENTIAL ELEMENT 4: CLASSROOM TALK

In planning for instruction, California teachers are expected to consult both the Content Standards and the English Language Development Standards to capitalize on using content to develop academic language. Inquiry-based activities provide rich, highly motivating language laboratories. The key to building on ELL experiences and leading them to read and write across all content areas is engaging them in purposeful, guided conversations about their lessons.

Pauline Gibbons (2003), one of the pioneers in content and language scaffolding, authored a groundbreaking paper in which she demonstrated how productive conversations can result by changing routine classroom discussions into genuine academic discourse. Gibbons observed fourth- and fifth-grade students working on the topic of magnetism. She described how teachers artfully used student responses to move dialogue toward higher levels of understanding and discipline-appropriate language. She discovered that applying effective strategies for instructional conversation resulted in student growth both in English as a Second Language and content knowledge.

According to Gibbons (2003), significant student gains occur under the following conditions:

1. Teachers and ELL students form partnerships through guided conversations in which students gradually appropriate the language of the discipline and use it to express their understanding. Although there is considerable linguistic and conceptual distance between teacher and students, teachers make discourse and linguistic choices that reduce that gap.

2. Teachers move ELLs along a continuum of oral social English to the school world of written language and from interpersonal talk to school-valued expository text.

3. Teachers signal a need to clarify ELL talk and provide clues for modifying language. "The teacher hands over to the student the responsibility for clarification, which results in increasingly explicit information from the student . . . comprehensible output" (p. 262). When repeating statements in more academic terms, ELLs are challenged to stretch language so that it conforms to conventions of the discipline.

4. ELLs take responsibility for making themselves understood to teachers. Students realize that the teachers' motivation is to develop effective speakers who can describe, explain, question, hypothesize, and persuade.

5. Instructional conversations are rehearsals for writing in journals or preparing reports.

Gibbons points out that to prepare ELLs for successful test taking, teachers must employ oral instructional conversation effectively to move ELLs from personal experience to academic English, from detailed oral expression to factual writing, and from superficial to deep understanding.

ESSENTIAL ELEMENT 5: VOCABULARY DEVELOPMENT

Vocabulary development represents a continuing thread for the academic growth of ELLs as they progress through the levels of English proficiency from beginning to advanced. Research shows a clear relationship between an ever-expanding student vocabulary and overall academic achievement. Success with standardized testing favors students with well-developed vocabularies. As they receive instruction, ELLs depend on their second-language vocabulary to understand concepts and generate written explanations of their readings, experiments, and observations for themselves, their teachers, and their fellow students.

Cummins (2001) maintained that ELLs progress in their academic careers by acquiring conversational fluency. ELLs add the most frequently used spoken words to their linguistic repertoire. They learn discrete language skills to comprehend new vocabulary to reach the ultimate goal of general and subject-specific academic language. In the early stages, vocabulary derived principally from Greek and Latin roots can pose a significant challenge. Reading materials become more complex, technical, and abstract, and they move quickly beyond the students' social experiences. Extensive reading provides more rich experiences than are typically found in using oral language.

A basic core of approximately 2,000 high-frequency words accounts for most of academic writing. There are many well-regarded, high-frequency word lists, ranging from general academic language to discipline specific. *Using English Words* (Corson, 1995) includes words such as *environment, affect, select,* and *species,* which first appear in kindergarten. An article titled "A New Academic Word List" (Coxhead, 2000) contains 800 terms from all disciplines arranged alphabetically. Bar-Tzur's (2004) "Vocabulary List for General Science" defines 357 terms, many of which surface early and continue to appear through the university level. The *EDL Core Vocabularies in Reading, Mathematics, Science and Social Studies* (Taylor, 1989) provides a rich source of terminology commonly used to write textbooks and examinations.

Instructors should be conscious of these word compendia, gauge their importance for ELLs, and emphasize words with the greatest benefit to students. The most profitable use of student time places the instructional spotlight on words that are most likely to appear across all grades, courses, and textbooks. Scarcella (2003) recommended that direct vocabulary instruction target both meaning and related issues, such as parts of speech, frequency, appropriateness to writing, which words commonly occur with other words, and pronunciation. Instructors should introduce vocabulary within the appropriate context and avoid requiring memorization of vocabulary lists devoid of content connections. These words should be used consistently during different lessons and be required in student speech and written work.

ESSENTIAL ELEMENT 6: TEXTBOOKS

The gap between best practices for working with ELLs and textbooks that pay little attention to ELLs poses a challenge to teachers. Textbooks must be systematically modified to meet ELL needs for learning content and the development of academic language proficiency.

Using the same textbook for English-proficient students and ELLs presents instructors with a pedagogical dilemma. The practice ensures that both groups will be exposed to the same standards-based content. During their standards-based examinations, all students will encounter similar content in English. Textbooks provide colorful illustrations, charts, and graphs, and they are a great potential source of academic language about real-world phenomena. However, because the text assumes proficiency in academic English, ELLs cannot possibly derive the same benefits without teacher intervention and guidance.

In her landmark work, *Teaching Science to Language Minority Students,* scientist and second-language acquisition specialist Rosenthal (1995) asserted that scientific writing can be dull, impersonal, and decidedly harder to understand than narrative fiction. The English classroom, in which the most direct teaching of language occurs, rarely exposes the ELL to expository writing with complex content. According to Rosenthal, textbooks deal with unfamiliar content and introduce new vocabulary constantly. Details are usually presented before general ideas and concepts. Dense passages require rereading for comprehension. Repetition or restatement of information seldom occurs.

When faced with fact-packed textbooks and the need to progress slowly and reread, even the most motivated ELLs complain of fatigue and frustration. Students with strong academic preparation in their primary language may still require two or three times as long to read textbooks and process information in English. Without careful instructional support, students' engagement with text and comprehension tends to be low. The following instructional strategies and approaches address challenges presented to ELLs by textbooks.

1. Provide primary-language support appropriate for ELLs at various levels of proficiency development. Depending on the instructional objectives of the program, primary-language utilization can incorporate classes taught in another language, bilingual instructional assistants, bilingual dictionaries, and other language editions of the textbook and tests. Group students who have a common primary language.

2. Adopt reading comprehension activities for individual students and groups. Target important habits such as previewing material, recognizing chapter headings, identifying introductions, reading first sentences in a paragraph, understanding visuals and graphs, summarizing, and answering end-of-chapter questions.

3. Classify textbooks as a genre with unique characteristics of expression. Identify such unfortunate textbook practices as placing visuals at a distance from related text or including interesting but extraneous material.

4. Enhance vocabulary development by explaining that words can have multiple meanings and be used differently in language. Emphasize commonly used words and teach vocabulary within an appropriate context. Avoid memorizing vocabulary lists without explicit content connections.

5. Analyze discipline-specific discourse patterns to reveal the differences between expository text and narrative. Have students practice reading, listening, and using common linguistic structures such as *if/then* and linking words (*then, next, finally,* and *after*). Teach them to explain events or phenomena using a logical sequence and the importance of concluding statements in oral presentations and written reports.

6. Use supplementary materials frequently to strengthen ELLs' understanding of major concepts or to link prior knowledge with new classroom experiences.

The challenges presented to ELLs by their English-language textbooks can be overcome successfully through a variety of instructional approaches that add depth to understanding and further the development of academic English language.

ESSENTIAL ELEMENT 7: TEACHERS' GUIDES

The previous section presented numerous textbook enhancement strategies. Despite these well-documented practices, even a cursory examination of teachers' guides reveals that few of these ideas have been adopted for chapter topics or recommended as methods for developing reading comprehension. Some publishers have responded to this problem by adding materials to teachers' guides for ELLs that are similar to sections for gifted and compensatory education students. Although such inclusions are welcome and long overdue, these suggestions and ideas often seem forced and disconnected from the major concepts presented in the textbook.

Recommended accommodations for ELLs found in teachers' guides fall into six broad categories. Common examples are offered here with commentaries.

1. Use of primary language

Examples: "Ask students for the word for 'lead' in their native languages." "Have students write the types of rocks in their native language in a journal."

Comment: Such ideas fail to address how teachers can use student-generated words in instruction, especially when the teacher is not fluent in the other languages or when primary-language instruction is unavailable. What ensures that students know this vocabulary in their own primary languages?

2. Word origins and pronunciation

Examples: "Mention that the word 'X' is of Greek origin and means 'Y.'" "Point out that when words with two or more syllables end with a 'y,' the 'y' sound is usually like a long 'e.'"

Comment: Telling about the word is not a significant approach to vocabulary development. Strong connections need to be made between words used within a unit and student applications of these new words in speaking and writing.

3. Study skills

Examples: "Challenge students to use the dictionary to look up 'Z.'" "Have students make up their own memory devices to remember facts."

Comment: Teachers must know how to help students build on their current language skills to review and write about what they learned. Little attention is given to the textbook as a specific genre with particular reading challenges or to understanding information presented in different forms.

4. Links to prior knowledge

Examples: "Have ELLs prepare topographical maps of the area where they were born or from which they emigrated." "Visit a construction site where machines are used and discuss observations in class."

Comment: There are no systematic ways to identify students' prior experience and knowledge. Prior knowledge is not valued as the key to gaining deeper comprehension of print.

5. Interactions with other students

Examples: "Pair up ELLs with English-proficient students to discuss experimental results." "Request that students review their experimental procedures with the class."

Comment: Insufficient guidance is provided for establishing the roles and expectations of ELL participation in heterogeneous groups.

6. Visual representations

Examples: "Challenge students to draw and label the parts of a volcano." "Arrange chairs to reflect the solar system." "Have students draw word webs."

Comment: These activities are adequate beginnings that can expand student language in all skill areas; however, more detailed instructions are needed.

If one compares the effective strategies for modifying textbooks for ELLs with the six idea categories discussed here—one from a methodological source, the others from teachers' guides—there is a degree of similarity among Items 1–3. Nevertheless, to operationalize these strategies fully, teachers' guides require further elaboration. For example, primary-language support exists when the teacher can understand and react to what the ELL student has produced in his or her other language. Vocabulary development is successful when ELLs can incorporate new vocabulary accurately into their oral and written production. Study skills result in independent learners. In the other three areas, teachers' guides fall far from the mark. To illustrate, reading comprehension ideally should focus on challenges presented by the textbook content itself. Also, little attention is provided to patterns of written and spoken discourse. References to supplemental materials other than those associated with the text series are usually omitted.

However well-intentioned teacher's guide suggestions may be, they offer inadequate support for developing academic language or conceptual understanding. The major burden still falls on the instructor to combine the pedagogical understanding of ELL strategies with content knowledge to ensure quality instruction. Following the teacher's guide alone does not lead to student mastery of standards. In most teachers' guides, the same set of suggestions is repeated chapter after chapter with little regard to topic, prior background, or English-proficiency level of students. Generally, discrete aspects of the textbook are emphasized with little concern for student comprehension of major concepts.

To evaluate properly the overall quality of a teacher's guide and any recommended strategies, teachers should ask these questions:

1. Is there any indication of ELL comprehension level of the unit's content? If ELLs did not understand the material, what should I do?

2. Do the recommendations correspond to the ELD levels of my students?

3. Are strategies used consistently throughout the teacher's guide?

4. Do the activities provide equal rigor for all students?

5. Is scaffolding instruction recommended for introducing new material?

6. Are strategies provided that lead to instructional conversations between ELLs and the teacher?

7. Do the activities capitalize on the visual and physical properties of inquiry?

ESSENTIAL ELEMENT 8: PROFESSIONAL DEVELOPMENT

A consumers' guide to help teachers make informed selections about professional development for ELLs would address the following important program elements:

1. The special challenges of spoken and written discourse, and vocabulary that needs to be included in the instructional design

2. Incrementally adding rigor to academic language as students progress to higher levels of ELD

3. Ensuring that the specific needs of ELLs are addressed from early stages until they master literary conventions and communicate effectively within the discipline

4. The ways in which materials for supplementing the text are most effectively used with ELLs

5. Efficient and supportive methods for evaluating and providing feedback to students about their written and oral work

Planning effective and worthwhile ELL professional development programs poses significant challenges. Consulting standard references offers little assistance because most of these publications ignore the issue of language minority students. Following are several issues to consider. No single program includes all of these features; most have additional topics, concerns, and issues. This list provides questions to consider in planning effective professional development programs for those who teach ELLs.

1. To what extent is the program based on developing academic English in a particular content area?

2. Is there a demonstrated understanding of the relationship between ELD and the content area?

3. Are activities designed to move students to higher levels of English proficiency?

4. Is there a strong focus on providing a rigorous, standards-based curriculum for ELLs?

5. Does the program make informed connections between ELD and standards?

6. Does the program address the needs of ELLs at all levels of English proficiency?

7. Does the program offer ideas for providing teacher feedback in all language skill areas, especially writing?

8. How well does the program address discipline-specific academic language challenges for ELLs?

9. Does the program help teachers to use textbooks and supplementary materials with ELLs?

ESSENTIAL ELEMENT 9: SHELTERED INSTRUCTION OBSERVATION PROTOCOL

Sheltered Instruction (SI) or Specially Designed Academic Instruction in English (SDAIE) is a means for making grade-level academic content accessible to ELLs and promoting their English-language development. Teachers skilled in SI use strategies such as visual aids, demonstrations, prereading activities, graphic organizers, and textbook adaptation to make content more comprehensible. Academic language is approached through specially designed activities that involve listening, speaking, reading, and writing. Teachers purposely add discourse in the content area to their students' linguistic repertoire. SI enjoys the most success with ELLs who have a formal educational background in their primary language and are functioning at the intermediate or higher level of English proficiency.

The world of SI for ELLs and their teachers took a major step forward when the California Science Project (CSP) developed the Sheltered Instruction Observation Protocol (SIOP). The SIOP is a tool for self-monitoring and/or peer coaching that enhances the effective delivery of content to ELLs. The document focuses on the following areas of teaching and learning: preparation, building background, strategies, interaction, practice/application, lesson delivery, and review/assessment. The SIOP Lesson Planning Guide complements the protocol. Both documents support a careful combination of ELD standards and content area standards.

The following example is from Item 15 from the instruction section of the CSP-adapted Sheltered Science Instruction Observation Protocol (SSIOP), which can be scored by an instructor or other observers during a science lesson.

The teacher engages students in a scientific conversation, which moves students from personal experience and everyday language to generalizations expressed in discourse patterns specific to the discipline.

The teacher includes the use of question types and strategies that specifically promote science process skills (e.g., observing, classifying, measuring, using numbers, communicating, inferring, predicting, collecting, recording and interpreting data, identifying variables, defining operations, making hypotheses, and constructing and using models) (see Figure 10.3).

Additional information on SIOP, articles on the project's accomplishments, and research on sheltered instruction are available from the Center for Applied Linguistics (Center for Applied Linguistics, 2002) at http://www.cal.org/projects/si.

Essential Element 10: Assessment

The incidence and frequency of standards-based testing to fulfill the requirements of the No Child Left Behind Act (NCLB) are on the rise at both national and state levels. Such assessments join a constellation of standardized tests designed for English-proficient students but that are administered inappropriately to ELLs.

One unintended consequence of NCLB and the new nationwide testing emphasis has been that science instruction has reentered the elementary school curriculum. Test blueprints reveal that students are expected to "know and express" and "show" their knowledge of specific scientific concepts from grade-level standards on a written multiple-choice test using scientific terms, discourse, and conventions. In response, the CSP developed and field-tested a set of criterion-referenced measures for ELLs based on the California Science Content Standards. The California English Language Development Test (CELDT) is the statewide standardized instrument for initial ELL identification that provides measures of annual English-language growth. CELDT offers common descriptors for ELL proficiency levels: beginner, early intermediate, intermediate, early advanced, and advanced. A complete description of these levels is available online at www.cde.ca.gov/ta/tg/el/.

CSP's commitment to this project arose from both extensive classroom experience and research that shows that it is difficult to obtain an accurate picture of what ELLs derive from instruction conducted in their second language (Sexton, 1999; Solano-Flores & Turnbull, 2003). The CSP also recognized the difficulty teachers face in working simultaneously with two sets of standards: content and ELD.

Figure 10.3 Sheltered Instruction Observation Protocol (SIOP)

I. PREPARATION	II. INSTRUCTION	II. INSTRUCTION
	STRATEGIES	**PRACTICE/APPLICATION**
• Write content objectives clearly for students. • Write language objectives clearly for students. • Choose content concepts appropriate for age and educational background level of students. • Identify supplementary materials to use (graphs, models, visuals). • Adapt content (e.g., text, assignment) to all levels of student proficiency. • Plan meaningful activities that integrate lesson concepts (e.g., surveys, letter writing, simulations, model construction) with language practice opportunities for reading, writing, listening, and/or speaking.	• Provide ample opportunities for students to use strategies (e.g., problem solving, predicting, organizing, summarizing, categorizing, evaluating, self-monitoring). • Use scaffolding techniques consistently (providing the right amount of support to move students from one level of understanding to a higher level) throughout lesson. • Use a variety of question types, including those that promote higher-order thinking skills throughout the lesson (e.g., literal, analytical, and interpretive questions).	• Provide hands-on materials and/or manipulatives for students to practice using new content knowledge. • Provide activities for students to apply content and language knowledge in the classroom. • Provide activities that integrate all language skills (i.e., reading, writing, listening, and speaking).
		LESSON DELIVERY
II. INSTRUCTION	**INTERACTION**	• Support content objectives clearly. • Support language objectives clearly. • Engage students approximately 90%–100% of the period (most students taking part and on task throughout the lesson). • Pace the lesson appropriately to the students' ability level.
BUILDING BACKGROUND	• Provide frequent opportunities for interaction and discussion between teacher/student and among students about lesson concepts, and encourage elaborated responses. • Use group configurations that support language and content objectives of the lesson. • Provide sufficient wait time for student responses consistently. • Give ample opportunities for students to clarify key concepts in L1 as needed with aide, peer, or L1 text.	
• Explicitly link concepts to students' backgrounds and experiences. • Explicitly link past learning and new concepts. • Emphasize key vocabulary (e.g., introduce, write, repeat, and highlight) for students.		**III. REVIEW/EVALUATION**
COMPREHENSIBLE INPUT		• Give a comprehensive review of key vocabulary. • Give a comprehensive review of key content concepts. • Provide feedback to students regularly on their output (e.g., language, content, work). • Conduct assessments of student comprehension and learning throughout lesson on all lesson objectives (e.g., spot-checking, group response).
• Use speech appropriate for students' proficiency level (e.g., slower rate, enunciation, and simple sentence structure for beginners). • Explain academic tasks clearly. • Use a variety of techniques to make content concepts clear (e.g., modeling, visuals, hands-on activities, demonstrations, gestures, body language).		

CSP's work capitalizes on the relationship between experiencing inquiry and talking and writing about the process using topic-appropriate discourse patterns and vocabulary for each grade level. The CSP believes that effective inquiry-based instruction provides ELLs with a contextualized, interactive opportunity for academic language development. Explicit teaching of inquiry process skills (e.g., observing; classifying; measuring and using numbers; communicating; inferring; predicting; and collecting, recording, and interpreting data) spurs growth in both science and English for ELLs.

The test items address a variety of K–12 standards in a format and style designed to minimize student confusion and maximize performance (Figure 10.4). Each sample contains the following sections: completed and labeled diagram, sentence completion with word bank, complete the visual organizer, write a paragraph, and an option to talk about it. Students are encouraged to draw on information from all sections of the item and their classroom instruction. Teachers and scorers are provided with separate scoring guides for evaluating student responses for content and ELD. More than 1,000 students have participated in the field test.

Developers, scorers, and field test teachers have increased their understanding about standardized testing and ELLs in a number of areas. Teachers have become increasingly sophisticated in using testing results when planning instruction. The CSP/EL assessment items provide additional subject-specific information for the development of academic language. The items also function as intermediate steps in preparing ELLs to take standardized tests that are designed for the general English-proficient population.

Based on our preliminary analyses of student responses, we have drawn the following conclusions:

1. Scoring guides alone are inadequate for making accurate determinations about content and ELD. Experienced and sympathetic scorers are needed to make reasonable judgments about ELL responses.

2. Students need to be taught to take advantage of and use all available information. They should understand that copying words, phrases, and ideas presented in the test items is not cheating. Test-taking skills and strategies need to be taught explicitly.

Figure 10.4   Examples From the California English Language Development Test (CELDT)

First Name, Last Initial _____ Grade Level _____
ELD Level _____ Date _____ ELD Level
(Circle): Beginner, Early Intermediate, Intermediate,
Early Advanced, Advanced, English Only
Teacher Last 4 Soc. Sec. _____
School/District _____

EARTH CHANGES AND AGRICULTURE

Diagram

The diagram shows a farm located in California. It is next to a river flowing through a wide flat plain.

Mountains   Farm   River   Plain

PAGE 1

First Name, Last Initial _____ Grade Level _____
ELD Level _____ Date _____ ELD Level
(Circle): Beginner, Early Intermediate, Intermediate,
Early Advanced, Advanced, English Only

Write a paragraph

Would you farm in the area shown in the diagram? Why or why not?

_____

_____

_____

_____

_____

PAGE 4

Complete the Sentences

Select the appropriate word that best completes the sentence.

erosion soil sediment flood shadow irrigate barrier river channel farm rain water

1. Water and wind act on soil to wear it away. This process is called _____

2. When a river rises and then falls, it deposits fertile material for farmers called _____ on the land near the river.

3. Farmers _____ their fields in order for their crops (plants) to grow.

4. Tall mountains may create a _____ that prevents rain from reaching a farm on the plain.

5. Water transports materials along the _____

Earth Changes

PAGE 2

First Name, Last Initial _____ Grade Level _____
ELD Level _____ Date _____ ELD Level
(Circle): Beginner, Early Intermediate, Intermediate,
Early Advanced, Advanced, English Only

Talk about it (Do this part with your teacher.)

What land conditions should a farmer consider when choosing an area to farm?

PAGE 5

First Name, Last Initial _____ Grade Level _____ ELD Level _____ Date ELD Level (Circle): Beginner,
Early Intermediate, Intermediate, Early Advanced, Advanced, English Only

Compare and Contrast

Use these words in the following chart.

erosion soil sediment flood shadow irrigate barrier river channel farm rain water

Why would this area (in the diagram on Page1) be a good place to farm? Why would this area be a bad place to farm? In the chart below add as many reasons as you can.

Good for farming (advantages)	Bad for farming (disadvantages)
The land is flat.	The land could flood.

PAGE 3

3. Directions for examiners must be clear, simple, and to the point. For example, it must be stated explicitly that students are to explain processes depicted in a diagram, not just describe superficial features.

4. In science and language instruction, extensive input and practice are needed to cause even small amounts of student production.

5. Writing is the key to communicating understanding and is the most accurate measure of academic language and content understanding. ELL students who can communicate in an accurate, simple, and clear manner have a solid base for more challenging work.

6. Words acquired within a particular context can have meanings that are quite different from their common uses in social conversations. Consequently, teachers need to introduce vocabulary within the context of the lesson, experiment, observation, or presentation.

This CSP developmental project is based on assessment research and best practice in second-language learning. It offers a model for other subject areas to assess ELL progress in the mastery of standards and development of academic language.

Summary

The things I want to fight for, and the things that no one will take from me, are the following: becoming a medical doctor, maintaining my language and culture, and being able to work together with people who speak other languages, or who come from a different cultural background than mine.

—Daniel Ruiz, seventh grader and
2003 winner of the CA Association for
Bilingual Education Student Writing Contest

Designing and implementing effective inquiry-based instruction for ELLs requires a reassessment of numerous elements of instructional practice. This chapter has drawn on the logical connection between the richness of an inquiry-based curriculum and the stages of second-language proficiency development to benefit the ELL population.

The nation's dedication to the academic achievement of ELLs continues to grow, but questions about relevant classroom practices remain to be answered. As the educational community continues to strengthen its commitment and refine its approaches, it moves ever closer to ensuring educational equity for language minority students from kindergarten through 12th grade and beyond.

REFERENCES

Amaral, O., Garrison, L., & Klentschy, M. (2002). Helping English learners increase achievement through inquiry-based science instruction. *Bilingual Research Journal, 26*(2), 213–239.

Bar-Tzur, D. (2004). Vocabulary list for general science. Retrieved September 22, 2004, from http://www.theinterpretersfriend.com/tech/vocab/vl/science.html

Bravo, M., & Garcia, E. (2004, April). *Learning to write like scientists: English language learners' science inquiry and writing understandings in responsive learning contexts.* Paper presented at the annual meeting of the American Educational Research Association, San Diego, CA.

California Department of Education. (1999). *English language development standards for California public schools, K–12.* Retrieved September 22, 2004, from http://www.cde.ca.gov/re/pn/fd/englangart-stnd-pdf.asp

Center for Applied Linguistics. (2002). *The SIOP model: Sheltered instruction for academic achievement.* Washington, DC: Author.

Corson, D. J. (1995). *Using English words.* Dordrecht, The Netherlands: Kluwer Academic.

Coxhead, A. (2000). A new academic word list. *TESOL Quarterly, 34*(2), 213–238.

Cummins, J. (2001). *Negotiating identities: Education for empowerment in a diverse society.* Los Angeles: California Association for Bilingual Education.

Dobb, F. (2004). *Essential elements of effective science instruction for English learners* (2nd ed.). Los Angeles: California Science Project.

Gibbons, P. (1993). *Learning to learn in a second language.* Portsmouth, NH: Heinemann.

Gibbons, P. (2003). Mediating language learning: Teacher interactions with ESL students in a content-based classroom. *TESOL Quarterly, 37*(2), 247–273.

Rosenthal, J. W. (1995). *Teaching science to language minority students: Theory and practice.* Clevedon, UK: Multilingual Matters.

Scarcella, R. (2003). *Academic English: A conceptual framework.* UC Linguistic Minority Research Institute Technical Report 2003–1. Retrieved September 22, 2004, from http://lmri.ucsb.edu

Sexton, U. (1999). *Guide to scoring LEP student responses to open-ended science items.* Washington, DC: Council of Chief State School Officers.

Solano-Flores, G., & Turnbull, E. (2003). Examining language in context: The need for new research and practice paradigms in the testing of English learners. *Educational Researcher, 32*(2), 3–13.

Taylor, S. E. (1989). *EDL core vocabularies in reading, mathematics, science and social studies.* Austin, TX: Steck-Vaughn/EDL.

Valadez, J. (2002). Dispelling the myth: Is there an effect of inquiry-based science teaching on standardized reading scores? Retrieved September 20, 2004, from http://sustainability2002.terc.edu/invoke.cfm/page/729

Yearwood, J. (2003). Teaching as gardening. In S. Nieto (Ed.), *What keeps teachers going?* New York: Teachers College Press.

CHAPTER ELEVEN

Museum Experiences That Support Classroom Inquiry and Teacher Professional Development

Linda S. Shore

> *There [are] attributes of museums that make them appropriate places for learning. In the first place, they display the genuine article, original paintings, actual tools and ornaments of ancient cultures, or the operating phenomena of nature on which physics and biology are built. Somehow this show of reality represents a basic honesty that has a surprisingly important effect on learning. A reproduction of a painting does not stir the imagination or lie as deep in memory as does the original.*
>
> —Frank Oppenheimer (1981a)

Teachers are caught between the gravitational influences of two seemingly opposing forces for educational reform. One set of forces is embodied by federal and state mandates that require increased accountability by educational systems: development of curriculum and professional teaching standards, and implementation of high-stakes student testing and teacher licensing procedures to ensure that these standards are met. The other force is manifested by ideas about teaching and learning that strive to make student learning more authentic, learner-centered, experiential, and inquiry-based. Numerous stakeholders, including content specialists, educational researchers, and teachers, support this kind of teaching and learning because they feel that it is at least as important for students to learn *how* knowledge is acquired as it is for students to learn the content knowledge itself.

However, these two forces for school reform need not act in direct opposition. Standards for student achievement can be advanced that hold educational systems accountable for the development of both content knowledge *and* inquiry skills. In fact, the national content standards articulated by professional organizations include the development of inquiry skills as a key objective of K–12 instruction. For example, the National Science Education Standards (National Research Council, 1996) state that

> students at all grade levels and in every domain of science should have the opportunity to use scientific inquiry and develop the ability to think and act in ways associated with inquiry, including asking questions, planning and conducting investigations, using appropriate tools and techniques to gather data, thinking critically and logically about relationships between evidence and explanations, constructing and analyzing alternative explanations, and communicating scientific arguments. (p. 105)

Similar inquiry standards have been developed for mathematics. The National Council of Teachers of Mathematics (NCTM, 1989) states that

> instructional programs from pre-kindergarten through grade 12 should enable students to recognize reasoning and proof as fundamental aspects of mathematics, make and investigate mathematical conjectures, develop and evaluate mathematical arguments and proofs, and select and use various types of reasoning and methods of proof.

Science and mathematics are not the exclusive domains for inquiry content standards. The National Standards for History (National Center for History in the Schools, 1996) developed standards for historical thinking that mirror the way historians approach research. The NCHS standards state that

> real historical understanding requires students to engage in historical thinking: to raise questions and to marshal evidence in support of their answers; to read historical narratives and fiction; to consult historical documents, journals, diaries, artifacts, historic sites, and other records from the past; and to do so imaginatively—taking into account the time and places in which these records were created and comparing the multiple points of view of those on the scene at the time.

Regardless of the discipline, engaging students in meaningful experiences that develop both their content knowledge and their ability to conduct and understand the principles of inquiry requires uniquely skilled teachers working in a well-equipped, resource-rich school environment. For example, consider what might be required to facilitate a science inquiry about sinking and floating. First, a science teacher would have to know enough about the physics of buoyancy to recognize student misconceptions when they arise, ask the right kinds of probative questions, offer alternative ways of collecting or interpreting data, and point out flaws in reasoning or experimental design. Second, this same science teacher would have to possess unique classroom management skills—for example, the ability to distribute a variety of fluids and breakable glass beakers safely to groups of students and still maintain decorum. The teacher would also need to design authentic assessment tools and interpret student work so that student achievement could be evaluated formatively and the lesson modified appropriately for future use.

Our science teacher would also need to have a work environment that was supportive of inquiry. At a minimum, this would include ready access to appropriate science materials, such as graduated cylinders to measure volume and balances for measuring mass. The environment would provide this teacher with exemplary lessons and unit plans that apply inquiry approaches to teach students about buoyancy. In the best of all worlds, this school environment would support a community of professional practice to enable this science teacher to reflect on his or her teaching and share the successes and challenges of his or her sinking and floating inquiry lesson with colleagues in a critical friends relationship.

The unfortunate truth is that few teachers are adequately prepared to facilitate inquiry in the classrooms. Many teachers, particularly in the sciences, are teaching out of their field (Seastrom, Gruber, Henke, McGrath, & Cohen, 2002). Consequently, they may lack the content expertise required to teach students topics described in the national standards and be unable to facilitate meaningful inquiry learning experiences. For example, the science teacher responsible for our sinking and floating lesson might have an undergraduate degree in biology and possess only superficial understanding of the physics of buoyancy. Few teachers have experienced science learning through inquiry as students or during either preservice or inservice preparation; thus they have few pedagogical models or predispositions toward inquiry upon which to draw. They tend to teach the way they were taught—through lectures, demonstrations, and other didactic, teacher-centered approaches (Kennedy, 1998).

Although teachers are responsible for the development of hundreds of children every day, teaching is ironically among the most isolating of professions. Rarely do teachers participate in professional, collegial networks that many experts on teacher education cite as critical to improving practice. Because inquiry teaching is a craft that requires years to master, it is important to share and reflect with like-minded colleagues dedicated to the improvement of teaching skills (Loucks-Horsley, Stiles, & Hewson, 1996). We can think of these networks as "guilds" that function like the craft guilds of the Middle Ages. Within these guilds, apprenticeships were critical. Journeymen mentored novices; veterans mentored journeymen; masters mentored veterans. Craft guilds operated on the assumption that it takes an entire career to achieve mastery. Such guilds are virtually nonexistent in the lives of teachers who wish to improve the craft of inquiry teaching and learning.

Mark St. John (2003), who has written extensively on the role that museums play in the development of teachers, describes the culture in which teachers work as one of need and isolation. Some teachers have significant content knowledge gaps. For them, developing the kind of rich disciplinary expertise held by scientists, historians, mathematicians, and so on is essential. St. John argues that teachers are constrained from acquiring this deep content knowledge because few schools and districts have or make this kind of expertise available to teachers. Many teachers, especially those working in poor urban environments, lack high-quality teaching materials and resources for inquiry learning. Moreover, although the teaching profession possesses a vast amount of pedagogical knowledge, teachers are isolated from this as well. Opportunities to share and reflect are unavailable in a majority of schools.

St. John framed the conundrum in this way: If teachers operate within a culture of isolation, then where will they find the expertise and resources needed to be successful? One answer may lie outside of the formal educational system and within the walls of more than 16,000 museums scattered in diverse communities across the country (St. John, 2003). If teachers require access to *disciplinary knowledge, pedagogical content knowledge, high-quality educational materials and resources,* and *teacher guilds,* then art museums, zoos, aquariums, history museums, science centers, botanical gardens, and so on are uniquely poised to fill this need. In fact, such institutions have been providing this kind of support to teachers for decades and are assuming increasingly prominent roles to support inquiry teaching and learning in schools.

In this chapter, the case is made for museums as important resources for the professional development of teachers responsible for providing their students with meaningful inquiry experiences. Although this chapter examines science teaching and learning, the arguments apply equally to other disciplines. Examples of how museums are providing learning opportunities to teachers of history, language arts, and math can be found at the conclusion of this chapter.

INFORMAL EDUCATION INSTITUTIONS AS RESOURCES FOR TEACHER LEARNING

To teach their students science through inquiry, teachers need to understand the important content ideas in science—as outlined, for example, in the standards (National Research Council, 2000). They need to know how the facts, principles, laws, and formulas that they have learned in their own science courses are subsumed by and linked to those important ideas. They also need to know the evidence for the content they teach—how we know what we know. In addition, they need to learn the process of science: what scientific inquiry is and how to do it.

At a recent educational research conference, a doctoral student described a case study in which a beginning high school science teacher was leading a class in an inquiry lesson on the topic of magnetism (Olson, 2004). The lesson began with students working in small "research" groups. Each group placed a bar magnet in the center of a large sheet of butcher paper and, using magnetic compasses, located and sketched the lines of magnetic force surrounding each magnet. At the conclusion of the activity, the teacher asked each group to report its observations to the rest of the class. The teacher ended the lesson with a demonstration. He placed a bar magnet on the projection surface of an overhead projector and sprinkled iron filings around the magnet. The iron filings lined up along lines of magnetic force demonstrating the connection between the invisible lines of force mapped by the students and showing the effect of these forces on tiny pieces of iron.

At first glance, this novice physics teacher appeared to have successfully facilitated an inquiry-based science lesson. He incorporated cooperative learning by dividing his physics class into small research groups, encouraged group investigation and exploration of the magnetic field surrounding the magnets, and had research groups summarize their key findings and articulate them to the class. However, when the doctoral student, a former high school physics teacher, examined the case study more carefully, he discovered profound errors in both content and pedagogy—errors that only someone with a very strong background in both physics content and pedagogy would have recognized.

First, the high school students had enormous difficulty mapping the field lines accurately. The compasses were either bent or demagnetized, causing the compass needles to point in completely random directions. Second, the lab tables had iron bars running beneath the student work areas. These iron supports influenced the few compass needles that were working properly. The doctoral student found that none of the student groups mapped the magnetic fields correctly even though all of them believed that their experiments had produced accurate results.

Finally, the demonstration that the novice teacher presented was deeply flawed. The novice teacher *believed* that all the magnets in the room, including the one used in his own demonstration, were bar magnets. He expected his magnet to display the same field depicted in the textbook used by this class (Figure 11.1). But when he sprinkled the iron filings on the projector and projected the image to the class, the iron filings produced an entirely different pattern (Figure 11.2). In the novice teacher's confusion and embarrassment, he announced to the class that

Figure 11.1 Magnetic Field of the Bar Magnet (Polarized North/South at Ends)

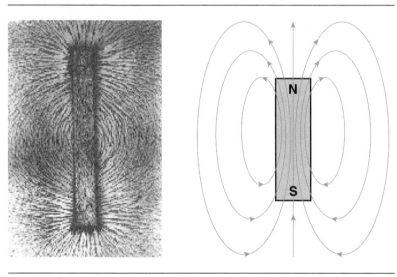

Figure 11.2 Magnetic Field of the Refrigerator Magnet (Polarized North/South Along Sides)

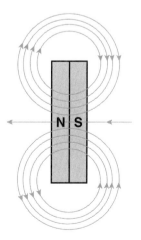

there was something wrong with his magnet. Before the students could study the image on the screen, the novice teacher quickly switched off the overhead, went to the blackboard, and drew what he and the students "had found." Neither the teacher nor his students had actually observed the magnetic pattern described in their textbook despite the fact that everyone in the classroom agreed that it was what they had witnessed.

I have seen this same magnetism lesson conducted by very skilled high school physics teachers at the Exploratorium. Here are some particulars that expert physics teachers address prior to and during the investigation. First, their craft knowledge cautions them that classroom compass needles are notoriously unreliable and need to be checked and possibly remagnetized. Veteran teachers also recognize that there are many other magnetic influences on the compass needles that needed to be taken into account, including the presence of nearby iron objects and the ubiquitous magnetic field of the earth. These accomplished science teachers even exploit the anomalies and external magnetic influences as opportunities for inquiry. I have observed physics teachers hiding iron objects under lab tables to intentionally create magnetic dilemmas and discrepant events that pique the interest of student groups.

Physics teachers with strong content knowledge also know that not all bar-shaped magnets produce the same field pattern. In this case, the novice physics teacher was not using the same type of bar magnet that was described in the textbook. Instead of using magnets polarized north and south on the *ends,* he had unwittingly used magnets polarized north and south on the *sides.* A physics teacher with greater knowledge of magnets would have immediately recognized the difference when students began making their maps. In fact, science teachers with more experience teaching through inquiry would have encouraged students to map the fields of a variety of magnets, such as horseshoes, bars, and cylindrically shaped magnets; pose questions; make comparisons; and generate possible explanations.

Clearly, the novice physics teacher in this example lacked sufficient content knowledge to facilitate successfully this student investigation of magnetic fields. But inadequate content knowledge about magnets was only one part of the instructional problem. He had enormous difficulty organizing and presenting the content in ways whereby students could conduct meaningful inquiries and learn from them. Shulman (1986) developed the idea of *pedagogical content knowledge* (PCK) to describe this ability to seamlessly integrate *both* content and pedagogical knowledge when teaching. In particular, PCK is the knack of transforming expert understanding into concepts that novices can grasp. Pedagogical content knowledge includes the ability to identify student preconceptions, select and use appropriate analogies and metaphors to clarify complex ideas, and recognize and exploit teachable moments when they arise.

To return St. John's (2003) earlier question, if teachers need a background that includes both strong subject matter preparation and pedagogical content knowledge to lead successful inquiry experiences, where is this kind of expertise and potential assistance housed? St. John argues that informal science learning institutions, such as science museums, zoos, and aquariums, whose mission is translating complex science content for general consumption, are ideal places to support science teachers. Informal learning centers that present inquiry experiences to the public are particularly well suited to serve as centers of teacher professional development.

To illustrate, consider the knowledge bases and types of expertise required by museum staff to develop an inquiry-based exhibit. Strong knowledge of subject matter is a prerequisite. A meaningful interactive, inquiry-based exhibit on magnetism could not be created without a thorough understanding of magnets. Pedagogical content knowledge is another essential ingredient. Exhibit developers must have an a priori understanding of the key concepts that laypeople will find difficult to grasp, and they must develop appropriate analogies and experiences to help visitors understand the main points. Museum staff must also be reflective about their craft. Did the public comprehend what the exhibit developer wanted to convey through the inquiry experience? If not, then how can the exhibit be revised to reach this goal?

Museums employ professionals with a variety of backgrounds and areas of expertise. For example, the Exploratorium staff includes physicists, biologists, people with doctorates in science education, and experienced science teachers who have left the classroom to work in informal education. Aquariums have marine biologists; botanical gardens have botanists; natural history museums have paleontologists, geologists, and anthropologists; and planetariums have astronomers. These institutions employ science, history, mathematics, and English educators who are experts in the pedagogy of their areas. Working in teams, these people are responsible for public education programs, exhibit design, and development of educational materials used in homes and schools. They also constitute the core staff of teacher professional development programs found in museums.

The following examples are illustrative of museum programs that help science teachers enhance both their subject matter and pedagogical content knowledge.

American Museum of Natural History

Educational outreach to the public, families, children, students, and teachers has been a core mission of the American Museum of Natural History in New York City (AMNH) since it was founded in 1869. The educational activities of the AMNH includes conferences, lectures, exhibitions, school support, special on-site programming, and an extensive and evolving library of Web-based resources for learners of all kinds. The AMNH also provides professional development for local teachers, specifically in the development of science content knowledge. As stated on the AMNH Web site, "Recognizing that science educators are positioned to pass on their knowledge exponentially, the museum created *Seminars on Science,* its flagship professional development program."

The Seminars on Science project sponsors 6-week summer institutes for teachers that are taught by museum research scientists and collection curators. Scientific inquiry occupies the heart of the courses. As described on the Seminars on Science Web site (AMNH, 2004):

> We believe in an inquiry-based approach to science education as supported by the National Science Education Standards. Our courses are modeled after the process of delving into a question, formulating a hypothesis, sharing it with others, and refining the answer in order to pose more questions. You'll come away from Seminars on Science courses with a first-hand understanding of how scientists pursue knowledge, and with hands-on experience that will enable you to engage your kids in inquiry-based learning.

Every week, teacher participants explore different questions, such as "Why are there ocean basins and mountains?" or "What makes a fish a fish?" Teachers are expected to participate as active learners. They conduct science investigations, share in online discussions with fellow teachers and AMNH faculty, and read essays and articles written by staff scientists and edited by museum educators. The program gives participants access to a rich collection of online learning tools designed to deepen their understanding of course content. For example, teachers have access to videos that accompany essays, interactive simulations, and a library of digital images.

Missouri Botanical Garden

Opened to the public in 1859, the Missouri Botanical Garden in St. Louis (MGB) is one of the oldest botanical gardens in the country. Today, the Missouri Botanical Garden's Education Division is dedicated to developing a scientifically literate citizenry. The Garden provides educational programs for more than 100,000 children and tens of thousands of adults every year. The MBG also provides professional development and other services to more than 2,700 teachers.

The Missouri Botanical Gardens offers an array of weeklong summer workshops for K–12 teachers to strengthen their inquiry teaching practices and their understanding of botany, earth science, ecology, and environmental science. Many of these workshops involve teachers in investigations that take place in authentic contexts such as the 20-acre Shaw Nature Reserve or within the botanical garden. For example, in the workshop "Ecology of Aquatic Environments," teachers from Grades 4–8 use both the Shaw Reserve and Missouri Botanical Gardens to investigate "pond, river, and stream ecosystems and learn about their biological, physical, and chemical characteristics" (Missouri Botanical Gardens brochure, 2004). In "Discover Botany," garden staff help teachers in Grades K–4 "use hands-on investigations and Garden collections to explore how plants grow, collect energy, reproduce, and help us live" (Missouri Botanical Gardens brochure, 2004). After completing workshops such as these, teachers are eligible to borrow classroom kits and educational materials that help bring these ideas back to the classroom.

The Missouri Botanical Garden also hosts professional development workshops designed specifically to meet the needs of local schools and districts. The Garden offers a menu of options that includes workshops listed under the categories Teaching Strategies (e.g., Inquiry-Based Science, Assessment Strategies for Hands-On

Science); Botany (e.g., Basic Botany for Teachers, Plants as Teaching Tools); Ecology (e.g., Using Your Schoolyard to Teach Ecology, Ecosystem Investigations); and Using Technology to Enhance Science Investigations (e.g., Journey North, GIS).

Fort Worth Museum of Science and History

The approaches described in the two previous cases provide direct support to help teachers increase the knowledge and skills needed to teach science through inquiry. Another method is to build capacity within schools and districts by working with teacher leaders and professional developers. The latter approach, found at the Fort Worth Museum of Science and History's Texas Center for Inquiry (TCI), provides science educators with in-depth experiences in science inquiry through institutes, workshops, forums, and follow-up coaching. TCI's mission is to help professional developers incorporate science inquiry into the elementary curriculum in ways consistent with the goals outlined in the National Science Education Standards and the Texas Essential Knowledge and Skills. The Center also seeks to create a network of people and institutions dedicated to inquiry learning and quality elementary science instruction (Fort Worth Museum of Science and History, n.d.).

Inquiry institutes and workshops offered by the Fort Worth's Center for Inquiry are adapted from professional development opportunities developed by the Exploratorium's Institute for Inquiry (IFI). The motto of both the TCI and IFI is "leadership in inquiry through inquiry." Workshop participants, who must apply in teams, are immersed in a variety of experiences that explore questions fundamental to the design of inquiry learning, are given opportunities to reflect on these learning experiences, and develop professional development programs to implement in their own schools and districts. For example, during TCI's 5-day "Introduction to Inquiry," participants explore the same science concept (e.g., What makes a top spin longer?) using a variety of different hands-on experiences, compare and contrast the results, and discuss their relative merits. Through firsthand experience with inquiry learning, participants discover how to develop testable questions, engineer good starting points for inquiry, and design learning experiences that foster conceptual understanding and critical thinking skills. Upon graduating from an "Introduction to Inquiry" institute, districts become eligible to send teams of teachers to the Museum of Science and History to participate in a 3-day workshop called "Building Capacity for Classroom Inquiry." Here, teachers discover how to infuse their own kit-based science curriculum and structured hands-on activities with opportunities for students to ask their own questions, conduct their own investigations, draw appropriate conclusions, and communicate their findings.

Informal Education Institutions as Resources for Inquiry Materials

> *Museums serve as [learning] centers in many different ways. They have their permanent exhibit collections and changing special ones. In addition, most of them produce written materials [and other documents]. At the Exploratorium, we have produced essays about the ideas related to [our exhibits] as well as catalogues, books, and magazines. Museums also create many visuals, including posters, reproductions, postcards, films, and television programs. . . . Many museums further have programs in which they take samples of their wares out to schools or community organizations. . . . I am both flabbergasted and inspired by the richness of the educational endeavors that center around a museum's activities and props.*
>
> —Frank Oppenheimer (1981b)

Anna, a beginning science teacher who was participating in the Exploratorium's professional development program, told an extraordinary story about her first day as a middle school teacher. She arrived at her new school one week ahead of the students to attend orientation meetings, fill out paperwork, and prepare her classroom. This was Anna's very first year as a science teacher, and she was excited to be teaching at an urban school serving traditionally underserved students. Anna, who held a bachelor's degree in biology, already had a small repertoire of activities and lessons from her preservice program that she was eager to present and refine. She dreamed of teaching her students not only science content but scientific inquiry as well.

Anna was horrified when she saw the classroom she had been assigned. The room was completely barren. There were no basic teaching materials, let alone supplies for infusing her curriculum with inquiry science. There were no pieces of glassware, measuring devices, or sinks. If she needed water, her closest supply was at the far end of a long corridor—in the student bathrooms. The classroom lacked supply cabinets or any other storage areas. Her science classroom was like a huge empty box with only a blackboard, a stack of required textbooks, and neatly placed rows of chairs and desks.

Anna immediately went to the main office to determine if her room assignment had been an error. If this was actually her classroom, then maybe someone could point her in the direction of the science supply closet where she could obtain the materials for appropriately stocking her room. Anna learned that this was her assigned classroom for the year, and that there were no additional materials or supplies available anywhere in the school. But all was not lost. A sympathetic school receptionist, overhearing Anna's distress, called the young teacher over. The receptionist opened one of her desk drawers, reached inside, handed Anna a gluestick, and earnestly said, "Let me give you this, honey. Trust me, this is the best stuff. You'll use it all the time."

Despite the absurdity of Anna's first day as a science teacher, scenarios like this occur again and again in this country. Lack of science supplies is one of the main reasons elementary school teachers offer for not teaching science (National Science Resources Center, 1997). This factor also contributes to job dissatisfaction, career burnout, and the high rate of attrition observed among beginning science teachers (Schneider, 2003). For those who remain in the profession, studies on the working conditions of teachers find that, on average, teachers spend more than $500 yearly to supply their classrooms with necessary materials. Novice teachers spend even more—an average of more than $700 (Wisconsin Education Association Council, 2002). Although many rightfully argue that no teacher should ever have to spend his or her own money or personal time to obtain the basic educational supplies that students need, teachers have done this in the past and are likely to continue this practice in the foreseeable future.

Another issue associated with teaching science as inquiry is the place where teachers can go for expert advice on selecting high-quality, inquiry-based activities, lessons, and student assessments. Museums and other informal educational institutions have become critical lifelines that connect many teachers to the "stuff" they need to teach inquiry. Museums and other institutions of informal learning are literally defined by the rich collections they house. Zoos have live animals; aquariums have fish; natural history museums have fossils and rocks; science centers offer interactive physics experiments. More importantly, museums are increasingly using their collections to facilitate authentic inquiry experiences among their visitors. Sensible teachers who need real science "stuff" to do inquiry turn to museums, zoos, natural history museums, and hands-on science centers for support.

Various science centers have responded to this need for "stuff" by literally transporting animals, fish, rocks, and fossils directly to classrooms. For example, the San Francisco Zoo sponsors the Mobile Zoo Outreach Program, in which a "zoomobile" transports animals and handlers to schools around the Bay Area. The purpose goes far beyond just showing off exotic animals to eager school-children. The zoo offers eight programs that incorporate the animals in activities that target California State Content Standards for the elementary and middle school grade levels.

Most informal science centers distribute instructional materials developed by museum content and pedagogy experts at a modest cost. For example, the Stupp Teacher Resource Center at the Missouri Botanical Garden in St. Louis circulates "suitcase science kits" supporting classroom inquiry on topics such as seeds, classification, and weather. Local teachers can also borrow botanical models and displays, CD-ROMs, and videos.

Although access to the stuff of science is critical, science teachers also need exemplary student inquiry activities, lessons, and unit plans, especially those that have been developed by people with content and pedagogical expertise and tested extensively in classrooms. A surprising number of inquiry lessons available to teachers through publications or posted on Web sites contain serious flaws in content and/or execution. If a teacher finds an untested activity, tries it with her students, and the inquiry lesson fails, the teacher is more likely to personally accept responsibility rather than blame the quality of the materials. Science teaching confidence is a precious commodity that is easily shattered by perceived classroom failure.

Museum educators understand the critical importance of field-testing teaching materials. To ensure that museum exhibits engage visitors successfully in meaningful learning experiences, displays are subjected to iterative cycles of prototyping, pilot-testing, and redesign. Museum educators apply the same practice and philosophy to the development of classroom materials. For example, at the Exploratorium, new activities are piloted with museum staff, revised, extensively tested with experienced science teachers, revised again, and then finally tested in classrooms with real students before being published in books or on our Web site (http://www.exploratorium .edu).

In this next section, I describe some innovative examples of what some informal science centers are doing to provide teachers with teaching supplies and curriculum materials that specifically support inquiry in the classroom.

American Museum of Natural History

Resources for Learning is a collection of more than 750 Web-based resources assembled by the American Museum of Natural History (AMNH) to "make their own collection of scientific and educational materials more readily available to teachers and their students" (American Museum of Natural History, n.d.). Resources on this Web site are categorized by type, such as student activities (resources that actively engage learners); curriculum materials (resources intended for teachers that provide a more structured class-room approach to a topic); evidence and analysis (resources that present the "real stuff" of science, the artifacts and specimens, data, tools, and methods that scientists use); and exhibition materials (science resources drawn from exhibits at the museum).

Under the collection labeled Oceans, one finds inquiry-based student activities such as "Just Add Water." In this elementary-level lesson, students build landforms out of modeling clay and fill them with water to create seafloor landscapes and develop topographical maps. In "Cartesian Divers," middle school students build neutrally buoyant divers out of balloons and plastic bottles and explore the relationship between volume and the diver's ability to sink and float. In all student activities, specific connections to National Science Education Standards both for content and inquiry are listed. There are links in the Oceans collection to other educational resources, such as curriculum units (e.g., Journey to the Deep Sea Vents), related AMNH field trip guides (e.g., Hall of Ocean Life Educator's

Guide), and reference lists for both teachers and their students (e.g., Ocean Life Book List).

Franklin Institute of Science

Philadelphia's Franklin Institute of Science offers programs designed to provide teachers with resources to infuse their curriculum with inquiry experiences that specifically satisfy the state and national science content standards. One of these, the Keystone Science Network (KSN), grew out of a major, multiyear collaboration among the museum, the National Science Foundation, the Unisys Corporation, the Commonwealth Department of Education, and selected school district and regional science alliance sites in eastern Pennsylvania. KSN was designed to support teachers' implementation of nationally distributed standards-based inquiry science kits by connecting a network of K–8 teachers with the kits and a plethora of online resources. The goal was to help teachers improve their subject matter knowledge and inquiry teaching practices. Specifically, KSN supported the science kit program Science and Technology for Children (STC), developed by the National Science Resources Center; Full Option Science System (FOSS), developed by Lawrence Hall of Science; and Insights, developed by the Educational Development Center.

The Keystone Science Network project has a Web site (http://www.keystone.fi.edu) where teachers can easily and quickly locate electronic resources reviewed and selected by museum staff to facilitate meaningful inquiry learning experiences. For example, a fourth-grade teacher who was implementing the FOSS kit on the Physics of Sound could access the KSN Web site and find a vast collection of links to strengthen her own understanding of sound, hearing, and wave mechanics. Science teachers and their students created some of the content-focused Web sites. "Sound: Wired@School," a site developed by fifth graders, includes animations, cartoons, and accurate explanations of key concepts such as the relationship between frequency and pitch, amplitude and loudness, and wave form and sound quality.

KSN also provides this fourth-grade teacher with the pedagogical support she needs to successfully lead her inquiry-based FOSS lessons on the physics of sound. Under a link called "Tips and

Comments," she will find advice and ideas for facilitating her FOSS sound lesson from other teachers in the KSN network. Another link, titled "Assessment Strategies," presents ideas for implementing and evaluating student learning through authentic, performance-based assessments created by experts across the country and reviewed by the education staff at Franklin.

Finally, KSN provides its network of teachers with "The Inquiry Curricular Companion," a set of links designed to support authentic, experiential science learning regardless of the content. Here, science teachers can locate connections to a vast library of images of inquiry taking place in other classrooms, reflections on inquiry teaching by colleagues in the network, samples of student inquiry projects, and links to other educational institutions and organizations that promote inquiry teaching and learning.

Resource Area for Teachers

An innovative illustration of how an institution outside the formal K–12 education system can help science teachers locate materials and lead classroom inquiry experiences is the Resource Area for Teachers (RAFT). Although RAFT is not a museum, it is an example of what museums could do for their communities. RAFT, which operates out of a huge warehouse near San Jose, California, has a mission based on the old saying (slightly paraphrased) that "one man's junk is another teacher's treasure." Local high-tech companies in Silicon Valley donate odds and ends to RAFT, where they are made available to teachers for little or no cost. For a few dollars, a teacher can take home a shopping bag full of such things as CD-ROMs, rolls of Mylar™, three-ring binders, bags of rubber bands, stickers, pens and pencils, plastic containers, and other miscellaneous objects that can supply a science teacher's bag of inquiry tricks.

RAFT also sponsors workshops in which K–12 science teachers discover how to use these low-cost supplies in meaningful and engaging student inquiry activities. As the RAFT Web site (http://www .raft.net) states,

Through interactive displays and hands-on workshops, RAFT transforms the ways teachers view our materials. Our members learn to see cardboard tubes as musical instruments, or as spectroscopes, or as kaleidoscopes. We show you how to take an object like a CD, and turn it into a science lesson about hovercrafts which defy friction, or a "Math Spinner" that makes multiplication fun.

INFORMAL EDUCATION INSTITUTIONS AS HOMES FOR TEACHER GUILDS

Laura Martin (1993), in reviewing the difficulty of changing teacher practices, describes a scenario familiar to those who design and implement teacher professional development programs that promote classroom inquiry. She describes the conclusion of a well-received 5-day workshop on inquiry-based teaching methods in which teacher-participants were asked to describe how motivated they were to apply these new strategies in their own classrooms. Almost all responded they were motivated at the very highest level. However, after a year of classroom observations were analyzed, the majority of these teachers failed to incorporate any of the new strategies into their familiar instructional routines. Many were unable to recall the primary purpose of the workshop, saying that they only remembered learning how to use some new math and science materials. Despite the enormous initial enthusiasm generated by their professional development experience, very few teachers adopted any of the inquiry practices during the following year.

Martin's (1993) discouraging account highlights a major challenge facing professional developers—namely, what can be done to overcome the resistance among teachers to changing their teaching practices? According to Martin, part of the problem is that professional developers tend to see individual teachers as the primary agents of change. The widely held belief is that simply providing teachers with a workshop experience designed to be deeply transformative will automatically lead them to reinvent themselves in the desired image when they reenter the classroom.

What this perspective neglects is the *social aspect* of learning. Whether or not teachers significantly change their practices relates as much to their social and cultural milieu as it does to their personal knowledge, skills, and beliefs. Here are some important questions that need to be considered. Does the teacher's workplace support inquiry? Does the teacher have access to colleagues who share similar goals? Does the teacher have opportunities to engage in meaningful discourse and reflection around inquiry teaching? Is there an apprenticeship structure in place so that colleagues with greater knowledge and experience support the shift to inquiry teaching? Does the school and/or district have the desire and capacity to support this kind of community of practice?

Although much has been written about the critical importance of school climate and culture in supporting inquiry, studies of the sociology of schools reveal that most teachers still spend most of their careers sheltered within classrooms walls and isolated from colleagues and administrators (Darling-Hammond, 1984; Lortie, 1975). Although there are exemplary schools and districts that support active professional learning communities, they provide the exception rather than the rule. Why are these teacher communities so scarce? In my experience, most administrators share a genuine interest and desire in establishing teacher communities within their schools. However, school districts simply do not have or make the financial resources available to support this type of initiative. To do so would require releasing teachers from the classroom to observe one another and share ideas, and providing appropriate inquiry resources and specialized work areas. Such activities represent a significant investment for school districts, many of which are already strapped with overcrowded classrooms and severe budget shortages.

The Exploratorium Teacher Institute Guild—A History

Although locating teacher communities within schools and districts is the ideal, it is possible for museums to partner with local districts and serve as homes to these "teacher guilds." In this section, I describe the features and outcomes of a 20-year-old "teacher guild" housed at the Exploratorium Teacher Institute. The primary purpose of the Exploratorium Teacher Institute guild is to induct and apprentice its members to reach higher levels of mastery. We partner with local school districts with the aim of developing similar science teacher networks within individual schools.

The Exploratorium is a hands-on, interactive science museum in San Francisco founded in 1969 by Frank Oppenheimer. His vision was a new kind of science museum—one that could help people of all ages understand science as a process and enable them to discover the nature of knowledge, inquiry learning, and human perception.

Today, the Exploratorium's mission is to transform science education in all places where science learning occurs: in schools, homes, and other museums. The museum has helped science teachers bring authentic science inquiry into their classrooms for more than 30 years. One of the museum's teacher professional development programs is the Exploratorium Teacher Institute.

The Teacher Institute (TI) began in 1984 when a group of local high school physics teachers asked for the opportunity to spend their summer at the museum and learn how to use Exploratorium resources to infuse their teaching with hands-on science and inquiry. Staff educators and physicists worked with these teachers to develop inquiry-based materials. These veteran teachers found the experience so rejuvenating that they returned the following summer and brought along their colleagues. Some of these physics teachers partnered with museum science staff and began developing and leading workshops for their less experienced colleagues. By the mid-1990s, the Teacher Institute had matured into a comprehensive professional development program offering summer institutes, weekend workshops, after-school sessions, a teacher library, and Web-based resources to both middle and high school science teachers.

The support given to TI alumni teachers is coherent and lifelong. Experienced teachers begin the program with a 4-week Introductory Summer Institute, where middle and high school science teachers become learners. They receive science content preparation through authentic science inquiry experiences. Exploratorium exhibits challenge teachers intellectually with unusual or counterintuitive physical phenomena. They offer a launching point for classroom activities that allow teachers to deepen their own science knowledge and experience inquiry-based teaching and learning. The teachers have access to a "machine shop," where they can build smaller versions of museum exhibits. These teacher-created exhibits are brought back to classrooms where, in a likewise manner, they become catalysts for inquiry for students.

After graduating from the summer institute, teachers become alumni of the Exploratorium Teacher Institute and are eligible to return for further content and pedagogical training during Saturday workshops, afterschool workshops, and 2-week advanced summer institutes. Alumni have lifelong access to museum staff, including science educators, scientists, artists, writers, and exhibit developers. Most importantly, alumni belong to an active community of other science teachers all dedicated to improving practice and infusing their science classes with authentic inquiry experiences.

During the late 1990s, TI alumni began reporting that their schools were hiring large numbers of beginning science teachers, and that more than half of these novices were leaving the profession after the first year. The alumni asked us to develop an induction program for novice science teachers and to include them in the larger TI alumni community. Simultaneously, many of our most experienced alumni, those in whom TI staff had invested a decade or more of support, were retiring.

These alumni were reluctant to "retire" from the Teacher Institute and expressed a desire to use the free time that retirement afforded to give back to their profession by supporting the upcoming generation of science teachers. These changing teacher demographics and the important retention issues led us to develop a program oriented toward new science teachers. In 1998, TI began to offer a 2-year TI Beginning Teacher Program for novice teachers in the Bay Area. Participants receive science content workshops, special pedagogy training, support group meetings, and in-class coaching. Retired alumni serve as the workshop leaders and in-class coaches. Other veteran teachers, who are still employed as full-time science teachers, serve as workshop leaders but lead afterschool support group meetings instead of providing in-class support.

The result of this 20-year history is that the Exploratorium houses a unique guild of science teachers from all stages of the career spectrum ranging from novices to experienced mentors. Like other professional guilds, such as professional communities of doctors, lawyers, scientists, and craftspeople, the Exploratorium guild is oriented toward a single purpose: the advancement of quality and best professional practices. Specifically, the TI guild is dedicated to the quality and advancement of best science teaching, which includes combining strong science content with experiential learning that mirrors the way science is conducted by practicing scientists. Almost 1,500 science teachers have been affiliated with the TI guild since its inception in 1984 with our original group of physics teachers.

The Exploratorium Teacher Institute collaborates with districts to ensure that we support our alumni to teach content that is consistent with local and state mandates. Science standards define the content of TI professional development. For example, when California adopted the State Science Framework in 1990, science teachers were required to teach science thematically. The curriculum was developed around interdisciplinary themes, such as "scale and structure," "cycles," and "evolution," and they were intended to teach students the overarching connections among biology, physics, chemistry, and earth science. The Framework emphasized science as a process and expected teachers to engage students in authentic inquiry. The Framework standards presented numerous and considerable challenges for secondary science teachers. First, because virtually no science teacher had ever been taught science through a thematic approach, teachers themselves needed to understand the connections among the big ideas. Second, teaching thematically required biology teachers to understand physics, physics teachers to know biology, and so on. Finally, most science teachers still were practicing didactic, teacher-centered instruction. The kind of authentic, inquiry-based teaching methods required by the Framework were utterly foreign to most science teachers. To help our alumni facilitate the Framework themes in their classrooms, the TI offered summer institutes on framework themes. Saturday alumni sessions were devoted to helping life science teachers learn physical science content and vice versa. Special online resources and library materials were compiled. The museum even worked with TI alumni to develop special exhibit collections devoted to the California State Science Framework so that the public would have a better understanding of what their children were learning in school. Within 4 years, hundreds of TI alumni had substantially broadened their science content knowledge, learned to teach thematically, and adopted inquiry-based teaching strategies.

Today, the state science standards no longer emphasize theme-based approaches. Instead, California has adopted standards that focus on specific science content and processes; for example, the sixth-grade content standards include the study of plate tectonics, ecology, and energy transformation; the eighth-grade standards focus on force, motion, the periodic table, and chemical reactions. In addition, high-stakes science achievement tests, mandated by No Child Left Behind legislation, began in 2004 and eventually will be administered to all students in Grades 5, 8, and 10 across California. The new state content standards and tests pose a new set of challenges for science teachers. Some science teachers are being asked to teach unfamiliar content. All teachers are struggling to balance the need to prepare students to pass the high-stakes science tests with requirements to engage students in authentic inquiry experiences.

The Teacher Institute is currently working with schools and district offices to address the challenges posed by the new state science requirements. The dynamic nature of the TI lends itself to the ever-evolving educational landscape.

CONCLUSION

There is about one informal science education institution for every 1,000 elementary school teachers in the United States and one such institution for every 100 middle and high school science teachers (St. John, 2003). The impact that these science museums, zoos, aquariums, planetariums, and natural history museums have in increasing the content and pedagogical knowledge of teachers, supplying schools with exemplary inquiry materials and resources, and providing local districts with professional teacher guilds dedicated to improving inquiry-based practice is enormous. Informal science centers across the country are becoming increasingly involved in this important work. As William Frascella, Director of the National Science Foundation's Elementary, Secondary, and Informal Education (ESIE) division argues, science museums have been a "sleeping giant" of science education support and reform that is awakening and realizing its potential (Frascella, 2003).

Although I described how informal science institutions play a critical role in supporting authentic inquiry teaching and learning in K–12 *science* classrooms, the same arguments apply to other kinds of museums and other subject areas. For example, history teachers incorporating inquiry in their curriculum need to possess a strong understanding of history, a working knowledge of the research methods employed by research historians, and strong pedagogical knowledge. Like science teachers, history teachers also need access to the "stuff" that researchers examine, such as documents, records, objects, and other materials. Throughout the country, there are museums dedicated to historical and cultural research and preservation that house historians, museum educators, and vast collections of artifacts inaccessible to most schools. Imagine the depth and quality of support that a history teacher could receive from a Civil War museum or from an anthropology museum. Likewise, consider what a professional learning community of history teachers supported by the staff of such institutions could accomplish together in terms of promoting inquiry learning.

A growing number of museums across the country support inquiry-based practices in history, math, art, and language arts. Like the science museums I described, these informal learning institutions are providing teachers with content and pedagogical knowledge, disciplinary expertise, materials, lesson plans, and opportunities for collegial interaction.

The Museum of Fine Arts (MFA) in Boston, Massachusetts, is helping local K–12 teachers improve their content knowledge through a series of evening workshops. "Art Deco: Making the Modern World" is a session that enables high school teachers to use the museum's extensive collection to learn about traditionalism and modernity—concepts targeted by the state's high school history curriculum standards. Another workshop, titled "Storytelling," helps elementary teachers use myths, legends, and traditional stories to enrich classroom activities. Middle school teachers can improve their own understanding of ancient Egypt and Nubia through the exploration of the MFA's renowned collection of ancient artifacts.

Art museums also provide teachers with opportunities to form relationships with other teachers to develop their inquiry teaching practices. The J. Paul Getty Museum in Los Angeles offers a 2-year program professional development program for local elementary school teachers that introduces meaningful and engaging strategies for developing their students' language and visual arts skills. The Getty's program, which supports the California Content Standards, is collaborative. Working teams of teachers share ideas and information with their peers and museum experts. Upon conclusion of the program, inquiry-based lessons that use art as the catalyst for learning language and visual arts have been developed and field-tested. The model lessons are disseminated on the Getty Museum's Web site (http://www.getty.edu) for use in other teachers' classrooms.

Even new museums are providing high-quality support to teachers. Shortly after the Bob Bullock Texas State History Museum in Austin, Texas, opened its doors in 2001, it began offering a variety of professional development programs. In a series of four 3-hour workshops titled "History Counts," math teachers measure and estimate at the La Belle shipwreck, interpret the geometry of trusses, and explore boom and bust cycles of the Texas oil industry. The museum also offers content and pedagogy workshops for art, science, and English-language teachers. All of the museum's workshops focus on content that satisfies the grade-level standards described in the Texas Essential Knowledge and Skills.

In 1974, Frank Oppenheimer testified before a congressional subcommittee on education to support federal funding for museums. He argued that such institutions are not "a frill for those who have completed their education." Oppenheimer urged the subcommittee to view museums as "libraries of experience" with the unique ability to provide students with opportunities for having a "firsthand acquaintance with art, history, and science" (Oppenheimer, 1974). At the time of his testimony, the Exploratorium was in its infancy and, like other museums, was just beginning to support local teachers. Now, 30 years later, museums like the Exploratorium have developed sophisticated professional teacher development programs and are partnering with schools and districts to promote authentic, content-rich, inquiry-based learning. At the Exploratorium, we are pleased to report that Oppenheimer's vision has been realized.

REFERENCES

American Museum of Natural History. (n.d.). Available: http://www.amnh .org

Darling-Hammond, L. (1984). *Beyond the commission reports: The coming crisis in teaching.* Santa Monica, CA: RAND.

Fort Worth Museum of Science and History. (n.d.). Available: http://www .fwmuseum.org

Frascella, W. (2003, November). *Views from the division of elementary, secondary, and informal education.* Presentation given at the second annual DFG-NSF International Workshop on Research and Development in Mathematics and Science Education, Washington, DC.

Kennedy, M. (1998). Education reform and subject matter knowledge. *Journal of Research in Science Teaching, 35*(3), 249–263.

Lortie, D. (1975). *Schoolteacher: A sociological study.* Chicago: University of Chicago Press.

Loucks-Horsley, S., Stiles, K., & Hewson, P. (1996). Principles of effective professional development for mathematics and science education: A synthesis of standards [Entire issue]. *NISE Brief, 1*(1).

Martin, L. (1993). Understanding teacher change from a Vygotskian perspective. In P. Kahaney, L. A. M. Perry, & J. Janangelo (Eds.), *Theoretical and critical perspectives on teacher change.* Norwood, NJ: Ablex.

National Center for History in the Schools. (1996). *National standards for history.* Retrieved May 20, 2004, from http://www.sscnet.ucla.edu/ nchs/standards

National Council of Teachers of Mathematics. (1989). *Principles and standards for school mathematics.* Retrieved May 20, 2004, from http://standards.nctm.org

National Research Council. (1996). *National science education standards.* Washington, DC: National Academy Press.

National Research Council. (2000). *Inquiry and the science education standards: A guide for teaching and learning.* Washington, DC: National Academy Press.

National Science Resources Center. (1997). *Science for all children: A guide to improving elementary science education in your school district.* Washington, DC: National Academy Press.

Olson, R. M. (2004, April). *A textbook case of induction.* Presentation given at the annual meeting of the American Educational Research Association, San Diego, CA.

Oppenheimer, F. (1974). Comments on the unique role of museums and the need for federal on-going support for their operation and expansion: Prepared statement presented to the Select Subcommittee of Education in consideration of H.R. 322. In *Writings by Frank Oppenheimer,* Exploratorium archives.

Oppenheimer, F. (1981a). Private correspondence with Lou Branscomb, Chair, National Science Board, IBM. In *Writings by Frank Oppenheimer,* Exploratorium archives.

Oppenheimer, F. (1981b). Untitled paper prepared for the American Association for the Advancement of Science (AAAS) meeting in Toronto. In *Writings by Frank Oppenheimer,* Exploratorium archives.

Schneider, M. (2003). *Linking school facility conditions to teacher satisfaction and success.* New York: National Clearinghouse for Educational Facilities.

Seastrom, M., Gruber, K. J., Henke, R., McGrath, D. J., & Cohen, D. J. (2002). *Qualifications of the public school teacher workforce: Prevalence of out-of-field teaching, 1987–88 to 1999–2000.* Washington, DC: National Center for Education Statistics.

Shulman, L. S. (1986). Those who understand: Knowledge growth in teaching. *Educational Researcher, 15*(2), 4–14.

St. John, M. (2003). *The national educational landscape and the design of museum based professional development programs.* Invited paper presented at the annual Informal Learning Certificate (ILC) Inquiry Workshop, Center for Informal Learning and Schools, Exploratorium, San Francisco.

Wisconsin Education Association Council. (2002). *Teachers spending their own money in class.* Retrieved May 12, 2004, from http://www.weac.org/News/2002–03/nov02/nssea.htm

Index